Pantaloons & Power

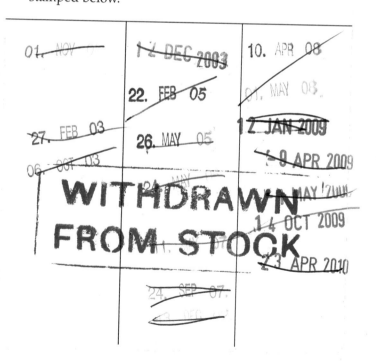

FIG. 3.   FIG. 4.

THE BLOOMER COSTUME.

Pantaloons & Power

A Nineteenth-Century Dress Reform in the United States

Gayle V. Fischer

The Kent State University Press
Kent, Ohio, and London

© 2001 by The Kent State University Press, Kent, Ohio, 44242

All rights reserved

Library of Congress Catalog Card Number 00-010253

ISBN 0-87338-682-5

Manufactured in the United States of America

06   05   04   03   02   01   5   4   3   2   1

Library of Congress Cataloging-in-Publication Data

Fischer, Gayle V.

    Pantaloons and power: a nineteenth-century dress reform in the
    United States / Gayle V. Fischer.

        p.   cm.

Includes bibliographical references and index.

ISBN 0-87338-682-5 (pbk.:alk. paper) ∞

1. Costume—United States—History—19th century.   2. Women's
rights—United States—History.   I. Title.

GT610.F57   2001

391'.2'097309034—dc21   00-010253

British Library Cataloging-in-Publication data are available.

For Peter

Contents

Acknowledgments

I would like to thank the following people for their comments, support, and assistance: Lois Banner, Persis Charles, Joshua Cole, Anne Epstein, Shelly Foote, Jean Friedman, Kathryn Wagnile Fuller, Andrea Hamilton, Joan Hoff, LuAnne Holladay, Lynn Hudson, Heather Kleiner, Maureen McCarthy, Laura Mason, Cynthia Nelson Meyer, Muriel Nazzari, Judith Papachristou, Thomas Prasch, Karen Rader, Bryant Simon, Valerie Steele, Stephen Stein, Steven Stowe, Amy Swerdlow, Patricia Campbell Warner, and my colleagues at Salem State College.

I would also like to thank the librarians and archivists at the following institutions: Cortland County Historical Society; Ellen G. White Research Center, Andrews University, Seventh-day Adventist Theological Seminary; George Arents Research Library at Syracuse University; Historical Society of Middletown and the Walkill Precinct; Lily Library at Indiana University; Madison County Historical Society; National Library of Medicine; New Harmony Workingmen's Institute Library and Museum; Oneida Community Mansion House; Oswego County Historical Society; Salem State College Library; Sarah Lawrence College Library; Seneca Falls Historical Society; and the State Historical Society of Wisconsin.

For emotional support, I thank Anita Gust Fischer, Michael I. Fischer, Samuel Maurice Fischer, Carol Ann Fischer Poliarny, Amy Fischer Suma-cewski, Benjamin Max Fischer Urkowitz, Edward Abraham Fischer Urkowitz, Peter Jacob Urkowitz, Steven Urkowitz, and Susan Spector Urkowitz.

Bessie Spector and the Indiana University Graduate School and Department of History provided financial support for this work in its early stages, for which I am grateful. A grant from Salem State College's Vice President's Faculty/Librarian Research Support Fund helped defray the costs of reproductions and copyright acquisitions.

Some of the information found on these pages has been published, albeit in different forms, in the following publications: *Communal Societies: Journal of the Communal Studies Association; Culture, Religion and Dress; Fashion Theory; Feminist Studies;* and *Mid-America*.

Pantaloons & Power

They know very well that their own fashions change
    With each little change of the season,
But Oh! it is "monstrous" and "dreadful" and "strange"
    And "out of all manner of reason,"
    And "out of all manner of reason,"
    If we take a fancy to alter our dress,
    And come out in a style "a la Bloomer."

—"The Bloomers' Complaint" (1851)

Introduction

Who Wears the Pants?

Advocates of pantaloons dress reform promoted a specific outfit for women —a dress with a shortened skirt and pantaloons. This reform had its roots in the antebellum period in the United States and continued in one guise or another until the last decades of the nineteenth century. The basic silhouette of the outfit remained unchanged from the 1820s, even as the details of the design and those who supported the outfit came and went. For a variety of reformers who identified fashion (and its attendant evils) as one of the ills facing nineteenth-century American society, the shortened skirt and pantaloons seemed a practical solution. However, like most nineteenth-century American reforms, the pantaloons dress failed to accomplish its mission or to leave a tradition on which later generations could build.[1]

President Thomas Jefferson opened the century on horseback; President William McKinley closed it riding in an automobile. Tremendous changes—political, social, economic, and cultural—marked the nineteenth century and affected dress reform. Industrialization swept the country; factories and canals grew in the East, while in the South the cotton gin made cotton a more profitable crop. Inventions such as the telegraph, the sewing machine, the camera, the typewriter, the telephone altered the way Americans lived. Several severe economic depressions occurred: the Panic of 1837 began when New York banks stopped redeeming paper money in gold and silver coins; nearly five thousand businesses went bankrupt during the panic of 1857; Black Friday in 1869 hurt both the economy and President Grant's reputation; and in 1893 a run on the U.S. Treasury fed a financial panic. By the 1850s, Jefferson's nation of farmers was becoming a nation of cities—141 cities had populations of eight thousand or more. While urban dwellers grew in number, transcendentalists and others experimented with new and different ways of living, such as the rural community Fruitlands. As the century progressed, people headed west, at first in their Conestoga wagons, later on the transcontinental railroads. Wars contributed to the changing landscape and often dominated the political scene: the War of 1812 encouraged Americans to build their own factories; victory in the Mexican War added five hundred thousand square miles of land to the United States; and more than half a million people died in the Civil War.

Revolutions personal and social cropped up everywhere. Some women struggled for their rights and occasionally made gains: in 1833 Lucretia Mott founded the Female Anti-Slavery Society; in 1839 Mississippi became the first state to grant property rights to married women; and in 1848 the first woman's rights convention met in Seneca Falls, New York. Medical sects such as Thomsonianism and hydropathy appeared and disappeared over the years. The century gave rise to a number of diverse religious alternatives: Joseph Smith founded the Church of Jesus Christ of Latter-day Saints; the Fox sisters claimed to be in contact with the spirit world; and eight hundred members of the Community of True Inspiration created the Amana Colony. In fact, religion changed profoundly in this period, sometimes adding another element to the confusion and at other times helping women and men understand and deal with the world around them. Conflicts north and south, controversy over slavery and Reconstruction, and friction over the destiny of Native Americans also reverberated throughout the country and throughout the century—leaving no one untouched.[2]

Given the people, the events, and the politics, it is not surprising that nineteenth-century America appeared dangerous and disorderly—a place in need of reform. A revealing poem asked, "And need We them! Need what? reforms?" The poet hit on some of the fears of nineteenth-century society—consumption, race suicide, drink, and death—before proclaiming "Reform and live!" Many took up this rallying call.³ The antebellum period especially seemed to be marked by rapid changes and the loss of a sense of identity, control, and values around which to understand life. As one historian described it, the "specter of social breakdown" haunted most antebellum Americans and spurred some to take up the mantle of reform.

Coinciding with the industrial revolution and the revolutionary political ideals and creed of romanticism of the early nineteenth century came a fundamental change in male apparel. The new fashions for men put cut and fit above ornament, color, and display. As cotton, calico, and muslin began to be widely used, fashionable women also modified their dress. Like the men, they abandoned powdered hair and wigs. The social and economic roles of men and women were beginning to diverge more sharply. Women's role was narrowing—becoming associated with domestic responsibilities to the exclusion of all else—and dress began to distinguish gender in more exaggerated ways. "Spheres" that had not existed in the same way in the eighteenth century also redefined men's roles. Sex-distinctive dress emphasized the physical and social differences between women and men and exemplified the prevalent "cult of true womanhood" ideology. The increased sexual stereotyping in dress defended the wearers from their fears about uncertain sexual identity, gender identity, and changes in society.⁴ At the same time, nineteenth-century antifashion rhetoric expanded on earlier criticisms of dress—that clothing should not blur gender distinctions and that immodestly clad women tempted men—and added new critiques with a special emphasis on health issues.

Throughout western history, clothing has defined people's roles, status, and gender. Dress has always been sex distinctive; the aspects that change over time are the specific gender distinctions and the meanings attached to styles of dress. Over the centuries, both formally and informally, gendered clothing has bolstered the institutionalized separation of the sexes. Historian Lois Banner suggests that the exposure of male legs in fourteenth-century Europe (a major change in dress style) coincided with a new resolve to dominate women.⁵ Until the nineteenth century, men's clothes had been as sumptuous and decorative as women's, but as the new century opened, male fashions began to show more sobriety and became progressively more somber and drab. In contrast, women's dress continued to be flamboyant. Most bifurcated garments (that is, garments divided in two, such as pants with two legs) belonged strictly to men, and only women wore skirts. The person who ostensibly had the upper hand, especially in marriage, wore the pantaloons. Bifurcation and lack of ornamentation became associated with masculine dominance in the public sphere and male superiority in general.[6]

When women's pantaloons dress reformers entered the world of antebellum reform, they were seen as participants in the nation's social breakdown rather than as part of the solution.[7] Fashion became the site that these reformers used to challenge long-held beliefs about women, their place in society, their health, and their spiritual well-being. They may not have gotten many women into pantaloons—this was not their true goal anyway—but they did manage to make women and men aware that clothing was not merely a covering for the body. On the contrary, clothing was (and is) a powerful cultural symbol that showed the constraints society applied to women. And at its core, dress reformers' challenge to conventional dress highlighted the role of clothing in the negotiation of power relations between the sexes. For women to take control of their appearance, to distance themselves from a primarily ornamental identity, primarily dependent on men and devoted to pleasing men, was intrinsically transgressive.

A number of women and men took up the banner of dress reform. They redesigned undergarments, condemned corsets and the practice of tight-lacing, sought alternatives to relieve the weight of clothing around women's waists, and questioned the morality of female gowns that revealed too much flesh. To call this dress reform a movement would be misleading, however, in its implication of an organized effort with a single agenda. Although some organizations played a role, it was for the most part the activities and writings of individuals that sustained the variety of nineteenth-century dress reforms.

Some dress reformers advocated that women wear pantaloons, more popularly known as bloomers. They incorporated ideas and suggestions from other dress reforms but concentrated their efforts on encouraging American women to adopt trousers. No other dress reform so shocked the American public. This book focuses on the nuances of that highly charged reform and its resonance in nineteenth-century society.

By the close of the eighteenth century, clear links had developed between how women and men were supposed to look and how they were supposed to lead their lives. Social, cultural, and religious strictures forbade bifurcated garments for women. Some women defied convention, cut their skirts short, abandoned the steel cages of their hoops and corsets, and stepped into trousers. It is difficult to imagine the anguish that must have accompanied the reformers' act—the doubt that plagued women who put on pantaloons for the first time. They wore trousers for a cause higher than their own personal and social ease. And while some women reveled in their new garments and wore them for the rest of their lives, some eventually returned to skirts. Thus it is amazing to learn how long this dress reform lasted.

Owenite followers, health reformers, Oneida Perfectionists, Strangite Mormons, Seventh-day Adventists, mediums, spiritual guides, woman's rights advocates, farmers, and travelers on the overland trail donned pantaloons and filled the rosters of this dress reform. White, middle-class women in widely varied contexts wore pantaloons and risked, at the very least, social ostracism. Many reformers had already transgressed laws and social custom in their choices of lifestyle, and their decision to wear pantaloons appeared to be yet another subversive act. In fact, when women adopted pantaloons in almost any form, they initiated a subtle shift in the perception of male and female power relations: the boundaries between the separate spheres began to crumble or at least to blur a bit—a result that was *not* the goal of most dress reformers. Sociocultural theories of gender identity emphasize the instability and fluidity of the categories "woman" and "man," and the pantaloons reform provides an excellent test case. This was an occasion when the rigidly oppositional classifications of "female" and "male" failed to operate as the prevailing culture expected.

To understand this reform, it is important to know not only the women who wore pantaloons but the reasons they braved public censure and adopted this new style. The simple explanations for this sensation point to the intersecting forces of politics, religion, health reform, and individual eccentricity—motivations that will be examined in depth elsewhere in this study. Although pantaloons were ostensibly a reaction to popular fashionable styles, a more accurate and nuanced interpretation of this dress reform reveals it as both a form of social control and a reaction against such control.

Fashion can be both a process and an end product. On the one hand, fashion is simply "the prevailing mode of dress" in a specific time period. On the other hand, one of the main characteristics of the fashion process is that styles change fairly rapidly.[8] Some wearers described pantaloons designs as a new fashion—just another change in styles. Others argued that reform clothing presented an alternative to both fashion and the fashion process, which commanded women to alter their appearance frequently.

Clothing at once reflects the public and private, being composed of layers—some intimate, some worn precisely to be viewed and interpreted by a social audience. Individuals might choose a garment for personal reasons—it makes them feel good, they like the way it looks, and so on—but to an observer, the same garment may have different meanings. Thus dress acts as a sometimes uncontrollable medium for expressing ideas, desires, and beliefs circulating in society. Further, fashion clearly reflects the changing social construction of human relations and manifests the many discourses about sexuality and power that existed in nineteenth-century society.

This book is organized in a rough chronological order. Chapter 1 examines nineteenth-century reform movements, with an emphasis on antebellum reform, the history of fashion, and the antifashion cultural critique of fashion. Reform and fashion were societal forces acting on all the women in this study. Antifashion allowed women and men an arena in which to express their opinions, but it did not require action. It became the umbrella under which women who did not choose to wear pantaloons could shield themselves and still criticize society.

Chapter 2 considers the first documented instance of women wearing pantaloons—in the Owenite community in New Harmony, Indiana. Though the Owenite women's practice was something of an aberration, their experiences in fact foreshadowed many of the struggles later reformers would face, and presented what would become commonplace among less militant women: pantaloons dress reform as a private practice.

Chapter 3 examines this legacy and how it was played out among other pantaloons dress reformers, including those in John Humphrey Noyes's utopian community, Oneida; Strangite Mormons; water-cure doctors; and some individual women. All created strikingly similar reform garb and seldom wore their costumes in public. The predominance of men who dictated pantaloons dress reform for women also echoes the pattern of New Harmony. Both are distinguished from woman's rights pantaloons dress reform.

Chapter 4 analyzes the turning point in this nineteenth-century dress reform—the moment when woman's rights leaders took it out of private spaces and into the public arena, politicizing reform costumes and linking them to woman's rights.

Chapter 5 returns to several of the dress reformers discussed earlier and evaluates the effect public dress reform had on private health and religious pantaloons dress reform: the National Dress Reform Association formed in the 1850s, and Seventh-day Adventists added dress reform to their agenda in the 1860s.

Chapter 6 focuses on women who struck out on their own. Between 1851 and 1879, a number of individual women tried wearing reform outfits, and their experiences illustrate class issues, urban-rural tensions, geographic influences, work in and outside the home, and sometimes individual eccentricities.

Chapter 7 summarizes the similarities and differences between pantaloons dress reformers. This chapter also explains why the reform ultimately failed in all settings. Despite that failure, however, the costume continued to be worn, usually as a gym outfit, and a variety of dress reforms continued to criticize fashionable dress after 1879.

The epilogue provides a brief history of trousers as an acceptable fashion for women.

A word on vocabulary: the terms denoting bifurcated garments have changed over time. In the interest of historical accuracy, this study employs the language of nineteenth-century women and men. First, "bloomer," a costume named after Amelia Jenks Bloomer, consisted of a short skirt and trousers. The definition later expanded to include gymnasium uniforms and bicycling outfits. "Bloomer" can also refer to the woman wearing the costume. "Breeches" are similar to trousers except that they generally come to just below the knee; as a colloquialism or in humor, breeches are synonymous with trousers. "Pantaloons" is a term applied to garments of different styles in different periods. By the late eighteenth century, the popularity of pantaloons began to supersede that of knee-breeches, and they became indistinguishable from trousers. Any distinction between pantaloons and trousers generally had to do with the fit, pantaloons being the tighter-fitting garment. "Pants" is a U.S. abbreviation for pantaloons, appearing as early as 1840, although it did not gain widespread usage until the twentieth century. "Pantalettes" were loose drawers or trousers with a frill at the bottom of each leg, worn by young girls in the second quarter of the nineteenth century.[9] The terms seem innocuous enough—even quaint, from a late-twentieth-century point of view. But they were the watchwords of both personal and social revolution for the women who tried to redefine an article of clothing. A great deal was at stake for those women and men who used women's clothing as conscious statements of belief.

REFORM!
"The Sibyl—For Reforms" And need
We them! Need what? reforms? Ah, bend
The voice that cries in thunder tones
From weak, consumptive man; the moans
That puny sons in echo give,
To parent sighs: "Reform and live."
"Reform and live!" loud speaks the grave,
"Reform and live!" the drunkard's lave.

—*Sibyl* (September 15, 1856)

Perfecting America

Antebellum Reform, Fashion, and Antifashion

Antebellum Reform

The widespread interest in reform that characterized much of the first half of the nineteenth century may have begun with Presbyterian minister Charles Grandison Finney and the religious revivals that proliferated across the United States in these years. Finney preached individual salvation at a number of revivals, replacing the concept of original sin with the idea of individual selfishness as the source of sin. According to Finney, sin could be rooted out of society. Members of the middle class found this message attractive, in part, because it seemed to reinforce their sense of themselves as earnest, pious, and respectable. Finney's words fell on particularly fertile soil in upstate New York, where "Perfectionism" also garnered a large following.

An 1830s evangelical movement that became particularly popular with New Englanders, Perfectionism taught that the Second Coming of Christ had already occurred and people could aspire to perfection in their earthly lives. Perfectionism—the ability of the individual to conquer sin and avoid temptation—cut across religious and secular beliefs, and the reform impulse arose in part out of the secular interpretation of Perfectionism: ideas for the improvement of American society. Reformers believed that, through education and models of good behavior, America could become a perfect society. The country suffered from numerous social evils that needed to be eradicated—dueling, crime and its punishment, the hours and conditions of work, poverty, and vice. Reformers rallied around various causes and social concerns—observances of the Sabbath, pacifism, temperance, woman's rights, and the abolition of slavery. Using their position as the guardians of morality and virtue in American society, women justified their entrance into reform movements. Via their belief in Perfectionism, middle-class women began to feel a sense of mission and to believe that they should work in society to pursue goals.[1]

In the first half of the nineteenth century, the disappointment with America's failure to live up to the expectations promised by the Revolution and republicanism prompted the establishment of approximately one hundred utopian communities devoted to political, class, gender, and religious concerns. The variety of alternative lifestyles chosen by communitarians suggested that any reform could and should be possible—including a change in dress. Many utopianists wanted to provide an example to mainstream society of a better way of life, in anticipation that the country would learn from them and change accordingly.

The thousands who flocked to utopian communities were inspired by a belief that all social evils and the weaknesses of human nature could be eliminated. The communities varied widely. Some were rooted in a religious faith that Christ's return was imminent and that the righteous should prepare for God's reign by living in accordance with biblical principles. Others were the product of an Enlightenment faith in the shaping influence of environment. Most emphasized economic cooperation; many engaged in radical experiments with diet, clothing, and family and sexual arrangements. Many communities tried to emancipate women from traditional household and child-rearing responsibilities and to elevate them to positions of equality with men.[2]

The same spirit and enthusiasm that encouraged the founding of alternative religions influenced the leaders of health reform and alternative medical practices. The health reform movement represented an effort to bridge the gap between health as a religious concern and the drift toward secular science. Health reform emphasized the individual's relationship to the natural laws established by God.[3] Reformers theorized that if women and men could be taught to live in accordance with the laws of God or nature, they could prevent disease. Dr. Mary Gove Nichols stressed the importance of God in the work of health reform—"the first duty we owe to God, to ourselves, our children, and the world, is to have Health." Some dress reformers saw themselves as missionaries seeking "opportunities to do good," while others severed their attachment to established religions and studied nature's laws as the basis for future societal perfection.[4] Historian Catherine Albanese has identified an ambiguous "nature religion," a system of thought that influenced the secular and the religious. Believers in nature religion questioned whether God "was the author of Disease." Their theory posited that God and nature "were congruent principles, mutual and intertwined in the living of life because they were very close to being identical." By living in harmony with nature, men and women could live the lives God wanted for them.[5]

The notion that God created the human form in his divine image led some health and dress reformers to argue that the body must be clothed in such a manner as to keep it in its "natural" state.[6] One dress reformer, inspired by a revelation, recognized that "the day has dawned, when many are seeing that the laws of Health come from God; the laws of Fashion from Paris milliners."[7] While they sought the body God wanted them to have, many health and religious reformers also drew on literature that blamed the Fall on Eve (woman) and linked sin, body, woman, and clothing. Both dress reformers and antifashionists would use this logic in their campaigns to change female dress.

A wide assortment of Americans took up the call and exhorted their fellow citizens along the path of health. "Nutritional moralist" Sylvester Graham traveled the country, speaking out against red meat, fats, salt, sweets, and white bread. He claimed these "sinful" substances caused sexual excess, disease, and insanity. Instead, he encouraged tooth brushing, frequent baths, looser clothing, and a vegetarian diet.[8] Health reformers insisted that individual women and men had to be held accountable and responsible for their own health. The general public did not sanction most of the more extreme ideas, but often incorporated the more moderate suggestions into their daily routines. Reformers also culled the most appealing approaches from the many health theories in vogue. Susan B. Anthony, for example, ate a simple diet, believed in breathing plenty of fresh air—always sleeping with a wide-open window—and used fresh water freely, starting each morning with a cold sponge bath.[9] The Strangite Mormons practiced their own variation on health reform, which prohibited alcohol, narcotics, too-small shoes, tight boots, and cinched waists.[10] Oneida Perfectionists boasted about the healthy lives they lived, but credited the community's relative freedom from disease to their spirituality rather than their healthful lifestyle, which included a balanced diet, exercise, and hygiene.[11]

Thomsonianism, Eclecticism, homeopathy, hydropathy, and phrenology could be counted among the most popular of the various medical alternatives introduced. The sects could be distinguished from one another by their therapeutics, degrees of professional education, methods of recruiting patients, relative appeal in rural or urban areas, and the class of their supporters. Yet their medical or health philosophies contained common elements even if their individual therapeutic practices differed. Most rejected "regular" medical practices and stressed hygienic principles. Many agreed on nature's ability to aid in the curing of disease, criticized the kinds and amounts of drugs used by regular doctors, stressed healthful living as a prerequisite for a strong physical constitution, and, in some instances, offered women a role as practitioners.[12]

The perception that many nineteenth-century women suffered from ill health reflects the important position women held in the health reform movement as objects of concern. Historians have grappled with the question of whether or not women were as sick as the numerous writings of health reformers, doctors, and others indicated.[13] It has been suggested that the assumption that women were unhealthy may have been self-perpetuating. Regardless of the extent of women's illnesses, health reform's stress on the individual's ability to prevent disease provided women with some measure of autonomy and control over their bodies. Health reform could be liberating for women, but it also made good health a measure of women's "respectability and self-worth."[14] As caregivers and maintainers of health, women became responsible for not only their own physical well-being, but that of their families and, indirectly, for society's well-being. The domestic sphere rose in importance as reformers attempted to standardize the household arts. At the same time, this focus on the home as the center for good health reinforced ideas about women and their place in society. This ambiguity is apparent in several places: health reform stressed self-control as the key to good health, yet made women monitor the health of others; it reinforced the emerging code of "true womanhood" as well as proposing alternatives to it; finally, health reformers attempted to guide women on the way to good health, but blamed them if they fell ill. Reformers held women accountable for many of their ailments, charging that women did not get enough exercise, ate the wrong foods, wore inappropriate clothing, and loved fashion too much. Conflicting notions about women and their role were not unique to health reform, however.

As an element in the design for better living, dress reform became an important part of many health reformers' agendas. Hydropathic thought replicated the larger health reform movement's message, and the message of many religions, with its emphasis on self-denial and self-control. The medical practice of hydropathy or water cure (an "irregular" sect) heralded the beneficent effects of pure water.[15] The hydropathic therapeutic system applied cold water (in the form of showers, baths, and compresses) to different parts of the body. Through personal examples of "right living," hydropathists expected to contribute to the common good. Dress reform fit into the ideology of water cure, and the isolated nature of hydropathic spas made them perfect environments in which to nurture "private" dress reform. Hydropathists encouraged women to restructure their place in society, and saw dress reform as a basis for arguing for new freedoms for women. Like many other antebellum reformers, hydropathists shared a belief that greater societal reformation would come through personal change.

Dress reform and an expanded role for women, closely resembling a domestic feminism, were carried into the public arena, although not necessarily into the formal male political sphere. The most important way the hydropathists aided dress reform was in their key role in the formation and continuation of one of the few formal dress reform organizations in the mid-nineteenth-century United States—the National Dress Reform Association.

While the ideal of good health managed to bridge some of the ideological differences among dress reformers, different definitions of what constituted a healthy woman and how a woman was to achieve good health prevented the reformers from joining forces and creating a mass dress reform organization. Social and intellectual historian Martha H. Verbrugge has argued that "definitions of health carried far more than biological information," and that they, too, were culturally constructed.[16] The diversity of ideas that dress reformers had about health and medical therapeutics reflected the larger discussion of health issues taking place in antebellum society.

The doctrine of good health and antebellum religious fervor came together in the Seventh-day Adventist Church. The roots of Seventh-day Adventism cannot be found in health reform, nor did health reform occupy a central place among the Adventists before the 1860s. The Seventh-day Adventists grew out of a faction of the Millerite movement of the early 1840s. When the Second Coming of Christ failed to occur in 1843, many Millerites returned to their former churches. Shortly after the "Great Disappointment," sickly seventeen-year-old Ellen Gould Harmon reported having ecstatic visions. In 1846 she married James White, a young Adventist preacher, who became her mentor as well as her husband. Ellen Gould White's visions influenced the Seventh-day Adventist Church, which she and James White organized.[17]

By the late 1850s, the institutionalization of the religion distinguished the Adventists as a separate religious community. First, members accepted Ellen Gould White's prophetic and authoritative role and her position as a leader in the church.[18] Second, Adventists observed the seventh-day (Saturday) Sabbath and distrusted evolutionists, Catholics, labor unionists, and evangelical Christians who observed Sundays. In the early 1860s, the Seventh-day Adventists embraced complementary reforms, as did many of their secular antebellum reform cousins. Ellen Gould White encouraged members to join temperance organizations and experiment with vegetarianism and water cures, and she discouraged the use of tobacco, tea, and coffee. The ideas of health reformers Sylvester Graham, L. B. Coles, and James Caleb Jackson influenced the Church, as did White's June 1863 vision, which elevated healthful living to a moral obligation. The vision impressed on her the intimate relationship between physical and mental health and the maintenance of one's body as a sacred duty.[19]

The religious experiences of the Second Great Awakening, the concept of the cult of true womanhood (also known as the cult of domesticity), and the desire to create a "Christian nation" motivated some women to enter reform organizations and, later, the woman's rights movement. This ideology dictated that true women should be the moral guardians of the family, because they were spiritually pure and, therefore, closer to God. Women remained pure and gained their own sphere because they stayed away from the degrading environment of the outside world. Men, who were by necessity exposed to the outside world and wise in its ways, became women's protectors. Although women's purity argued for strict seclusion from the corruptive elements of the outside world, that very corruption obligated women to intervene in the male-run world for the good of their men, the community, the nation, and humankind. Thus, the more women accepted the tenets of the cult of true womanhood, the more they were forced to step outside them.[20]

A public debate over the proper role of women in the antislavery movement, especially their right to lecture to audiences composed of both sexes, led to the first organized movement for woman's rights. In 1840, Lucretia Mott and Elizabeth Cady Stanton traveled to England to attend the World Anti-Slavery Convention. When they arrived, they learned that women would not be allowed to participate. Both were upset and frustrated. Writing over the next few years, Mott and Stanton recognized that women had to fight for their own rights, and they decided to host a gathering of sympathetic activists to explore the status of women in society and develop the issue of woman's rights. About three hundred women and forty men attended the first convention at Seneca Falls in 1848. Stanton read a Declaration of Sentiments, modeled after the Declaration of Independence, that began, "We hold these truths to be self-evident: that all men and women are created equal."[21] During the two days of meetings, the convention adopted and passed unanimously twelve resolutions—except the ninth, which demanded for women the right to vote. Many delegates worried that people would think it ridiculous. It is not surprising that the health crusade also converged with woman's rights, although it never became central to the campaign for rights.[22]

The world of antebellum reformers was a small one; the paths of some reformers crossed often. Susan B. Anthony did not follow Sylvester Graham's vegetarian regime strictly, but knew of it and ate little meat, following a simple diet of fruits, vegetables, and grains. She used some hydropathic cleansing methods and seldom called a doctor. When necessary, Anthony preferred a woman schooled in homeopathy.[23] The Oneida Community members were not Grahamites either, although they too ate an abundance of fruits and grains and little meat.[24] Lucy Stone dined on a version of the Graham health diet, and the Grimké sisters often stayed at vegetarian boardinghouses when on the lecture circuit.[25] Seventh-day Adventists Ellen Gould White and James White visited hydropathist James C. Jackson; later, Jackson became involved with their health empire.[26] Robert Dale Owen, son of New Harmony founder Robert Owen, was Jackson's patient; abolitionist, reformer, and politician Gerrit Smith also counted Jackson a good friend.[27] Although John Humphrey Noyes never met Robert Owen, he did read Owen's works. Seventh-day Adventist newspapers reprinted Smith's essays; his daughter, Elizabeth Smith Miller, and his cousin, Elizabeth Cady Stanton, added another connection. Helen C. Noyes (and probably John

Humphrey Noyes) was acquainted with Mrs. Gerrit Smith and Elizabeth Smith.[28] And yet, although nineteenth-century reformers often knew one another and had some causes in common, dress reform would not be one.

The public figures or leaders in the dress reform cause shared many of the characteristics that marked their contemporaries who led other antebellum reform movements, chief among these being their involvement in more than one reform. As with many antebellum reforms, in the beginning, the leaders of dress reform tended to be white, middle-class, from the Northeast, and male. The followers of dress reform were a more diverse collection of women and men than the leaders; this tended to be true of other antebellum reform movements as well. Historian Anne Firor Scott points out that members of moral reform groups, temperance societies, and abolition organizations "were unwilling to join the women's rights movement." Many dress reformers shared this reluctance.[29]

Some dress reform groups refused to be identified not only with the woman's rights movement but with other dress reformers as well. The two reforms with which pantaloons dress reformers did commonly identify were health reform and religious alternatives. Within these two large categories, different reformers stressed one religious ideology over another or one aspect of health reform over another. Thus, even within the context of larger reforms, dress reformers could not always find points of agreement.

When pantaloons dress reformers argued for a change in women's dress based on health, comfort, convenience, rights, or religion, they addressed issues that did not greatly concern women devoted to fashionable dress. Such reformers were in many ways women ahead of their time—or women out of touch with their time—and failed to recognize that the majority of women in the United States did not consider fashion or their status oppressive. Still, fashion became the site that these reformers used to challenge long-held beliefs about women, their place in society, their health, and their spiritual well-being. They may not have succeeded in getting most women into pantaloons—this was not their goal anyway—but they did manage to make women and men aware that clothing was not merely a covering for the body but a cultural symbol that showed the constraints applied to women. And at its core, pantaloons dress reformers' challenge to conventional dress highlighted the role of clothing in the negotiation of power relations between the sexes. For women to take control of their appearance, to distance themselves from an identity as primarily ornamental, primarily dependent on and devoted to pleasing men, was intrinsically transgressive.

Pantaloons dress reform could be empowering for women, but the opportunities and choices it offered women could also be self-limiting. Two principles that characterized the ideology of pantaloons dress reform (and other antebellum reform movements)—self-denial and self-control—emphasized the individual's ability to bring about societal change through personal example or one's own labor. In a deeply personal but highly visible way, dress reformers wanted to destroy fashion's hold, open up economic opportunities for women, and improve female health. Yet, at the same time, most dress reformers did not want women to seize male privileges and rights. Of course, in trying to change how they looked, women were in fact attempting to seize such a privilege or right. This ambivalence points to both the empowerment and the powerlessness of women—a quandary of dress reform in all of its permutations.

Nineteenth-Century Fashion

Beliefs about how men and women should look were part of a powerful system of values about appropriate female and male behavior. Thus dress reform had less to do with fashionable clothing and more to do with perceptions about woman's place in society, who would determine that place, and how it would be maintained. Dress reformers saw evidence of this value system in the sex-distinctive dress of the U.S. population. Around 1827, fashion plates and descriptions of costumes began to appear in a variety of magazines.[30] Illustrations tended to emphasize elaborate extremes that attracted attention and drew subscribers, and for women far from urban centers, fashion publications were valuable. The absence of copyright laws in America until the end of the nineteenth century allowed American magazines freely to reprint French fashion plates. The extreme, elaborate styles shown in the plates could not be worn by the average, busy, middle-class woman for everyday wear; she usually wore a simplification of the styles displayed in magazines.[31]

It is worth noting that styles become fashionable and unfashionable so unobtrusively that it is often difficult to determine the height of a style and when it begins to fade away. The period known as the "Directoire and Empire" lasted from about 1790 until 1815. After the French Revolution, a great change in European and U.S. costume seemed to take place. However, many of the modifications had already begun to occur prior to 1790. Most women had given up panniers (a stiff petticoat or underproper) in the 1780s, simple cotton fabrics gained popularity, and attention was paid to the "simplicity" of children's clothes as a possibility for adult clothing designs. This early look at children's dress for ideas on adult apparel would reappear in the context of dress reform. At the close of the Revolution, however, women's clothing represented a devotion to the new republican-democratic order and turned to classical Greece for inspiration. In France, the more extreme followers of the new styles discarded their undergarments and exhibited a new form of freedom, one that sympathizers in the United States did not take up. By 1804, the corset had returned, as did the desire to wear more concealing clothing. According to costume historian Douglas A. Russell, this period marked the break from aristocratic court styles and the beginning of middle-class styles.[32]

The period from 1815 to 1840 is usually deemed the "Romantic" period; the distinguishing features of fashionable dress included full skirts worn short enough to allow ankles and feet to show, narrow waists emphasized by large belts, light colors, and immense balloon sleeves for shoulder emphasis. Hair might be dressed high in a "giraffe" and covered by an exaggerated and ornate hat. The waistline remained high until about 1836, when it returned to a "natural" level. Rumors about tight-lacing began in this period, although corsets in the Romantic era differed little from earlier ones—not until the end of the 1840s did boning become a regular feature of corsets.[33] Extremes continued to mark the ideals of woman's appearance in the late twenties and early thirties; large, exaggerated hats and sleeves complemented tiny feet and hands.

The prevalence of foreign "exotic" elements (often ambiguously referred to as Middle Eastern) in nineteenth-century U.S. fashionable dress was a way of adding a "thrill," something different to familiar fashions, and followed a trend already established in England and France.[34] Long shawls, especially "genuine India cachemire" shawls, as well as imitations, frequently accessorized fashionable gowns in the 1830s and 1840s and proved popular among Western women, although the expense of real cashmere shawls often meant that only the richest Americans could afford to purchase them. Earlier in the century, Dolly Madison had popularized the turban as fashionable headwear for women in the United States.[35] Turbans of the "Turkish form" and the familiarity of other articles of Middle, Near, and Far Eastern apparel may have laid the groundwork for the introduction of "Turkish trousers," first as a masquerade costume, later as a reform garment.

By the 1840s, women's clothing had changed. First the waist came down; then the sleeve fullness slipped to the elbows and finally disappeared altogether. By 1842 skirts, supported by very full crinolines, had grown even larger than in the late 1830s. Concern with a woman's physical condition and appearance, as well as her clothing, entered the fashion dialogue with greater frequency. Harriet Beecher Stowe remarked, "when we see a woman made as a woman ought to be, she strikes us as a monster." Stowe further noted that rounded women often "make secret enquiries into reducing diet[s], and . . . cling desperately to the strongest corset."[36] The new fashionable ideal stressed women's delicacy and fragility, not a strong, healthy body.[37]

During the 1840s, some of the more extreme aspects of women's fashions (large hats and full sleeves) disappeared, and contemporary social commentator John Murray extolled the virtues of women's fashionable dress. "Female attire of the present day," wrote Murray in 1847, allowed women to "dress quickly, walk nimbly, eat plentifully, stoop easily, loll gracefully; and, in short, perform all the duties of life."[38] Darker colors and fuller skirts suggested modesty, respectability, and sobriety. (Few of Murray's peers would have agreed with his interpretation of female attire. His evaluation implied that female clothing satisfied the wearer and served a utilitarian purpose.) Compared to the fashions of the Romantic period, the dresses worn by women and featured in fashion plates in the 1840s did appear "simpler." If the Panic of 1837 and the depression that stretched from 1839 to 1843 are taken into account, it seems logical that fashions of the 1840s would be plainer and more modest. While it is possible that the depression contributed to what Murray referred to as the "simplicity" of women's clothing in the 1840s, it is not very likely. Theorizing that the depression simplified women's fashions becomes more problematic when one takes into account the increased amount of fabric required for a dress in the 1840s.[39] If expense proved to be a problem, women sometimes used the fabric from older dresses or remade them to keep up with the latest styles as much as possible. The availability of certain materials may have favored one style over another, but this was not the only factor involved in the fashion process.[40] Doubtless the depression did influence fashion and who bought clothing, but it cannot be assigned a direct cause-effect relationship in the design of fashionable dress. A reasonable solution might be to keep the cost of clothing down by simplifying the styles, yet fashion is rarely discussed as a "reasonable" phenomenon, following the logic of supply and demand.[41] Whatever the cause, women's dress in the 1840s appeared to many contemporary observers to be simpler and more demure than in the previous decade. Clothing in the forties was designed to make women look as small as possible, and the "demure line" was repeated in the simplicity of trimmings or absence of trimmings on skirts that continued to grow wider.[42] However, by the end of the decade, the invention of the sewing machine led to an increase in skirt ornamentation.[43] The moderate bell-shaped skirts again hung down to the ground, and feet, barely visible, poked out from beneath six or seven petticoats. According to costume historian James Laver, "there never was a period when women . . . were more completely covered up."[44] Shoes had no heels, dresses had tight sleeves that restricted arm movements, and poke bonnets, which grew increasingly smaller in the 1850s and 1860s, adorned "demurely parted hair."[45]

Not much time passed before the "feminine" fashions of the forties gave way to the new styles of the 1850s. The basic silhouette remained the same, but gowns became more ornamental in the "age of the crinoline" (approximately 1850 to 1870). At its most extreme, rows of ribbons, ruching, fringes, or flowers trimmed fashionable skirts. These outrageous skirts could be supported by as many as seven starched petticoats fastened at the waist, and rolls of horsehair stiffening in the lining. The clothing worn by women in the 1850s seemed to emphasize femininity and female powerlessness. Most women did not make this connection, nor did they voice complaints about stylish fashions. One could easily assume, however, that this pinnacle of absurdity and discomfort inspired some adverse response. Some women complained about the sheer number of layers of fabric (up to twelve or more) wrapped around a woman's waist, if one included shifts, corsets, petticoats, crinolines, skirt bands, belts, and jackets. Without corsets helping to support the torso, women would have had a terrible time supporting the weight, sometimes as much as twenty-five to thirty-five yards of cloth just in the skirts without the petticoats.[46] In the 1840s, some women and men had begun to connect female dress with woman's lower position in society, but heedless of any undercurrents of discontent, fashion continued to evolve.

In 1856, the introduction of the crinoline relieved many women from the weighty burden of petticoats and outer skirts. The first crinoline consisted of gauzelike fabric that could be stiffened by starch. Then came "a 'cage' petticoat made of steel wires," or hoops. As the number of petticoats

Juvenile Fashions for September.

Although ostensibly a fashion plate for juvenile clothing, this illustration also allows a glimpse at female fashions. It is worth noting the similarity between the girls' and boys' clothing. It is difficult to distinguish the sex of the children based on their clothing alone. A nineteenth-century audience would have looked at the toys for clues to the sex of the children. *Godey's Lady's Book and Magazine* (September 1850).

necessary to support the more decorative outer skirt decreased, the width of the skirt increased.[47] The skirt "either just cleared the floor or actually touched it" and rendered a woman's feet almost invisible. The swaying crinoline, however, often offered a glimpse with an accidental flip of the hoop. More than just feet could be exposed in such instances; legs and underwear might also be seen, and evidence suggests that women commonly wore a shift or a shift and petticoat under the hoops in an effort to keep the skirt from swinging too much.[48] By the 1850s, the underwear worn beneath the crinoline consisted of "drawers," bifurcated garments "drawn" or pulled on.[49] Sloping shoulders, a small waist, and curves characterized "the upper part of the silhouette which, all together, resembled a pyramid or a spinning-top upside down." Beneath the bodice, a corset molded the body to create the popular curvy shape that sat atop the full skirts.[50] During this period bodice styles varied enormously in every detail. Gowns could be made in one or two pieces. A skirt and bodice made separately could allow a woman to wear more than one bodice with a single skirt, perhaps one for day and one for evening wear. Before the Civil War ended, the metamorphosis of the crinoline into the bustle had begun, and by 1868 the transformation of the silhouette was complete: a close-fitting dress with a long skirt looped up over a relatively tight underskirt had replaced the immense bell-shaped skirts.[51]

Young children's clothing appeared the most androgynous of all the gendered clothing in the nineteenth century. Toddler girls and boys wore short, loose-fitting dresses until about two or three years of age. Until five or six, some children wore dresses or suits with short skirts. Both girls' and boys' skirted styles bore a strong resemblance to women's dress of the period, usually reflecting current fashions in sleeve, neckline, and so on. However, boys did not dress *exactly* like girls.[52] While the basic silhouette remained the same for both sexes, descriptions of children's clothing in fashion magazines made it clear that subtle differences between female and male styles existed.[53]

Although fashion seemed to impose major changes in women's dress throughout the nineteenth century, after 1840 it dictated only subtle alterations in men's clothing styles.[54] By the 1840s, most adult men had rejected colors and ornaments in their clothing, except for vests and neckties, preferring neutrality and austerity. In addition, various types of ornamentation had become feminized and were no longer considered acceptable for men, i.e., the connotations of "Dandy," or even "Beau Brummel." During this decade, the institutionalization of the plain, dark, somber three-piece suit for men was nearly complete. The transition had been going on for quite some time (some date the origins back to the Puritans), but by the 1850s the ensemble had been established as respectable middle-class men's wear.[55] The "feminization of fashion" followed the larger societal trend toward separate spheres and preserved gender-specific and separate fashions. Men gave up their claims to ornamentation, colors, and lace, and adopted a more uniform style of dress, thereby making fashion and all of its accoutrements the sole province of women. The standardization of male clothing in the 1840s appeared to improve on earlier styles, and these changes could be interpreted as dress reform on a massive, informal scale. However, the same was not true of women's clothing. The conservative styles of male clothing reflected the masculine ideal of "solid integrity and economic reliability." Feminine fashions highlighted the role of woman as an object of beauty and a dependent.[56] Few women would have defied the "almost omnipotent" "goddess," fashion, and her "exacting . . . demands." Woman became "simply the butterfly of fashion."[57]

Two significant developments in the 1850s had less to do with changes in style and more to do with the economics of clothing sales and production. The emergence of haute couture (high fashion or a "house" of fashion) changed how women's dresses were sold, and technical innovations lowered the prices of many luxury fabrics. Individual dressmakers had serviced the needs of elite women prior to the establishment of Charles Frederick Worth's first "house" of fashion in France in 1858. Worth's reputation quickly became international; Edith Wharton wrote that every wealthy American lady included a stop at Worth's *Maison* when on the Grand Tour. Her trunk filled with Worth gowns, the society dame led the new season when she returned home. Worth had changed how clothing was marketed. Women no longer visited dressmaking workrooms; instead, they made appointments at beautifully furnished, luxurious salons. Worth's contribution to the world of fashion should not be underestimated. He wielded a great deal of power over female fashionable apparel—and in the realm of women's pantaloons dress reform, men would also exercise considerable control. Fashion houses were clearly for the elite; the technical innovations in the production of textiles and finished garments also made a larger variety of fabrics and clothing available to "ordinary people." The fashions of the 1850s strengthened separate gender roles; an arena of fashion appeared exclusively for the wealthy; and industrialization made possible the replication of haute couture styles for middle-class women.[58] These factors contributed to the unanticipated arrival of dress reform.

Antifashion

Antifashion, which used the authority of clergy, medical practitioners, and journalists to disseminate criticism of dress, was not a nineteenth-century phenomenon. It could be traced back, without too much exaggeration, to the first fig leaf.[59] It did, however, take on unique nineteenth-century characteristics. Just as changes in American society seemed to indicate disorder, almost every change in fashionable dress met with disapproval and sometimes fear. Accounts in newspapers, periodicals, medical journals, and popular fiction indicated that a vocal contingent of the public objected to fashion: condemning the crinoline as "indecent"; opposing the skirt's "dirt, danger, [and] discomfort"; abhorring tight-lacing; and complaining about extravagant trimmings.[60]

The amount of attention given to apparel may seem curious at first, but in Western culture dress has seldom been a mere veil covering and protecting the body. Woman's outward appearance—her clothed body—had ties to gender and moral character. If a woman, through her apparel, transgressed gender lines (e.g., wore a "male" garment), she constituted a threat to the "natural" order and produced near-hysterical reactions. Although violating rules of gender-appropriate clothing produced the most agitated responses, issues of immorality and dress were the more immediate concerns of nineteenth-century antifashionists. In the nineteenth century, a "modestly" dressed woman expressed harmony, order, and self-sacrifice (it is no accident that these could be counted among the republican virtues), and "immodest" dress signified self-indulgence, disorder, and wastefulness (those elements that seemed to be corrupting society). If fashion's role was to define clearly the standards and rules of beauty and true womanhood, then antifashionists were to insure that women did not stray from these standards.

On the surface, women had a simple task: dress modestly, yet fashionably. The task would have been simple, if fashion had clearly followed the rules it defined. Alas, numerous contradictions and ambiguities permeated fashion discourse. To present the image of the "true woman," the "real" woman needed corsets, padding, and makeup; this was fashion's paradox—a woman achieved "true womanhood" by disguising herself. Fashion magazines and aesthetic standards of beauty encouraged women to mold their bodies, paint their faces, and groom their hair in the latest styles and, at the same time, openly criticized them for their observance of these rituals. Historian Karen Halttunen summed up a common midcentury perception of fashion as an entity that undermined all moral self-improvement. In a variation on this issue she wrote about the "mask" of antebellum woman's fashions that sought to ameliorate the "hypocrisy" of American society. The irony, Halttunen argued, was that the fashions, which attempted to counteract societal hypocrisy, actually contributed to it. Even as a woman assumed "simplified" fashions, she took on the role of a fashionable woman who was by definition insincere and a woman who had successfully learned how to manipulate clothing for her own ends. Thus, fashion and its role in deception added to the fear and distrust circulating through middle-class society.[61]

Louisa May Alcott's short story "Behind a Mask" played to the theme of fashion and deceit, and the alternate title, "A Woman's Power," expressed the genuine fear that lay behind much antifashion rhetoric. The antagonist entered Alcott's tale as a new governess in an English country estate. The members of the family "all felt a touch of pity" for the young "pale-faced girl in her plain black dress, with no ornament but a little silver cross at her throat." The young woman clearly did not follow fashionable dictates, nor did she try to do the unpardonable and imitate the styles of her "betters"; thus she endeared herself to her employers. However, alone in her room, the governess removed "the long abundant braids from her head, wiped the pink from her face, took out several pearly teeth, and … appeared herself indeed, a haggard, worn, and moody woman of thirty at least."[62] A mask of innocence effectively hid a scheming woman who fooled a "respectable" middle-class family.

During the Civil War, the Grand League and Covenant of the Ladies resolved to "impress upon others how *unwomanly* it [was] to make outward display a paramount subject of thought," especially while the nation fought a bloody rebellion.[63] Denying their desire for clothing gave northern women the opportunity to prove their loyalty and support for the soldiers. Women who paid attention to fashion spent time thinking about themselves—a trait deemed unacceptable and narcissistic—yet women were expected to present a particular "picture" of womanhood. They were expected to engage in a balancing act, taking an interest in fashion to maintain their looks, without becoming too interested in the process.

As the nineteenth century advanced, a discourse of health began to replace earlier arguments about social graces when attacks on fashion were made. The argument that fashion harmed women's physical well-being emphasized deleterious effects on their reproductive organs. This preoccupation with women's dress and reproductive capacity reflected a focus on women as bodies in need of control and care. In a period of medical history when available knowledge failed to explain the causes of disease, fashionable dress presented one "logical" source for disorders unique to women.[64] Dr. Atlee, president of the Pennsylvania Medical Society, expressed a concern over the connection between apparel and women's ill

health. Women wearing long skirts (or "caricature[s] on nature," as he liked
to call them) could be compared to "pea-fowls strutting the streets and taking a scavenger-like promenade, gathering filth and exhausting strength."[65]
Regular physicians were not the only ones to accuse of women of destroy-
ing their health with their dress. Hydropathist James C. Jackson maintained
that a woman could not wear long skirts and keep "her uterus [in] its proper
place" because the "direct and primary effect" of long skirts deranged and
displaced the uterus, which induced "diseased conditions."[66] He further
charged that "wearing dresses as most women do, tight about their waists,
is a powerfully provoking cause of a class of diseases known in polite phrase
as FEMALE AILMENTS," otherwise known, less politely, as "uterine difficulties."[67] Health reformer and exercise advocate Dio Lewis scorned the popular beauty standard that favored a "fragile, pale young woman with a lisp"
over "one in blooming health."[68]

The list of crimes perpetrated by fashionable dresses continued to fill
medical journals, popular magazines, daily newspapers, and pamphlets.
Some detractors noted that cumbersome long frocks made locomotion uncomfortable and forced women into sedentary positions and lifestyles. Others recorded instances when the length of a woman's gowns hindered her
free movement, forcing her to avoid carrying heavy or awkward objects for
fear of becoming entangled in her skirts. Doctors mentioned that when
women actually did move, their long heavy skirts forced them to walk awk-
wardly, using upper leg muscles rather than their knees. An argument
against braies centuries earlier resurfaced—friction within the pelvic cav-
ity might result from an awkward gait and cause sexual-function diseases
or sexual stimulation.[69] Mental illness was also connected to fashionable
dress—the practice of frequently changing their outfits supposedly rendered women mentally unstable. A love of fashion could also be diagnosed
an illness. And just as a fallen uterus, shortness of breath, or pinched nerves
had to be cured, so too did the desire for new clothing. The urge to rid
women of their passion for fashion implied that there was something wrong
with women's enjoyment of dress. In 1869 the *Chicago Post* compared "fashionable women" to "savage nations that only hunt, fish, and make war, and
eat their enemies, and sometimes one another" because both "took to trinkets and ornaments." The *Post* further wondered what "savage," fashionable women might do with the vote.[70] Not only did fashion stand accused
of making women sick, but contemporary commentators and modern historians agree that it made illness, delicacy, and fragility fashionable.[71]

Health reformers concentrated their attacks on "harmful" aspects of fashionable dress and paid less attention to the aesthetics that made looking sick fashionable. According to them, fashionable dress led to a lower birthrate and, ultimately, the end of the white middle class. Fashion made women who managed to produce children into poor mothers who raised physically and mentally diseased descendants. Long skirts and tight bodices, insisted Dr. G. S. Whitman, "have done more, and are yet doing more, to deteriorate our race, than any one thing of which we are guilty as a nation." The belief that fashionable gowns made white women "unstable and incapable of" bearing and rearing healthy children encouraged critics to speak out forcefully against female dress.[72] No article of women's clothing was free from criticism. Wearing tight dresses; "whalebones, excess of apparel around the hips, and too little on the chest and shoulders"; and crinolines could cause "a vast number of chills, the consequences of which [were] almost always mortal." "Died of thin shoes" was carved on at least one headstone. The opinion that "fashion kills women" seemed valid.[73]

Historians have often fallen into the trap of agreeing with contemporary nineteenth-century doctors and antifashionists about the health consequences of dressing fashionably. Modern historians, however, have tended to concentrate on the corset. In the middle decades of the nineteenth century, despite prevalent antifashion rhetoric about tight-lacing, at least one group of dress reformers actually put most of their efforts into outer garments. Only in the 1870s did most dress reformers focus on undergarments, primarily corsets. Late-nineteenth-century dress reformers took up the cause of tight-lacing with a vengeance, and it is these reformers who have captured the attention of modern historians. Sociologist Jennifer Craik and historian Valerie Steele have done an excellent job of explaining the "corset controversy"—which only superficially concerns this study.[74] The amount of time historians have devoted to the corset leaves the impression that the corset constituted the most important issue for dress reformers. However, although pantaloons-wearing dress reformers also advised women to take off their corsets, they saw corsets as only one component of unhealthy dress. Antifashionists spent more time on the issue of tight-lacing than pantaloons dress reformers did, but they too did not become "single-minded" until later in the nineteenth century. Antifashionist arguments reflected many of the types of reform that influenced pantaloons dress reform. Health preoccupied antifashion discourse, and religious ideals also consumed a great deal of attention.

Finery in general had been considered a vice in many Christian religions; however, modesty in *male* apparel was seen as a duty for women because Eve introduced sin into the world. Just as social conventions expected women to have a certain "look" without artifice, theology charged women with being pure and appearing pure. Thus women had to clothe their bodies in such a way as to suggest modesty. If women failed to dress modestly they bore responsibility for two sins—their own failure to dress according to God's laws and the sin of sexually arousing men through immodest dress. The cult of domesticity may have lauded women's moral superiority, but in the case of fashion, women who willingly exposed their bodies and excited men also proclaimed their inferiority. The complaints of woman's rights activists about fashion mirrored society's distrust of fashion, but the feminists stressed the sexism of fashion. Elizabeth Cady Stanton agreed with others that "every part of a woman's dress has been faithfully conned from some French courtesan" and was "a direct and powerful appeal to [man's] passional nature."[75] The "fallen woman" also symbolized the dependence of all women on men, and the prostitute's power to influence fashion degraded all women by association.[76]

Once again, the antifashion literature suggested that women could never get it right. Clergy, physicians, and even woman's rights activists seemed to agree. "Shamefully indecent" hoops and long skirts "excited" men, charged a writer to the *Revolution,* adding that hoops were "invented to conceal pregnancy, and no virtuous woman ought to wear them."[77] Every time a woman lifted her skirts off the ground in order to move about, her exposed legs elicited leers and comments from men.[78] For centuries, critics had argued that women raising long skirts and exposing limbs captivated men—this argument was not new in the nineteenth century. In spite of the history against them, women continued to wear long skirts into the twentieth century. Meanwhile, leading hydropathist Dr. R. T. Trall disapproved of the gender distinctiveness of fashionable dress because it eroded female modesty. Trall reasoned that since the dress of women differed dramatically from that worn by men, men could never forget that they were with women. "The low-dressed neck, the bare arms, the wide expanse of crinoline, the trailing skirt, the lace-edged petticoat, the fanciful shoe, and the fantastic bonnet—do they suggest, and they suggest, were they ever intended to suggest, any idea to a man except that the wearer is of the opposite sex?"[79] Thus the "damned if you do, damned if you don't theme" continued—fashionable dress was tied directly to sensuality and deliberate attempts to control men through suggestive apparel. Angelina Merritt succinctly summed up attitudes about women and dress: "devotion to fashions" rendered women "unworthy of their immortal natures."[80]

Although antifashion commentators focused on the clothing choices of middle- and upper-class women, they commented on the morality of working-class women as well. Linus P. Brockett envisioned a scenario in which working women who loved fashion would discover that they could make more money with "a single smile" than by working for a month. Working women's love for clothing would drive them to a life of sin: eventually, the smile would lead to greater and greater transgressions and before she knew it, the young working woman who loved "finery and ease" would find herself a victim of the worst kind.[81] Fashion's high price tag was yet another reason detractors found to denounce it. Cost sharpened the distinction between the social classes. Although the styles worn by upper-, middle-, and working-class women did not differ significantly, the cut and fabrics they used did. Before the advent of mass production, wealthier women had skilled dressmakers make their clothing. Because working women could not afford this luxury, their clothing did not fit in the same way, nor did their clothes reflect the subtle changes in cut that occurred from year to year. Few women of any class possessed the skill to cut and fit stylish dresses. The well-made dress became a sign of class status. Working-class women also wore inferior or more durable fabrics, and to nineteenth-century society these subtle distinctions in dress were clearly visible.[82] Another underlying argument related to the expense of clothing seemed inherently contradictory: on the one hand, clothing could have a leveling effect—by spending enough money a woman could look like she belonged to a certain class. On the other hand, the cost of dress could further divide the classes by placing high fashion out of the reach of all but the very wealthy.[83] Some observers suspected that working women's desire to dress above their station had more to do with wanting to marry up the social scale than it did with loving fashion.[84] It is not clear what working-class women thought about fashion; it is clear that wealthier women used dress to maintain class distinctions.

Antifashion and dress reform, especially pantaloons dress reform, were distinct. The voices of antifashion did not organize and did not usually offer any practical advice on how to change fashion. Dress reformers generally worked with like-minded associates to provide women with a functional alternative to current styles. Yet antifashionists and dress reformers did share many anxieties about female apparel. They emphasized fashion as a woman's problem. Women received severe criticism for their interest in dress and found themselves in the difficult position of balancing society's expectations of how they should look with not showing too much interest in fashion. They should place little value on fashion, yet follow it religiously. Antifashion attitudes could police women in ways that ultimately would be unacceptable. Regulating morality through dress, for example, made women responsible for controlling men's sexual desires by not wearing "sexy" clothes.

Antifashion was not new, but in combination with nineteenth-century reform ideas and apparel styles, it offered possibilities for action that had not been previously recognized. This would be the primary distinction between antifashion and dress reform: antifashionists limited themselves to words—they spoke from the pulpit or lyceum, wrote numerous articles and books, and unleashed their disapproval of women's clothing; pantaloons-wearing dress reformers also engaged in verbal battles about apparel but also took the next step—radically altering their own clothing. In 1860 Ada Clarke accurately assessed the "ineffective" attacks that "everyone [had] read"—"the vituperation of the hooped skirt, long dress, small bonnet"— and that brought about no change in female apparel.[85] Thus, antifashionists spoke as dress reformers acted.

Perfecting America

Antebellum reform activities make it clear that white, middle-class, Protestant women and men were not a monolithic group in the nineteenth century. The forces motivating reformers varied as did the reforms they chose to join, and dress reform drew interest from groups with an assortment of agendas.[86] Many antebellum reformers, including pantaloons dress reformers, employed the strategy of self-determination and did not attempt to change state or national laws. Instead, they tried to modify the public's behavior by using their own lives as examples.[87] Isolated groups and individuals who never came together with a shared philosophy or strategy to change the dress of American women made up the reform movement. No single organization or person involved with dress reform consolidated all of the many, varied reasons for advocating pantaloons. This characteristic of pantaloons dress reform is one of the features that differentiated that movement from other antebellum reform movements. All dress reformers (and many other reformers) agreed that something had to be done about women's fashions, and some held in common ideas about health, women's status, or religion. Most did not. No allegiance to one broad dress reform philosophy or ideology united this disparate group.

Although many of the pantaloons dress reformers refused to be identified with any general dress reform ideology and with other advocates of the reform, their sense of themselves as individual reformers who owed nothing to other dress reformers was a false notion. It was perhaps natural that reformers in this age of evangelical and millennial enthusiasm would take up dress reform, both as an outgrowth of their all-encompassing reformism and because a unique dress could symbolize allegiance to the reform cause. Antebellum reform, fashion, and antifashion, however, do not adequately explain why some women in the nineteenth century defied custom and tradition and put on trousers—one leg at a time.

No more ribbons wear, nore in rich dress appear. . . .
This do without fear, and to all you'll appear
Fine, charming, true, lovely and clever
Though the times remain darkish—
Young men will be sparkish,
And love you more dearly than ever.

—*New Harmony Gazette,* June 28, 1826

The First Dress Reformers

New Harmony, Indiana, 1824–27

The union of several reform impulses, the feminization of fashion, and pervasive antifashion sentiments created an environment ripe for a change in women's dress. Yet in southern Indiana, far from the "Burned-over District" in New York—the hotbed of reform—the first radical attempt to alter female apparel went largely unnoticed. A man—Robert Owen—led this effort to put women in pantaloons. Immediately the question of why women in the nineteenth century wore pantaloons becomes more complex.

New Harmony

The community at New Harmony, Indiana, was Robert Owen's "halfway house" on a journey to a "new state of existence." The son of a Welsh ironmonger and saddler, Owen had put some of his humanitarian and socialist ideas to work for the first time in the small company town of New Lanark, Scotland. There, workers could buy food and clothing at cost, children were encouraged to attend local schools, and medical and other services were provided free of charge. Although he accomplished a great deal at New Lanark, Owen's efforts at reforming legislation proved frustrating. As he worked to improve working conditions, Owen realized that the entrenched, traditional institutions of marriage, church, and private property interfered with the creation of a "new moral order." He decided that Scotland was not the appropriate place to try his experiment and looked across the ocean to the United States.[1]

Owen learned that the land, buildings, shops, and farms of the Rappite (Harmony Society) colony on the banks of the Wabash River in New Harmony, Indiana, were for sale and purchased the property and its holdings.[2] In February and March of 1825, he addressed the House of Representatives, visited with congressmen and prominent citizens, and invited the "industrious and well-disposed" to come to his community and begin a "new state of society." A heterogeneous assortment of people answered his call. Residents of several states, cranks, the curious, those attracted by the prospect of life without labor, and freethinkers combined to form a group short on skilled and enthusiastic workers. By October 1825, the population numbered nine hundred. Owen explained to his followers that a transitional stage had to precede the new moral order; therefore, on May 1, 1825, the Preliminary Society of New Harmony was formed and its constitution adopted. Under Owen, neither the Preliminary Society nor the Community of Equality, which followed, were true communal societies— Owen retained ownership of the land and buildings.[3] After seven weeks, Owen left for Scotland to attend to business and family affairs; he returned six months later.

In January 1826, Owen and "his boatload of knowledge" were met with an enthusiastic greeting from the inhabitants. Pleased with the community's progress, Owen decided the time had come to end the Preliminary Society and begin the Community of Equality. The constitution had lofty and worthy ideals that strongly emphasized equality among members. All were to be considered as one family with no one held in higher or lower esteem because of occupation. There was to be "similar food, clothing, and education." As soon as "practicable," all were to "live in similar houses" and be accommodated alike.[4] Two weeks after the constitution was adopted, members rejected self-government and asked Owen to direct the affairs of the community until January 1, 1827.

The first months of 1826 also saw the formation of splinter communities. Conflicting ideas about New Harmony's organization and a desire for more religious activity contributed to the growing friction within the "commune." Some of the agitators formed new societies. Owen cooperated and even gave them land. He regarded the new associations as "prunings from the original vine and as evidence of the tendency for new communities to emerge as his ideas and principles became rooted."[5] The splintering continued until there were eight "major" communes; then some of these divided until there were ten communities at New Harmony. When Owen left for England on June 1, 1827, he remained optimistic; however, the communities soon dissolved.[6]

The failure of New Harmony has been attributed to Owen's absences in the early days, to admitting anyone who wished to enter the community, to the lack of a religious conviction, to discrepancies between the stated goal of equality and the inequality experienced by some members, and to Owen's inability to be practical.[7] Although deemed a failure as a communal living arrangement, New Harmony's accomplishments—including the introduction of trousers for women—continued to be felt throughout the nineteenth century.

Costume of Equality

Robert Owen had decided that a rational society should have few distinctions in dress, and the rules of the Community of Equality stated, "There shall be similar food, clothing, and education, as near as can be furnished, for all according to their ages."[8] One way Owen expressed his commitment to an egalitarian society was by criticizing extravagant dress. He viewed opulent clothing—its costs and competitiveness—as divisive and contrary to true equality. Frequent visitor and former minister Robert Jennings agreed. On at least one occasion, Jennings preached that equality "was essential to the happiness of society" and that "all distinctions arising from extravagance in dress and external appearance have no solid foundation." He recommended eliminating all distinctions.[9] Owen announced that New Harmony had relinquished worldly "trammels" and abolished class and gender distinctions with an original style of dress. As a community devoted to economic development as well as to equal rights, Harmonites defended the cost-effectiveness of reform dress, attacking extravagant apparel because its price grew with each ornament, design detail, or yard of luxurious fabric. In addition, New Harmony's financial struggles made plain, uniform dress a practical as well as ideological reform.

Robert Owen worked actively to introduce a new plain dress into his utopian society and was successful to some degree. Clues to Owen's thinking on dress can be found in the *New Harmony Gazette* (later *The Free Enquirer*), in Robert Jennings's sermons, and in the rules of the community.[10] Commentaries on fashion appeared infrequently, but the articles published are significant. A poem summing up the community's stance on fashion appeared in 1826:

> No more ribbons wear, nore in rich dress appear....
> This do without fear, and to all you'll appear
> Fine, charming, true, lovely and clever
> Though the times remain darkish—
> Young men will be sparkish,
> And love you more dearly than ever.[11]

A passage of a letter from a Philadelphia physician condemned the use of corsets. Owen's son, Robert Dale Owen, wrote an article on "Fashionable Incarceration," in which he proclaimed the wearing of a corset to be an "immoral" and "sometimes a criminal action."[12] R. D. Owen's disdain of fashion's "follies" is further evidenced in his delight in "the absolute freedom from all trammels, alike in the expression of opinion, in dress, and in social intercourse" found in New Harmony.[13] Owen found dress a convenient instrument for pursuing his socialist ideas; uniform clothing could immediately enhance and proclaim equality of sex and status. Robert Owen supported negative critiques of fashionable dress, especially female apparel, and was committed to an egalitarian society. It is not surprising that he chose a visual symbol to reflect the community's denunciation of worldly affectations and distinctions between the sexes.

Karl Bernhard recorded a description of the "particular costume adopted for the society" in his travel diary. The men wore "wide pantaloons buttoned over a boy's jacket, made of light material, without a collar," and the women wore "a coat reaching to the knee and pantaloons, such as little girls wear among us."[14] In all likelihood, Bernhard was describing a skeleton suit, a distinctive style for boys that reflected the special status boyhood had attained. In the late eighteenth century and early nineteenth century, young boys might wear a skeleton suit—a pair of ankle-length trousers buttoned to a sleeved jacket, usually of matching material. It was introduced as an intermediate stage of attire for young boys, between infant and adult clothing, and it differed from men's clothing and from the clothing girls of the same age might wear.[15] Although both women and men changed their attire to resemble children's dress, they did not wear the same costume, and the changes in male apparel were not as dramatic or radical as the alterations in women's clothing—a pattern that would be repeated in other dress reforms throughout the century. Men wore a basic outfit of trousers and jacket—similar to the pantaloons, shirt, and jacket they already wore. Their instructions did not include the adoption of a completely new type of dress, as the women's did. (This is one of the few instances when men reformed their clothing to any degree.)

Despite the gender distinctions, Sarah Pears claimed that it was "rather difficult to distinguish the gentlemen from the ladies." Did that mean that men looked like "little girls" or that both sexes were childlike in appearance? Not everyone favored the new costumes; Pears not only refused to wear it or to allow her daughters to wear it, she also ridiculed the outfit in her letters. She wrote, "The female dress is a pair of undertrousers tied round the ankles over which is an exceedingly full slip reaching to the knees, though some have been so extravagant as to make them rather longer, and also to have the sleeves long." She recorded hearing a fat person in the "elegant costume" compared to a "feather bed tied in the middle."[16] Frances Wright, a prominent member of New Harmony, had her own ideas about how a costume for equality should look. She wore a "garment of plain white muslin, which hung around her in folds that recalled the drapery of a Grecian statue."[17]

Despite the seemingly androgynous nature of the New Harmony clothing, it failed to live up to Jennings's predictions about external appearance and sex equality. Wearing the new costume did not grant equality to Harmonite women. In 1825 Thomas Pears noted, "Women, not actively employed, are not considered as members." To be considered actively employed, women were required to perform domestic duties for members of the society, not including their own families. Sarah Pears wrote harshly about the conditions women faced at New Harmony, focusing on how overworked they were. In return for cooking, sewing, and washing, women were given credit toward purchases in the community's businesses.[18] However, if women limited their domestic duties to their own homes, they did not receive this remuneration. Despite reformed dress and "restructured" society, traditional values that depreciated women's domestic work were upheld. Only when such work occurred outside the home was it acknowledged as contributing to the greater good of the society, and only then were women considered members of that society.

The Owenite costume superficially addressed the issues of women's equality and rights, but it did not wipe out traditional stereotypes about women or help grant them rights equal to men's. The patriarchal system in New Harmony determined what part women could and could not play within the community. Owen's attitude in the following incident is just one example of how traditional stereotypes about women were maintained in New Harmony. During the summer of 1826, the society agreed to hold meetings three times a week. An objection was raised that "the females would hardly have time to get done with supper to meet there so early and so often." Owen "had been endeavoring to ascertain the cause why so much difficulty is experienced by the females of this community in the performance of their domestic duties." He suggested the women were talking too much and "by coming to these meetings for instruction they might perhaps get rid of the desire and the occasion for so much useless talk."[19]

By 1827 the connection between pantaloons and gender equality had been forged and would become the most important recurring theme in dress reform's history, even though Owen and Harmonites used uniform dress to symbolize an equality that did not exist in the practical day-to-day life of the commune. A "masculine" dress for women could be threatening, but in New Harmony the radical change failed to live up to fears about women in pantaloons. Women did not look like men, nor did they play at being men. Trousers did not destroy visual gender distinctions, did not open up new economic opportunities for women, and did not change the prevailing ideology about femininity. It can be argued that at New Harmony pantaloons symbolized a new form of female exploitation—not female emancipation. But the costume, and the lip service paid to equality, presaged the connection between dress reform and woman's rights.

Robert Owen did not wholly succeed in wiping out interest in fashion among the Harmonite women. Sarah Pears noticed that "the young girls . . . here think as much of dress and beaux as in any place I was ever in."[20] Nor did Owen convince all the community women to wear the new costume, although he adamantly and sometimes cruelly coerced some women into doing so. Owen spent relatively little time in the Indiana community, but when he was present his demands seemed harsher than if he had been there on a regular basis. He used tradition and division of labor as well as direct pressure to force women to behave in a manner he found acceptable. Nowhere was this more apparent than at a double wedding that took place in New Harmony. The bridal parties with their "bridesmaids and groomsmen were all dressed in the new costume, which is of black and white striped cotton." Having only recently adopted the costume, the brides and grooms had "but one apiece." One of the brides "had been working in the boarding school kitchen all the preceding week, and had done a great deal of scrubbing in hers." Since her costume of equality was stained and dirty, "she, poor girl, had first dressed herself very nicely in bridal white." Owen and the bridegroom, however, persuaded her "to lay aside these trappings of the old world, and to draw from its depository amongst the dirty clothes this elegant suit in which she was married." The ordeal of giving up her bridal white for a soiled outfit, no matter what it symbolized, caused the young bride "many tears."[21]

The first dress reformers made it quite apparent that there was nothing inherently liberating about trousers. In fact, any type of clothing, be it a tightly laced corset, a long skirt, or loose-fitting trousers, could be used to imprison the wearer. Repeatedly the issue of dress highlighted the significant differences between Owen's motivations and those of the women who had to embody his ideas. There is no evidence that Owen himself wore the male reform costume, and available illustrations of Owen indicate that he wore contemporary mainstream male garments.

New Harmony was not oblivious to society's reactions. Robert Owen was accused of advocating free love because he condemned the marriage institution as it existed in larger society. Owen did not support sex outside of marriage, but a state of "natural" marriage in which both parties were equal. Nevertheless, he was accused of being a free lover. Perhaps a legacy of New Harmony, which continued until the end of the nineteenth century, was the accusation of loose morals and the epithet "free lover" hurled at women who wore pantaloons reform dresses. For example, when the women of the North American Phalanx appeared in short dresses and pantaloons it confirmed their neighbors' suspicions—the Phalanx was a free love community. To allay this fear, the women wore long dresses outside Phalanx grounds.[22]

The design origins of the New Harmony costume are unclear. The evidence suggests two possibilities. The first is Karl Bernhard's remark that the dress was "such as little girls wear." Perhaps Owen thought the simple style of children's dress reflected his principles better than any of the limited number of adult fashions with which he was acquainted. Or, he may have seen his followers, especially the women, as children, in need of guidance and control. Also suggestive is a notice in the *New Harmony Gazette:* "The dress of the higher ranks of Arab women is borrowed from the ancients. A zone placed immediately below the bosom, serves to confine a loose robe, open in front, so as to display a pair of rich pantaloons."[23] Aside from the ornamentation, this description sounds remarkably like pantaloons and short dress costumes, and knowledge of Eastern clothing styles may indeed have been instrumental in the New Harmony design. Two decades later, Oneida Community pantalettes and short dresses would be attributed to children's dress, and the woman's rights freedom suit would be connected to Middle Eastern clothing.

With the dissolution of the Community of Equality, knowledge about the short dress pantaloons costume for *adult women* seemed to disappear, contrary to Miner Kellogg's assertion that the New Harmony costume lasted "as a fashion long after the disbanding of the community."[24] The New Harmony dress reform did not precipitate a tradition of women wearing bifurcated garments in mainstream society after 1827. One explanation for why the costume did not stimulate a larger dress reform movement may be related to its limited use within the boundaries of the New Harmony village. Sometime in the 1830s and 1840s, some women did begin wearing outfits similar to New Harmony's when exercising in private. But European spas, not New Harmony, are usually credited as the source for these exercise outfits. Given the wide distribution of Owen's ideas and the attention Robert Dale Owen and Frances Wright garnered, some accounts of the Harmonite dress reform experiment must have circulated, especially among later communitarians interested in socialism.

There is no evidence, for example, that John Humphrey Noyes encouraged his followers to dress in the Owenite costume. However, Noyes's familiarity with the writings of Robert Owen influenced many of his ideas, so it is possible that Noyes incorporated Owen's ideas about dress into his own, although Noyes's ego may not have permitted him to credit Owen with creating the Oneida Community's short dress.[25] Other mid-nineteenth-century dress reformers did not mention New Harmony as a source or inspiration for their own pantaloons reform costumes either. Still, evidence suggests that New Harmony's dress reform experiment had far-reaching influence. Because the Harmonite community earned a reputation as a haven for free love and other radical ideas, it is possible that the Owenite costume suffered from association—later pantaloons dress reformers may have preferred to distance themselves from New Harmony and its attire. It is also plausible that the reformers knew little about the Owenite garment because the outfit was short-lived and the number of Harmonites who wore the apparel may have been small. It is also true that dress reformers preferred to credit themselves with originating the style.[26] The evidence does not prove that the Owenite costume directly influenced later pantaloons reform garments. However, coincidence does not adequately account for the similarities in the descriptions of the Harmonite outfit and reform garments introduced almost thirty years later.

New Harmony may not have directly influenced subsequent dress reform; however, three features of the Owenite experiment appear in the mid-nineteenth century. Dress reform as a private practice began in 1824 with the closed community of New Harmony and continued to characterize dress reform before 1851. Robert Owen first introduced pantaloons and short dresses; other male leaders followed his example. Thus, the role of charismatic men as champions of reform dress marked pantaloons dress reform from its inception. Evidence supports the proposal that men had a direct and compelling influence on women's efforts to reform dress; with few exceptions, women in communal societies, private spas, and resorts changed their attire with the encouragement of male leaders. Robert Owen expected female costumes to announce to outsiders that New Harmony had discovered a new, more equitable way of life; this goal also linked reform apparel to woman's rights. Through Harmonite women's clothing, Owen made a statement differentiating himself and his community from mainstream societal values.

Simple Dresses

Dress reform continued in closed environments after the Harmonite dress ceased to be worn. However, no one chose to wear a New Harmony–type costume of pantaloons and tunic until John Humphrey Noyes proposed short dresses to his followers at Oneida in 1848. Instead, the preferred approach in utopian societies was simplified dress. Most communitarians would have been uncomfortable allowing women to wear trousers—even within the confines of a closed society—because such costume departed fundamentally from acceptable ideas about female and male dress. Furthermore, in both religious and secular communal societies and among the general public, the Bible's explicit message clearly warned women and men to maintain gender-distinctive clothing. Almost no one was immune to such biblical admonitions: "The woman shall not wear that which pertaineth to a man, neither shall a man put on a woman's garment: for all that do so are abomination unto the Lord thy God" (Deut. 22:5). Since men had been wearing some form of breeches since about 1400, five hundred years later trousers seemed a "natural" and exclusively male garment.

Simple styles and unadorned garments became the acceptable means of expressing dissatisfaction with popular modes, and many communal societies simplified clothing as a way to reflect their religious beliefs. There was no consensus between religious and secular associations on what simplified outfits looked like. For one group it was plain "sunbonnets and calico." Kaweah community women stopped "wearing corsets and bustles" and called it a reform.[27] Some communes wore "fossilized" dress—clothing that did not change with each season or even with new generations—which remained the "uniform" for decades. Because most nineteenth-century utopianists agreed that female apparel needed more improvement and women, more than men, found too much pleasure in dress, modifications to women's clothing occurred more often. Sometimes, in an effort to streamline clothing, communities adopted the ancestral ethnic dress of their homelands. At Economy, members donned the traditional "honest" dress of "German peasants,"[28] and Amana communitarians dressed in German "peasant" costumes "of two hundred years ago."[29] From time to time, the changes made to fossilized apparel resulted from necessity and not from fashion's dictates. In contrast, Beverly Gordon noted that the Shakers evinced a practicality that enabled them to adapt to the changes occurring in mainstream fashions. When synthetic dyes became readily available, Shakers purchased them. When it became cheaper to buy cloth from mills rather than produce their own, the Shakers did so. And as clothing styles changed, Shaker styles also changed, albeit at a slower rate.[30]

Although pantaloons and short dresses disappeared until the Oneida Community resurrected them in 1848, an undercurrent of dress reform activity continued. Insular communities that reformed clothing stressed simplicity and plainness; outsiders also emphasized the superiority of modest, austere dresses. Abolitionist Sarah Grimké considered the "gew-gaws and trinkets" and the "ribbons and laces" with which women of the late 1830s "bedecked" themselves as obstructions to the elevation of women. Although Grimké's Quaker dress was "simple and convenient," she did not advise other women to adopt the style. She reasoned that individual women had to adopt a design they found comfortable.[31] Years later, Dr. James C. Jackson criticized people who understood the problems with women's fashionable dress yet strenuously urged "*simpleness* in dress," instead of a more radical reform.[32]

The clothing styles of women, men, and children do not explain the absence of pantaloons and short dress reform in the two decades between the demise of the Owenite community and the creation of the Perfectionist society, Oneida. Apparel changed during this period as it has always done. Some people approved of and happily wore the new fashions, and others railed against them. Nothing about the clothing itself stimulated a desire for reform or the lack of such a desire. New Harmony's reputation and Robert Owen's notoriety may have severely limited the costume's appeal, making the pantaloons outfit impossible for women to wear until the community's connection with it had faded from popular memory.[33] Between 1827 and 1848, men and women continued to share an interest in clothing, and few called for a dress reform for either sex. Before 1848, women had few opportunities to wear any form of bifurcated garment; perhaps by the middle of the century, women who had grown comfortable wearing underdrawers began to consider the garment's viability as an outer garment.

The absence of conspicuous dress reform activity in this period is the most plausible explanation for why New Harmony's costume has been overlooked in the larger history of dress reform movements. However, dress reform did not disappear. Throughout most of the first half of the nineteenth century, communal societies continued to practice some type of dress reform. However, since they did not recommend a radical alteration in dress, it may have seemed to outsiders that no reform took place.

During this period when radical dress reform appeared fallow, antifashion commentators inadvertently kept the cause of dress reform alive. Their ongoing and much-publicized disapproval of fashion aided the reappearance of radical reform dress by keeping many clothing issues before the public.

The Fate of Early Dress Reform

The first reform costume vanished for several reasons, the most obvious being the negative legacy left by the Owenite community's experiment with pantaloons for women. Ultimately, however, the feminization of fashion would play a part in the reappearance of reform garb. Until men gave up their interest in apparel, clothing, whether male or female, did not seem to need radical reform. Fashion proved to be a powerful foe to antifashionists and dress reformers who failed to recognize the importance large numbers of women placed on dressing in the latest mode. Dress reform continued along the antifashion path for two decades, until John Humphrey Noyes suggested an alternative costume for women, and utopian societies continued to be the most common site for private dress reform experiments. The supportive atmosphere necessary for women to change their clothing radically could also be found in other closed environments, such as private hydropathic spas and health resorts. Women usually limited their use of pantaloons to a private setting, preferring not to wear their unusual clothing in public. In this dress reform, public and private blurred—early reformers constructed their own definition of "private space," not necessarily a domestic space, but an all-female space or a place of like-minded people.[34] And in 1848, antifashion changed from an intellectual exercise characterized by written critiques into a practical reform, as women cast aside yards of fancy ribbon and sumptuous fabric and embraced trousers.

The role of reform costume in the Owenite community complicates the observation that pantaloons reform dress was intrinsically radical. The initial, and emotional, response to pantaloons for women in the first quarter of the nineteenth century was that the garment was radical. Yet, clothing has no meaning without cultural context. A pair of trousers is a pair of trousers. When women wear those trousers in a society that not only frowns on such behavior, but actually prohibits it, then the act of donning unsanctioned apparel has the potential to be radical and transgressive. The contradiction in the Owenites' actions, whether they acknowledged it or not, is that dress reformers were serious transgressors. The Owenites' apparently "small step" outside women's prescribed circle of behaviors might lead anywhere.

Female apparel now
Is gone to pot I vow, sirs,
And ladies will be fined
Who don't wear coats and trousers;
Blucher boots and hats
And shirts with handsome stitches,—
Oh dear! What shall we do
When women wear the breeches?

—Broadsheet, 1851

Pantaloons in Private

Health and Religious Dress Reform
before Freedom Dresses

American women did not experience an epiphany in 1848 and reach into their husbands', brothers', or fathers' wardrobes, grab the first pair of pantaloons they found, and put them on. Such a shared experience might have explained the increase in dress reform activity around this momentous year—a year that included the discovery of gold in California, the passage of the Married Women's Property Act in New York, the woman's rights convention in Seneca Falls, and the establishment of the utopian religious community of Oneida. Although 1848 was marked by many activities, a universal agreement among women to change fashionable dress was not one of them. Nevertheless, some women did begin wearing pantaloons in 1848. Why? Most did so in answer to the call to reform female apparel. For centuries, almost everything women wore became associated with a negative characteristic. Trains, hoopskirts, and sumptuous fabrics were associated with female vanity. Crinolines were condemned as impractical. Corsets raised critiques about ill health. Some women and men decided that the time had come to act.

At this point, dress reform did not center on a single philosophy or ideology. Advocates argued that they did not wear the same (or even similar) costumes, although at least one branch of the fragmented movement focused on a single style of clothing. The most striking aspect of this moment in the history of dress reform is the active involvement of men in dictating new dress for women—particularly charismatic religious leaders such as John Humphrey Noyes of the Oneida Community and James Jesse Strang of Beaver Island, Michigan. Women did not always have a choice or say in wearing pantaloons, any more than they were able to resist current fashion trends. A closer look at men's idiosyncratic relationship to dress reform reveals the hybrid nature of that reform's history.

Hydropathists, Private Advocates, and Communes

In the first half of the century, dress reformers agreed on little except short dresses with pantaloons, and they all wore reform costumes in private or closed environments. Given the timeline of dress reform's appearance in different milieus, it seems reasonable to suppose that as organizations and individuals learned about preceding costumes they adapted their own. However, all dress reformers vehemently denied this scenario, insisting that they knew nothing about other efforts before they created their own "unique" reform outfit. Proponents of water cure or hydropathy, the occasional bold individual, and communal societies all tried to stake claims on this contested turf.

Dr. Lydia Hammond Strobridge, Dr. Lydia Sayer Hasbrouck, Dr. Mary Gove Nichols, and Dr. Harriet Austin—women prominent in both hydropathy and dress reform—published books, lectured, and even wore the dress long after dress reform ceased to be a political issue.[1] These female reformers, perhaps more than any others, equated the need for dress reform with woman's inferior position in society. They also closely related women's subordinate status in society with women's poor health. Although women actively participated in dress reform at water cures, Dr. James C. Jackson claimed the distinction of introducing the pantaloons costume to women. When Jackson "induced Miss Theodosia Gilbert to make and wear" pantaloons reform dress in 1849, he insisted that he "knew not that a woman in the world had adopted it."[2] Jackson and his adopted daughter Harriet Austin, are thus often recognized as the originators and the first advocates of a *healthful* pantaloons reform outfit, which later came to be known as the "American Costume."[3] Jackson also fostered the founding of the National Dress Reform Association (NDRA), which adopted the American Costume as its own. Gilbert, an investor in Jackson's Glen Haven Water Cure, altered her fashionable dress in the "fall of '49, and wore [the reform garment] as a working dress" for a year. It is probable that she confined her clothing experiments to the spa, because there was no widespread knowledge of her particular outfit. It is difficult to conclude if Gilbert's apparel influenced subsequent reform garments. However, the location of the spa in central New York state placed it close to other sites of dress reform agitation, suggesting the possibility that gossip spread about Gilbert's pantaloons dress.[4]

The evidence suggests that despite his claim to originality, Jackson may have known about the earlier Oneida experiment. In his autobiography, he would credit Lucretia Jackson, his wife, and Austin, with attempting to produce a "physiological dress" that was "at once comfortable and tasteful" and "aped" men's wear. In the 1850s, however, Jackson did not acknowledge Lucretia Jackson or Harriet Austin's contributions. Instead he asserted his own position in the development of the reform outfit, perhaps intending to increase the garment's credibility by insisting that a professional medical man created it.[5]

Some women, discontented with contemporary fashionable styles, experimented privately with alternative clothing. Few women defied social custom and included pantaloons in their experiments—pantaloons would have been difficult for individual women to wear even in the privacy of their own homes. Dress-reforming women faced a contradiction; modesty dictated that if women wore shorter skirts then their legs must be covered, but pantaloons, which seemed the logical solution, were considered indecent when worn by women. Nevertheless, the private home became one of the spaces where women altered their attire without publicly joining a larger reform movement. The women who wore short dresses and pantaloons exclusively at home also assisted in the maintenance of the nineteenth-century sex/gender system by not challenging it openly.[6]

There were exceptions, however. Mary E. Tillotson, an active reformer and member of the NDRA, recalled that in 1842 she had been suffering from "dispepsy" for five years and "was just able to walk from bed to chair." It seemed likely that her weak condition would remain a permanent feature

The *Water-Cure Journal* published a number of illustrations depicting variations on the pantaloons reform garment. Anyone interested in water cure would have had easy access to information on the style by simply reading the journal. *Water-Cure Journal* (January 1852).

of her life. However, in 1843 (a point in her life when she wrote with "scientific" or phonetic spellings) she and her sisters designed "a soft, loos, lite suit that tha named 'grandmother suit' [*sic*]." This was five years before the Oneida short dress and eight years before the freedom dress. According to Tillotson, she did not learn about other reform garments that resembled hers until 1851, after which she shortened her skirts an additional twelve inches.[7] Tillotson was not the only individual to create a short dress with pantaloons for personal use.

In 1849, a follower of the water-cure doctrine entered the ongoing discussion about the ill effects of fashionable dress and offered her preference to the current styles. "Perhaps I might be allowed to suggest a style which I adopted myself some time since. . . . Stout calf-skin gaiters; white trowsers [*sic*] made after the Eastern style, loose, and confined at the ankle with a cord; a green kilt, reaching nearly to the knees, gathered at the neck, and turned back with a collar, confined at the waist with a scarlet sash tied upon one side, with short sleeves for summer, and long sleeves for winter, fastened at the wrist; a green turban made in the Turkish mode."[8] The author did not make it clear when she invented her costume, but it is likely that hydropathic denouncements of fashionable dress encouraged a number of women, on their own initiative, to devise substitute styles.[9] The widely disseminated artists' renderings of the Middle East may have suggested that trousers, an element of Middle Eastern women's dress, be incorporated into reform garments. In addition, some women may have become familiar with the style of short skirts and pantaloons if they had seen it or a similar style used as a private exercise dress for women.

In 1859, E. M. Richards declared that he had "advocated (in private)" the adoption of dress reform "years before Mrs. Bloomer wrote in favor of it"—an easy claim to make, but one originating from an unusual source. Richards described himself as the discoverer of sensible dress: while "hundreds of miles away from civilization" at a Hudson Bay Co. fort, he "got the idea of the Reform Dress" after witnessing the clothing of the "daughters of the forest." The Native American women Richards saw wore clothing manufactured with English fabric, but not fashioned in the styles of "Regent's Park or Broadway"—practicality and utility took precedence in the designs. So impressed was Richards that he immediately became a champion of dress reform. However, only years later, in the pages of the *Sibyl,* did he propose a design based on the earlier Native American dress.[10]

Yet another branch of dress reform was sprouting in experimental communal societies like New Harmony—territory situated somewhere between the private home and the public space. Outsiders did not initially object to pantaloons outfits because few thought communes had any far-reaching influence on society.

Communal experiments—including Hopedale, North American Phalanx, Brook Farm, Modern Times, and Ruskin Commonwealth—were known to have tried reform styles. It is difficult to determine how many of the more than one hundred utopian societies in the nineteenth century experimented with some type of clothing reform. Information on the conditions under which alternative apparel was introduced and worn in communal settings is often limited to observations by visitors, with few commentaries by the wearers.[11] The communes did not choose a universal pattern or dress code; each established its own guidelines. But whatever the nature of the community, clothing, although not necessarily pantaloons reform garments, became an important facet of its life. Members of some colonies negotiated formal agreements that clearly outlined appropriate apparel. Other associations informally approved "acceptable" garments.[12] John Codman noted the relaxed endorsement at Brook Farm (from 1841 to 1855) of "women who chose" to make "a short gown with an undergarment, bound at the ankles." He compared the costume "to the dress worn by Mrs. Bloomer."[13]

The reasons utopian communities instituted changes in dress were as varied as the ways they introduced reform wear into their circles. Practicality and physical freedom, however, led the list. North American Phalanx women wore pantaloons reform apparel when they worked in the kitchen or at one of the mills, which they said made the physical labor easier to bear.[14] Brook Farm women who chose to wear short reform skirts and pantaloons stressed that the outfit enabled them to "walk well and work well."[15] Reform apparel supposedly allowed women to move as freely as they thought men moved; this in turn made it possible to break down the sexual division of labor. Unhampered by long, full skirts, women— theoretically— could engage in any employment. (Being able to do the work of men did not, in fact, mean that women also enjoyed the privileges available to male members.) Utopians also sanctioned reform clothing for its symbolic value: it set members of the commune apart from mainstream society and signified allegiance to a particular community.

Most communal societies originated as male constructs, with women often defined by their relationships to men with authority, as we will see in greater detail with Oneida and Beaver Island communities. The patriarchal ideology pervasive in male-defined communes often limited and regulated the clothing choices available to women.[16] The dress reform experiences of the Icarian women dramatically illustrate the direct effect men had on dress reform. The community had experimented with uniformity of dress, but some women wanted to try the short dress and pantaloons costume. They shortened their skirts and stitched trouser leggings. Ridicule by the men "summarily snuffed out" the women's efforts.[17] This incident suggests that men had more control over dress reform in the commune than may be readily apparent if one focuses exclusively on the wearers—women. Pantaloons reform dress "is indecent," concluded one critic, not because "it removes the separation wall . . . between the sexes," but because "no woman should voluntarily 'stand in the breech.'"[18]

Men, however, could "break down, and rudely" the sex/gender system that clothing helped maintain.[19] As late as 1940, the *New Yorker* cast doubt on the origins of the freedom suit and questioned whether the idea for short dresses and pantaloons could have come from a woman at all.[20] Women in such supposedly egalitarian societies could not attempt dress reform on their own without recrimination, but if men introduced or endorsed it, it was acceptable. Ridicule was one of the most powerful tools available to men in regulating dress reform inside and outside closed communities; it forced women to change their clothing back to conventional and male-sanctioned dress. Although codes varied within utopian societies, women sometimes freely chose (without a backlash) to wear reform apparel. However, some male leaders permitted little choice. Within the communal setting, women in pantaloons did not threaten the sex/gender system or the sexual division of power because men, not women, promoted the use of trousers for women. What or whom were the men reforming? And why?

The Oneida Community and "The Dress of Children"

Oneida developed during the religious enthusiasm sweeping over western New York in the 1830s and 1840s. In the Oneida Community, John Humphrey Noyes ruled with a firm hand, and his dominance as a forceful leader ordered life there. Members tended to treat the founder of their Madison County commune as a god, shaping their behavior by the "desire for the approval of Father Noyes."[21] Small wonder: Noyes exercised virtually complete authority, not unlike the traditional patriarch's control of his dependents,[22] and he based that authority on divine inspiration— "from God to Christ; from Christ to Paul; from Paul to John Humphrey Noyes; and by him made available to the Community."[23] He affected others by his very presence, as a mother's revelations to her daughter showed. "Why did you live that way? What was there about him?" enquired the daughter. The mother responded, "Don't ask me to explain it. I can't. All I know is that when you were in his presence, you knew you were with someone who was not an ordinary man."[24]

Noyes based Oneida theology on Bible Communism and Perfectionism, the belief that people could become the "perfect followers of Christ." Rejecting the consequences of original sin, Perfectionism asserted that men could be freed from sin and attain in life the perfect holiness necessary for salvation. Communitarians believed that God and humanity were dual in nature—composed of both male and female traits. Thus, spiritually the sexes existed as one in their innermost life with Christ. Noyes asserted that secular culture and society had corrupted the meanings of femininity and masculinity and that women would not be enslaved at Oneida as they were in contemporary society.[25] Religious ideology as well as secular political theories influenced Oneida's unique lifestyle, which included the social practices of "complex marriage," "male continence," "mutual criticism," and "stirpiculture." In "complex marriage," all community adults considered themselves married to one another, and "male continence," patterned after withdrawal except that men did not ejaculate, became the Community's favored form of contraception. Oneida communitarians utilized "mutual criticism," a system in which everyone had their faults told to them by the community members. "Stirpiculture," Oneida's experiment in selective breeding, eventually consumed much of Noyes's attention.[26]

In day-to-day activities, Oneida's gender-specific roles remained remarkably similar to those of mainstream society.[27] Oneida insisted on the rights and importance of women, but this was not understood to mean that women and men were equal. The proper relation of the sexes, the community argued, was stated by Paul: "the head of every woman is the man." This was God's plan for woman, that man "take care of her and see that she is 'holy and without blame.'"[28] In general, women looked to men for inspiration, even though roles might be reversed in particular relationships because of age or spiritual maturity. In the eyes of the Community, a woman trying to act like a man, breaking her subordinate connection with man, or becoming independent was abhorrent.[29] Given the Community's Pauline view of man's role as the caretaker of woman—and given Noyes's godlike authority on top of that—Noyes would be the only person to dictate a change in women's dress. In fact, he included "short dresses" for Community women in the Oneida plan for creating a heaven on earth.

Shortly after moving his community of followers to Oneida, New York, in 1848,[30] Noyes first introduced the topic of an alternative outfit during a discussion of women's contemporary dress. In the eyes of these religious dress reformers, women's outward appearance could also reveal who they were within. Francis Wayland-Smith recalled that in the early years of the

A young Oneida woman with a Community invention; she does not look pleased with it. She is wearing the Oneida "short dress" with pantalettes and has her hair cut in the manner advocated by John Humphrey Noyes. Courtesy of the Oneida Community Mansion House.

Oneida Community, "in an effort to make the separation from the world as distinct as possible, its fashions of dress and personal adornment were discarded."[31] Thus, reform dress could symbolize simultaneously a break from the secular world and a spiritual awakening.

Purging the "dress spirit," woman's vanity, became one of Noyes's underlying motives for introducing the short dress. Oneida shared with mainstream society and other religious groups a contempt for fashion, especially women's pursuit of it, and punished women who overstepped the bounds of correct behavior with respect to clothing. As a child, Corinna Ackley Noyes recalled visiting John Humphrey Noyes and sitting upon his knee when he opened a desk drawer. In that drawer, lying atop a bed of cotton, lay the "dazzling, beautiful" brooches of all the Oneida women.

Later, C. A. Noyes learned that the jewelry "had been temporarily banned to crucify the women's vanity." Only after conquering the "dress spirit" did J. H. Noyes return the brooches to the "offenders."[32]

Noyes decided that women spent too much time thinking about clothing, and attempted to eradicate the practice. Pride in dress was considered a particularly female vice, in part because the *need* to wear clothing could be traced back to Eve: "Eve was the cause of the institution of dress.—She opened the gate for sin and shame and death to come into the world, and after that invasion dress was necessary. But because dress was introduced in this way, is a reason why women particularly should renounce all pride in it. Its very existence is a reminder of their mother's fault."[33] From the Oneida, and Christian, perspective all finery was a signifier of Eve's sin, and display in dress was a sign of vanity and pride. Triumphing over the dress spirit aided women on their journey to a higher, heavenly civilization and elevated them spiritually and socially. Charlotte Leonard prayed that she would "not follow too much the fashions of the world." Instead, she hoped to dress "simply and modestly" and sought "to please God always" in her choice of apparel.[34] Harriet Matthews believed her prayers had been answered when she joined the garden workers and cut her hair short. Matthews understood the convenience of short hair in her new occupation and had this been her only consideration would have readily cut it earlier. However, pride in her long hair prevented her from doing so, and only when she overcame the "dress spirit" and committed herself to "pleasing Christ" did she cut off her hair.[35] Annie Hatch also had long hair in which she took pride and which she did not want to cut. Father Noyes made it clear to her that her "salvation" hung in the balance if she refused to cut it. Fear for her eternal soul made Hatch "shake in [her] shoes."[36] Although no written rule required short dresses or short hair, Noyes made sure that a woman who refused to follow the practices knew she risked everlasting damnation.

Vanity and pride were not vices unique to women. Men also transgressed the lines of acceptable clothing. Noyes acknowledged that at one time men had been slaves to fashion, but quickly pointed out that this changed in the nineteenth century, when men dressed "mainly according to convenience and utility."[37] Furthermore, there was a gender difference in sartorial transgressions. Criticism of male fashion often implied a warning against, not a condemnation of, feminization and was expressed as ridicule.

Noyes wrestled with the dilemma that while human beings must clothe themselves to transcend their fallen condition, clothing itself was impure, especially where women were concerned. Unadorned short dresses, accordingly, became a transitional costume to be worn by women until the true social state where sin and shame no longer existed could be attained. In the coming Millennium, "the vast burden of falsities in outward life will be cast off ... among the things cast off will be the falsities of *dress*." Women and men would no longer look to Paris for fashions but to "the New Jerusalem."[38] Women and men would then return to the original garb found in the Garden of Eden, "the dress-no-dress of nature." However, in the imperfect world of the mid-nineteenth century, women bore the burden of dress for both sexes. The "dress-no-dress" found in the Garden of Eden was not nakedness but an idealized, celestial nudity.[39] It is interesting to note that in 1996 Christian nudists quoted Genesis, "naked and not ashamed," when they explained their penchant for nudity. They also argued, as Noyes did, that clothing came into existence only after the forbidden fruit was eaten in the Garden.[40] In the 1850s, Oneida members were not prepared to resume the "dress-no-dress of nature" or to become nudists.

The Community women's understanding of themselves centered on the belief in "the truth that 'man is the head of woman,' and that woman's highest God-given right is to be 'the glory of man.'" In this context a woman's chief ornament, her "meek and quiet spirit," made her pleasing in the eyes of God, for Jesus had said, "'The life is more than meat and *the body than raiment*.'" Thus women understood dress to be a covering and a "necessary institution," but it was sinful to take pride in it. Plain short dresses and pantaloons enabled women to reject the worldly excesses of fashion and express their obedience to God.[41] At Oneida, most women wore pantaloons for religious reasons and to express their communal support, and after Noyes had applied some pressure.

Noyes had written repeatedly that current woman's dresses denied that she was "a two-legged animal," but was instead "something like a churn, standing on castors!" In contrast to mainstream critiques, Community criticism of clothing focused on the way dress made the "distinction between the sexes vastly more prominent and obtrusive than nature ma[de] it." What was needed was a costume for women that would "break up effeminacy" and allow them to take "part in many kinds of industry usually considered masculine." What it would look like generated much discussion. Noyes proposed an alternative costume for women to wear—"the dress of children—frock and pantalettes." He valued youth and lectured his followers that one way to keep young "was to keep up our attractiveness." He pointed out that the "virgin state" had proven to be the most attractive condition for women and recommended that women "find a way to keep [them]selves in a virgin state all the time."[42] The short dress in this context may also have reflected a common deviant sexual reaction in Noyes and some of his male followers, namely that women dressed as children became sexually exciting.[43]

Historian Louis J. Kern had a different interpretation of Oneida short dresses—he proposed that the purpose of the costume was "prophylactic" rather than sexually stimulating. According to Kern, John Humphrey Noyes used the short dress "to control the female and to protect the male from his sexual desires, which threatened to be inordinately excited by female seductiveness."[44] Kern, relying heavily on the numerous negative assessments of reform apparel's aesthetic appeal, suggested that the homely costume rendered women sexless or at the very least unattractive to men. While many observers did remark on "how unspeakably ugly [short dresses] were on some of the women," the Oneida men "think that it improves their [Oneida women's] looks."[45] Kern thus reiterates the most common complaint about mainstream dress—immodesty for the sake of seduction—which insisted that women were responsible for the effect, usually sexual excitement, that they had on their male observers and should not wear clothes that exposed the body. John B. Ellis, a nineteenth-century cultural critic who found the Oneida Community and its ideology thoroughly reprehensible, subjected the Community's female apparel to some of his scorn. His description seems to support Kern's interpretation. Ellis noted that the short dress was "peculiar," but rather than focusing on the garment he turned his attention to the women who wore it. The Oneida outfit "requires a decidedly pretty woman to look well in it," he judged, "the majority, being any thing but pretty, are rendered simply ridiculous by it." However, unlike Kern, Ellis did not assume that "ridiculous"-looking women were sexually undesirable. Instead, he commented on the irony that "healthful" uniforms did not rid Oneida women of their "peculiar air of unhealthiness"—brought on by "sexual excess."[46]

Inspired by the discussion of a new costume for women, two of the Community's most prominent women, Noyes's wife, Harriet Holton Noyes, and one of his favorite lovers, Mary Cragin, set about making a new costume. H. H. Noyes and Cragin, along with Harriet Noyes Skinner, the founder's sister, did not have to search hard to develop the idea of a short dress with trousers, because John Humphrey Noyes had already discussed such a costume "in the upper room of an Indian log house . . . the writer assisted in the clandestine preparation of two short dresses for Mrs. C[ragin] and Mrs. N[oyes], who proposed to experiment on the fashion described in the Annual Report. . . . It is impossible to appreciate the heroism that was then required, to appear in the semi-masculine attire. . . . The style adopted . . . was the plain, loose pantaloon."[47] When the three women appeared together before the Oneida "family" in their new short dresses, the responses ranged from shock to acceptance. It took courage for the women "to appear in the semi-masculine attire" because a change in dress could be disturbing, even if encouraged within a receptive environment. Perhaps, when the women made their appearance, they feared being laughed at for looking like children because they had styled their new clothes after children's dress. If women altered their clothing to resemble the styles youngsters wore, then it was more likely that they would be identified with children rather than seen as "semi-masculine" and thus closer to men in the social and spiritual hierarchy.[48]

With the encouragement of John Humphrey Noyes, other women followed the example of the female leaders until frocks and loose pantalettes became the typical attire of women in the Community. Using the patriarchal power of the father over his wife, children, and other dependents, Noyes linked women to children through their appearance—essentially "dressing" them to keep them subordinate. Not surprisingly, the recommendation that men also adopt a distinctive costume based on children's clothing never received support. Efforts were made to simplify contemporary male apparel, which allowed men to renounce popular dress—a symbol of bondage to worldly values—and eased the burden for the women who made the garments.[49]

The original story, promoted by Noyes himself, emphasized that Cragin and H. H. Noyes, of their own devices, decided to create a dress to rid themselves of "effeminacy."[50] J. H. Noyes preferred to recognize the Community women as the initiators. In doing so, he implied that women had a strong voice in the Community, especially in matters of direct concern to women. However, Noyes never distanced himself too far from the short dress's introduction.[51] Without J. H. Noyes's urging and authority, the

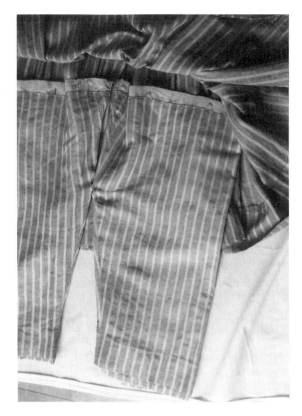

Detail of Oneida short dress pantalettes. Note the buttonholes at the top of the pantalettes— this garment obviously copied little girls' pantalettes, which tied around the knee or buttoned to under-drawers. Courtesy of the Oneida Community Mansion House.

other Community women might not have followed Mary Cragin and Harriet Noyes's example and changed their outfits. No official rule ever made the short dress compulsory, yet Community women would have had a difficult time opposing Noyes. The Oneida women were not overtly forced to wear "the dress of children," although Noyes made his displeasure known if his followers hesitated to comply with a Community practice. After female followers accepted Noyes, Oneida, and its religious ideology, it apparently pleased many of them to dress in an outfit that proclaimed their allegiance.

However, there is no indication that Perfectionist women themselves wanted to follow the silhouette of children's apparel. Oneida costumes consisted of short dresses and "pantalets" in contrast to other reform garments, which included "trowsers" or "pantaloons." Fashioned after little girls' pantalettes, Oneida pantalettes were two fabric tubes that either buttoned to underdrawers at the knee or tied on just above the knee. Thus, women attired in Oneida reform costumes with "true" pantalettes unquestionably wore a child's garment. Rather than empowering the wearers, an article of clothing or style worn exclusively by children made them appear infantile or childlike.[52] Oneida Perfectionist Harriet Worden remembered with pleasure that short hair and short dresses made women appear so youthful that "visitors often [mistook] our middle-aged women for girls, and our young women for children."[53]

In some ways children's clothing seemed an obvious choice for Oneida, since the Community hoped to institute gender-neutral clothing: sexual distinctions in children's clothing did not become obvious until about the ages of five or six. In actual practice, fabric, trim, and headwear often revealed the sex of children even when they wore similar garments, and although worn by both sexes, young children's clothing tended to follow feminine lines. More importantly, Oneida men did not wear the reformed and supposedly gender-neutral costume that the women wore.

The dress portion of the outfit mirrored adult women's fashions and other reform frocks, since "a long dress abridged, cut off a little below the knee" or "cut just long enough to fall two inches below the knee," made up the upper portion of the costume. The Community short dress consisted of a bodice and a skirt that hung only two or three inches below the knee, supplemented by wide, straight, untrimmed pantalettes reaching to the ankle. The same pattern continued to be used on dress after dress for years with few alterations in the style. The dress could be made of any material and of any color, but the women favored brown and blue for outdoor wear and white for evening. Generally, they made the dress and pantalettes from the same material. No stays or crinolines supported the dresses.[54] Every Oneida woman made her own clothes and, within specified parameters, followed her own taste in making the short dress. In addition to being responsible for their own clothing, women were assigned the task of making, mending, and laundering the apparel of male Community members.[55]

Women at Oneida augmented their childlike reform garments by cutting their hair—a decision that directly confronted Saint Paul's teachings that women use long hair as a covering. But Father Noyes helped the women reinterpret Paul's message by placing it within a historical context. In the present age in the United States, Noyes pointed out, the same customs regarding modesty did not exist. The current fashions that coiled long hair into a bun "covers less of the nakedness of the person, than the short hair of men." Reassuring women of the propriety of the act, Noyes encouraged them to cut off their hair in the "simple mode of little girls, down in the neck." Adult Oneida women ended up looking like little girls with short dresses, pantalettes, and short hair.[56]

Some female followers, however, chose not to wear the short dress. Jessie Kinsley recalled the "very stout Mrs. Toby" and her "great hoops," which she wore over "spreading long skirts, while every other woman at the O. C. wore pantalets and short dresses."[57] Pierrepont Noyes remembered "Lady Allen" and "Lady Thayer" and several other women "who represented a female dignity that I recognized but could not understand." These women wore "fancy lace caps, long dresses and old-fashioned hoopskirts."[58] The absence of these nonconformists from the Community's official documents is perhaps best explained by Oneida's commitment to a shared communal experience in which members subordinated the "I-spirit" to the "We-spirit." If these women acted on an individual impulse they would not be encouraged, even if tolerated. J. H. Noyes may have preferred to let these women wear what they wanted, given their small number, rather than calling attention to their actions.

During the first years of communal living, Oneida women were in the process of adopting and making their short dresses and seldom wore them outside their community. But Noyes had no intention of keeping the attire a secret, and the commune's publications referred to it frequently. Prior to 1851, Oneida's detractors were more concerned with the sexual practices taking place on commune grounds than with what women were wearing. It would not be long, however, before the connection between short dresses and free love and campaigns for woman's rights was made, and the public took another look at the female clothing worn at Oneida.

Another Charismatic Leader

In June 1851, James Jesse Strang and several of his Latter Day Saint (Strangite Mormon) followers were charged with counterfeiting, trespassing on federal lands, and obstructing the U.S. mail. District Attorney George Bates, determined to discredit the Mormon witnesses, battered the Strangites with questions about their allegiance to "King" Strang and their disregard for laws that did not come directly from him. The deposition of Sarah McCulloch dramatically illustrates the faith Strang's followers had in him. Before reproducing the records, Bates inaccurately and maliciously described the Mormons in attendance as a "motley crowd" with the ladies in full bloomer costume, and Strang in his "pontifical robes."[59] Although we must be skeptical of the accuracy of the transcription from which the following is drawn, McCulloch's assertions nevertheless demonstrate Strang's charisma:

> Question—"Mrs. McCulloch, you are an educated, accomplished lady born in Baltimore, and reared in the very best society. Can it be that you are a Mormon?"
>
> Answer—"Yes, sir, I have that honor, sir."
>
> Q.—"Can it be possible, madam, that so accomplished a lady as you are can believe that that fellow Strang is a prophet, seer and revelator?"
>
> A.—"Yes, Mr. District Attorney, I know it."
>
> Q.—"Can it be possible, Mrs. McCulloch, that you are so blind as to really believe that that fellow who sits there beneath you—that Strang, is the Prophet of the Lord, the successor of him who bore his cross among the jeers and sneers of Mount Calvary?"
>
> A.—"Yes, you impudent district attorney, and were you not a darned old fool you would know it too!"[60]

The jury acquitted Strang and his disciples. Ironically, Sarah McCulloch would, a few short years later, rail against his command that all women wear the "Mormon" costume, becoming one of his most outspoken detractors. Although Bates recalled the Strangite women as wearing "bloomer costumes," few, if any, would have been wearing the costume at this early date.

Mormonism

In the 1820s, Joseph Smith found golden tablets with "The Book of Mormon" inscribed on them. His supporters believed that he had been specially chosen by God to restore "true" Christianity. A teaching central to the Mormon doctrine, as revealed to Smith, was that the Latter-day Saints were living in the final dispensation of the Gospel: a time of preparation for the resurrection of the ancient Saints and the return of Jesus Christ to begin his millennial reign in God's kingdom on earth. The headquarters for the Church of Jesus Christ of Latter-day Saints was established eventually in

Nauvoo, Illinois, which initially welcomed Smith and his followers and granted them a good deal of autonomy. Many of the distinctive features of Mormon theology date from the Nauvoo period: the plurality of gods, baptism for the dead, marriage for eternity, and plural marriage. Smith also created the controversial Council of Fifty, permitted the establishment of a Masonic Temple (a secret organization), and borrowed from Masonic rituals to establish the secret rituals of the Mormon temple.[61]

One of the secrets of the Nauvoo Mormons was a sacred white garment referred to as "the garment of the Holy Priesthood." Participants in a religious ceremony devoted to theological instruction wore the garment. At this ceremony one received "endowments" as a step toward being accepted into the Celestial Kingdom.[62] Although originally designed as an undergarment for the endowment ceremonies, the garment was worn beneath regular clothing (and next to the skin) every day afterward. The sacred garment probably resembled today's contemporary long underwear or a union suit. Unlike most religious apparel, which made church affiliation visible, it was secret and invisible to the casual observer, allowing the wearer alone "to keep the faith."

The innovations and the secrecy Smith introduced to Mormonism eventually worked against the religion in Illinois, turning public opinion against the Mormons as well as creating internal dissension. The Mormon secrets turned to rumors, and popular gossip in Illinois hinted at Mormon conspiracies to disrupt the economic and political life of the state. After Joseph Smith was killed, a number of groups broke away from the main body of Mormons. One group became the Reorganized Church of Latter-day Saints and stayed faithful to the Book of Mormon but rejected Smith's ideas about gathering, secret temple rituals, and the doctrine of plural marriage. Although this group survived, it did not prosper to the same degree as the Mormons who journeyed to Utah under the leadership of Brigham Young. Another splinter group—the Strangite Mormons—experimented with reform dress.

James Jesse Strang and Strangite Theology

By the time he was thirty, James Jesse Strang had worked as a farmer, taught school, given temperance lectures, practiced law, dabbled in politics, edited a newspaper, and served as a postmaster. He married Mary Abigail Perce in 1836, and together they had four children. Seven years later, Strang and his family followed the lead of many others in the country and moved west to Burlington, Wisconsin. Shortly thereafter, Mormon missionaries persuaded him to visit Joseph Smith's community in Nauvoo, Illinois. In February 1844, Strang received religious instruction, was baptized, became a Mormon church elder, and was given a ministry in Wisconsin. Strang spread the word of Smith's Church—but he also had some ideas of his own that he wished to plant.[63]

Joseph Smith was assassinated in June 1844 and Strang—a Mormon convert for only about six months—insisted on his right to succeed Smith. Strang claimed to have had a divine vision at the very hour of Smith's murder, to have received a letter from Smith written nine days before his death, and to have unearthed three ancient brass plates: all of these signs purportedly recognized him as the new leader of God's chosen people. The struggle for the succession ended in the triumph of Brigham Young and the excommunication of Strang. Not one to accept defeat easily, Strang returned to Wisconsin and continued to assert his position as he gathered a small body of believers around him—the Strangite Mormons.

On August 25, 1846, Strang had a vision that described Big Beaver Island in northern Lake Michigan as the future home of the Strangite Saints, or Strangite Mormons. The island, twenty-five miles from the mainland, offered Strangite Mormons isolation from powerful outside forces and protection from their detractors and enemies as well as a place to live and prosper and practice their faith freely. The settlement on Beaver Island, including the village of St. James, grew. In the summer of 1849, more than 250 Strangite Saints had located there, and by 1850 that number had more than tripled. "King Strang" was "prophet, seer, revelator, translator, and first president of the Church, governing by revelation of the word of God, and deriving his authority solely from God."[64] Beaver Island became a theocracy, and Strang apparently became its autocrat. He acted as the "supreme master in every sphere of human thought and action," with no tolerance for insubordination.[65]

The Beaver Island Kingdom had numerous rules and regulations. Prohibitions against the use of tea, coffee, tobacco, and liquor stressed the importance of temperance and tested individual self-control. Men and women were discouraged from engaging in gambling, prostitution, and other lewd acts. The Sabbath was celebrated on the seventh day, and everyone physically capable was expected at services. The Saints paid one-tenth of their earnings into a public fund. Strang's presence was felt in every aspect—social, domestic, economic, and political—of his followers' lives.[66]

A reversal in the original Strangite religious doctrine that sanctified monogamous marriage to a new acceptance of Strangite polygamy became a recurring point of dissension within the Strangite community. Existing primary evidence does not make it clear why Strang changed from his vehement antipolygamy stance to his acceptance and practice of polygamy. Strang may simply have developed a sexual attraction to Elvira Field that he felt compelled to act on. Joseph Smith's acceptance of plural marriage and the Utah Mormons' polygamous practices may also have made it easier for Strang to rationalize his desire to be married to more than one woman. On the other hand, women had difficulty finding suitable husbands, and polygamy allowed them "a wider range for the selection of husbands," according to Strang.[67] Finally, Strang also believed that polygamy restrained lasciviousness and lust. Although polygamy would be the subject of much debate, the practice of multiple marriages directly affected only a few Strangite families.

Polygamy is not central to the issue of dress on Beaver Island; however, it helps establish Strang as a forceful, controlling leader capable of instituting major theological and social changes into his community without prior discussion.[68] The polygamy controversy is also worth mentioning because, without exception, the wives of blatantly antipolygamist Strangite men led the opposition to the "Mormon" dress. Although many problems plagued the Strangites on Beaver Island, the community flourished, growing to 2,500 by 1854. Their political leverage enabled them to elect Strang to the Michigan legislature twice. Life on the island also included a great deal of violence and conflict. Gentiles opposed the Strangite Saints on the issues of fishing rights, suspected thefts, and the stifled liquor trade with island Indians. Strang and his followers found themselves in court and jail at nearby Mackinac Island as well as in Detroit, charged with everything from murder and treason to general moral depravity. Strang's "autocratic rule" irritated some of his own followers—as his assassination by two dissatisfied Strangite Mormons on June 16, 1856, made all too clear. After the murder, most of the Strangite Saints evacuated the island and settled on the mainland in Wisconsin or Michigan; in fact, Strangite Mormonism is still practiced by a few followers.

The Strangite Mormons shared many things with the Utah or Brighamite Mormons, including the names "Church of Jesus Christ of Latter-day (or

'Latter Day' in the case of Strangites) Saints," "Saints," and "Mormons." Although similarities existed, Beaver Island Mormons and Utah Mormons were two distinct religions. Both the Strangite and Brighamite churches accepted as doctrine the life and works of Joseph Smith, and both practiced polygamy at one time. Beaver Island and Utah Mormons established "kingdoms" that were spiritual as well as temporal and political. The "kingdom" also caused their enemies to speculate about the possibility of treason against the U.S. government. Both enacted laws and punishments that recalled the harshness of the Old Testament—including using the whipping post rather than a jail cell. Although adultery was a crime punishable by death in Utah and on Beaver Island, neither community enforced this draconian rule. Both groups endured persecution at the hands of hostile Gentiles. The Strangite Mormons actively sought members, and sent missionaries throughout the United States, but the better-organized Utah missionaries attracted more converts.[69]

No official rule ever made short dresses compulsory in the Oneida Community. In contrast, Strang eventually *ordered* his female followers to wear Mormon dress. There is no "hard" evidence that Strang knew of Oneida's short dress outfit, but it is plausible that he learned of the Community and their clothing in his travels east. The closed religious community with its authoritative male leader may have reinforced Strang's philosophy, and its female costume may have suggested possibilities that he had not yet considered. Strang was born in New York but left the state in 1843, five years before the Oneidans experimented with dress; therefore he could only have learned of the costume after his conversion to Mormonism. It is conceivable that knowledge of Noyes, Oneida, and its dress code for women influenced Strang's desire to introduce such an outfit to Strangite Mormon women. Strang, like John Humphrey Noyes, controlled all ecclesiastical, secular, and civil affairs within his kingdom; only his endorsement would permit women to wear an outfit that included pantaloons.

Reform Dress, Charles J. Douglas, and the Mormon Dress

In a rather odd turn of events, the first time a Strangite Mormon woman wore an outfit ordained by Strang, it was a disguise. Strang, his legal wife Mary Perce Strang, and their children traveled east in 1849 to recruit settlers to Beaver Island; Strang also wanted his second and (at that time) secret wife Elvira Eliza Field Strang to accompany him. Strang disguised his young wife as a man, his "male" secretary. Elvira Field Strang, transformed into Charles J. Douglas with a short haircut and dressed in men's clothing, met Strang in New York and traveled with him spreading the word about Strangite Mormonism. Elvira Field Strang's disguise did not fool everyone: rumors circulated about "his suspicious curves," and observers saw the Strangs kissing and touching intimately. Mary Perce Strang became aware of her husband's interest in another woman through his curious references to "Charley Douglas" in his letters.[70] At the conclusion of the eastern journey, Strang acknowledged Elvira Field Strang as his wife in polygamy and reversed his earlier stance against the practice. Mary Perce continued to live for a short while on Beaver Island and then returned to Wisconsin. Her letters suggest that she continued to love Strang even as they lived apart. Ultimately, Strang had three more wives in addition to Mary Perce and Elvira Field.

Although Elvira Strang wore pants as "Douglas," this did not directly translate into a new costume with pants for Strangite women. Strang introduced a "new Mormon" outfit to his female followers, but the accounts of this event (many written years later) often disagree with one another, making it difficult to follow the chronology of pantaloons dress reform on Beaver Island. The first reference to a distinctive costume worn by female Strangites can be found in the diary of Stephen Post, a Mormon elder. Writing about his trip to the island for a conference in 1850, Post described Elvira Field Strang's "odd" costume: "She was dressed in pantalets—long loose trousers gathered closely about the ankles—covered by a skirt that came down to her knees."[71] Post also learned that this had become the typical style of dress for Beaver Island women. Two facts make this reference particularly fascinating. First, if Post is correct, then Strangite Saints adopted the reform outfit almost a year before Amelia Bloomer first wore the famed "bloomer costume," which suggests that Strang learned about pantaloons for women at Oneida. Second, in May 1851, the Strangite newspaper the *Northern Islander* carried a brief article about "short dresses." It is unclear if the piece was reprinted from another newspaper or if Strang wrote it. The content of the article can be read in two ways. The article mentions "several ladies" who appeared in Syracuse, New York, in bloomer costumes and notes that Syracuse is a town "for all kinds of foolish and odd freaks to take root in." The article continues in this vein, laughing at an outfit similar to one already worn on the island, which seems odd given that the Strangites expressed pride in their reform. If the commentary was reprinted, this implies that the Strangites monitored reactions to the costume in the Gentile world, perhaps as a way of differentiating their own clothing experiences. Or maybe, for them, the secular dress was worth mocking because it was worldly—not divinely ordained. Only the blessing of a king could consecrate what would otherwise be freakish. Despite conflicting or puzzling evidence and stories, it seems reasonable that by the summer of 1852 the "Mormon dress" was commonplace, but not universal, on Beaver Island.[72] In 1852 Strang, perhaps following the lead of John Humphrey Noyes, did not initially institute strict dress regulations. A few years later, however, he no longer tolerated the informal dress code and formalized rules about dress.

Apparel and Ornaments

Strang ruled his followers with authority, and nowhere is this more clearly evidenced than with the Mormon dress. At a conference in 1855, Strang made remarks "concerning the apparel of the sisters," in which he showed the necessity of conforming to the "pattern that God [had] given" and ordered the women to wear "full-length calico-pantalets, covered by a matching straight-waisted dress reaching down to the knees."[73] His directive corresponded with the conclusion of his translation of the brass tablets, which were later published as *The Book of the Law of the Lord*.

Chapter 39, "Apparel and Ornaments," began with the injunction, "Ye shall not clothe yourselves after the manner of the follies of other men; but after the manner that is seemly and convenient, shall ye clothe yourselves."[74] The chapter then details objections against female dress and provides some specific clothing instructions. King Strang's motivations for changing female attire paralleled those of other contemporary dress reformers. Both *The Book* and the *Northern Islander* reiterated arguments that had been in circulation for decades (some for centuries). Strang and Strangite writers railed against the indecency and vagaries of fashion, which demanded that women sacrifice "convenience, health, and sometimes life."[75] From time to time, the island newspaper reprinted the fashion opinions of commentators it agreed with; several of "Mrs. Swisshelm's" comments even found their way into *The Book of the Law of the Lord*— unacknowledged. For example, Swisshelm wrote, "I notice they [women] are awfully deformed, too, as a general rule, having great lumps on their backs, like dromedaries—."[76] *The Book* similarly remarked on skirts "padded out to the uncouth style of a camel's hump."[77] A February 14, 1856,

Northern Islander article, commenting on hoopskirts, facetiously invited those sisters "who have itching eyes for Gentile customs" to make haste and adopt the new outrageous fashion or "they will be too late" and the fashion will have passed. Briefly, chapter 39 lists the problems with "fashion" as follows: ornamentation is extravagant; constantly changing styles invite wastefulness; unhealthy, and possibly even deadly, fashion encourages depravity among those who follow it; some styles are simply ugly and should not be worn; and high fashion promotes class dissension. All of these arguments could be found in most dress reform and antifashion material, but in 1855 they became a part of official Strangite Latter Day Saint doctrine and heralded a new order for the Beaver Island community.

The apparel chapter did not simply outline the objections to Gentile fashions, but also made it clear that the Saints "shall clothe themselves according to my [Strang's or God's?] Commandment."[78] The "law" distinguished between clothing worn for public gatherings and formal worship—this dress was a "matter of divine appointment"—and everyday wear. Although apparel for "common uses" did not have the distinction of being a "positively divine appointment," it continued to be regulated by Commandment. Within limits, Saints could "exercise [their] own taste in common apparel"—for women this meant customizing Mormon dress. When proselytizing or traveling among Gentiles, Saints could "imitate, to some moderate extent, their [Gentile] foolish and ridiculous styles," in order to avoid being singled out or made the object of ridicule. Oneida women also wore worldly fashions when they left the confines of their community, which suggests another link between the Strangite and Oneida dress reforms. Because of the hostility often directed at their followers and their beliefs, it is not surprising that Strang and Noyes would want to minimize visual differences outside of their havens. Not coincidentally, fashionable dress also made it easier to attract new converts.

Why did Strang wait to formalize a dress code? It is possible that he hoped to replicate Noyes's success at Oneida, where most of the women wore short dresses and pantalettes without being ordered to do so. That Strang had to put a law in place suggests that his influence was not as strong or widespread as he wanted and that he found it necessary to institutionalize his authority. An underlying motive for reforming Beaver Island Mormon dress may then have been greater social control. Strangite theology came from the mind and life experiences of a mortal man who always retained an awareness of his own ambitions and desire to rule without opposition, and Strang used uniformity in dress to gain greater control over his followers, especially the women. A uniform was never adopted for universal wear on Beaver Island, with the exception of formal gatherings, and then only those who had specific duties wore prescribed robes.

Uniformity or similarity in dress did, however, become standard on the island. The difference between uniforms and uniformity is significant as well as paradoxical. Wearers of uniforms are usually encouraged to give up their individuality and act primarily as "occupants of their uniformed status"[79]; thus it would seem that if Strang wanted to control every aspect of his followers' lives he would have commanded uniforms rather than uniformity. Yet Strang did not use uniforms to strengthen his authority because to do so would have pushed his followers too far—as the resistance to Mormon costume showed him. Standardized apparel enabled Strang to limit and regulate the clothing choices available to women and reinforced his dominance, without his having to go to the extreme measure of uniforms. (Although the sources are contradictory, apparently men did not have to follow the same strict rules women did.) The pervasive nineteenth-century understanding that women had a special attachment to clothing that adversely affected them probably influenced the gendered Strangite dress regulations. Strangite women could not alter their apparel of their own volition without recrimination.

The Dress Rebellion

One biographer, recognizing the powerful repercussions that can result from taking clothing choices away from women and men, described Strang's 1855 order commanding "all the women of his kingdom to wear 'bloomers'" as his "fatal mistake."[80] Another historian concurs and suggests that the Mormon dress had much to do with bringing about Strang's "overthrow."[81] As with most issues and events that occurred on the Strangite Beaver Island, the record of women's reactions to the new clothing regulations is conflicting and confusing, with some accounts praising the outfits and others condemning them. Writing to H. A. Chaney in 1877, Wingfield Watson observed that the Strangite women seemed to "genuinely like" their Mormon outfits. He also recalled that after Strang's death the women stopped wearing the garment "with many a regret."[82] Given the persecution women suffered if they did not wear the Mormon dress, it is not surprising that Watson heard only favorable remarks.

Although most female Saints wore the Mormon dress, King Strang's command to women to wear short skirts and pantaloons did not meet with universal approval or compliance. Some women, echoing the opinions of non-Mormon dress reformers, objected to the costume because it was "ugly" and "unbecoming." Others may have used the dress to vent their disapproval of Strang's authoritarian leadership and his position on polygamy. Still others resisted because they believed Strang had overstepped his place and was interfering with the private "feminine sphere." The most vocal Strangites who complained about the Mormon costume and continued to wear long dresses were Mrs. McCulloch, Mrs. Bedford, Mrs. Johnson, Mrs. Wentworth, and Mrs. Orson Campbell. Those male Saints who could not (or would not) make their wives obey Strang's command were treated as Gentiles by the community. After some husbands failed to make their wives comply or actually supported their wives in wearing long dresses, Strang "declared in public that the law should be obeyed, if he had to wade ankle deep in blood."[83] Women who did not wear the Bloomer costume, or their husbands, might be publicly whipped—often by Strang himself—or publicly humiliated. They might become the victims of nonsense lawsuits filed by Strang, or their homes might even be burglarized. In order for Strang to maintain control over his followers, it became important that he suppress individual impulses—in this case, the rejection of his regulations on uniform dress for women.

A brief article that appeared in the May 1, 1856, issue of the *Northern Islander* summed up Strang's attitude toward the apparel, the women who wore it, the women who did not wear it, and what purpose he thought Mormon dress served in the Strangite community. It began, "The Mormon ladies have their own style of dress—convenient and very beautiful." After additional praise for the dress itself, the tone of the column changed as Strang addressed the "lady who deems it beneath her dignity to wear a Mormon dress." Strang attacked the reputations of disobedient women and made it clear that he considered these women beneath contempt. Not content with a general reprimand, Strang singled out one malcontent in particular. Although no name was mentioned, the article's details would have made identification easy for readers. The woman attired in a long dress had stolen, confessed to the theft, but never made restitution. Her crimes continued: she had committed adultery, her husband had publicly whipped the lover, and she had been cast from the island community. Strang seemed to laugh bitterly at women with low morals who rejected the Mormon dress, and stated that such women would be a disgrace to the outfit and should not be permitted to wear it. Yet despite the bravado of such statements, it is clear that Strang did not want any woman—immoral or chaste—to defy his orders.

Several scholars theorized that Mrs. Thomas Bedford was the woman singled out in the *Northern Islander* report.[84] Thomas Bedford, characterized as rebellious and outspoken, liked to do as he pleased without regard to the king's orders. He and Strang were antagonists, suing and countersuing each another. Apparently, when Bedford could not or would not force his wife to wear the Mormon dress, he was "given 39 lashes with a willow whip."[85] It is more likely that Bedford received the whipping for spreading tales that put in Strang in a poor light, but the wife's violation of the dress code proved to be the practical avenue of punishment. The flogging sealed Bedford's hatred of Strang. On the morning that Bedford's countersuit against Strang was to be heard, the justice of the peace stopped briefly at Bedford's home. There, he saw Mrs. Bedford wearing a long dress and sewing another. The justice informed Bedford that since his wife dressed as a Gentile, the couple would be treated as Gentiles. Thus they had no case against Strang, and the justice dismissed the suit. The irate Bedford then began to conspire with others, including Alexander Wentworth (whose wife also refused to adopt Strangite Mormon dress), on Strang's assassination.

Mrs. Sarah McCulloch—who in 1851 had testified as a follower of Strang—"refused to wear the bloomer costume of obedient daughters of the Church" and encouraged other women to oppose it as well.[86] In keeping with Strangite punishments, her husband, Dr. Hezekiah McCulloch, suffered the consequences of his wife's actions and found himself the target of a Strang lawsuit. McCulloch had joined Strang in the early days and become a trusted officer; however, a weakness for liquor—expressly forbidden on the island—contributed to his loss of status and Strang's disapproval.[87] The story goes that when the sheriff arrived to assess McCulloch's property for the trial, McCulloch turned to Strang and said, "Now it is you

SCENES IN AN AMERICAN HAREM.

BRIGHAM YOUNG AND HIS FAMILY ON THEIR WAY TO CHURCH.

This drawing of Brigham Young and his wives, some of whom are dressed in deseret costume, offers an intriguing look at the outfit. However, given the controversial nature of the Mormon lifestyle, it is likely that the artist wished to connect the two "deviant" practices—polygamy and bloomers—in the minds of the reader. *Harper's Weekly Illustrated Newspaper.*

and I for it; you will destroy me or I shall destroy you."[88] Weakened and disgraced, McCulloch nevertheless tried to undermine Strang's power before joining the other conspirators in plotting his murder. On June 16, 1856, Strang's assassins shot and beat him and left him barely alive—James Jesse Strang died on July 9, 1856.

Deseret Costume

Utah Mormons had long stressed a practical approach to clothing, but little is known about what has come to be called the "deseret costume" worn by Latter-day Saint women on their travels to Utah and in the early settlement period. More is known about their religious undergarments and "everyday" dress.[89] In an excellent study, Ruth Vickers Clayton examined Mormon clothing practices of the mid-nineteenth century. Clayton focused on the fashionable clothing worn by Mormon women and men between 1847 and 1887 and discovered that their dress became an important cultural symbol, and that *fashionable* clothing symbolized to the world that Mormon colonization of the Great Salt Lake region had prospered.[90] In contrast to many other nineteenth-century religions with negative appraisals of fashionable clothing, the Mormons thus allowed, and even enjoyed, fashionable styles as long as they did not incorporate extremes.

Their approval and sanction of fashionable attire make it difficult to understand the Latter-day Saint experimentation with reform dress. According to Susa Young Gates, a daughter of Brigham Young, sometime in the 1850s her father and Eliza R. Snow indirectly encouraged Mormon women to find a "stabilised dress." The design they came up with, the "deseret costume," consisted of "bloomers and full skirts, without hoops, trimming or trains." The unattractive, "hideous" dress did not appeal to many of the women, and within a few years they returned to "beautiful colours and pretty clothes."[91] The information on the deseret costume is sparse, and the information gleaned from the pages of Susa Young Gates's and Clarissa Young Spencer's memoirs is unreliable. Neither woman had firsthand knowledge of Mormon reform garb, and thus any conclusions drawn about the costume must be speculative.[92] Since the Mormons believed that, as God's elect people they were destined to achieve the best possible life through building God's kingdom, it is not surprising that they would have chosen fashionable dress, a visual symbol of success. However, their brief experimentation with reform garb suggests that the Mormon leaders may not have been entirely comfortable with fashionable dress, which could encourage "Madame Vanity."[93]

In contrast to some other religious leaders, Brigham Young stated that he did not mind seeing women adorned, nor did it bother him that women liked to adorn themselves, but he wanted the adornment to be the workmanship of Mormon hands. In their early years in Utah, the leaders of the church encouraged home industry, in part to save money, but also to reduce the Mormons' dependence on the outside world. Young suggested that Latter-day Saint women should make contributions to such worthy causes as the emigration of poor Mormons from abroad, instead of wasting their money on "useless articles that do no good to the body of the persons who use them."[94] The Utah Mormons seemed able to accept women's "dress spirit" as long as it did not distract them from their more important religious and community activities.

It is possible that the deseret costume influenced the Strangite Mormon dress; however, it is not likely that the deseret outfit had any other far-reaching effect. Like most of the early reform garments, it was worn in private. The relative isolation of the Utah Mormon culture and the westward trail ensured that few people beyond the Latter-day Saint Mormons would see it. In fact, the myth surrounding the garment's use and popularity was out of proportion to the small number of women who actually wore it. To those outside the Church, deseret and Mormon costumes hinted at sexual improprieties because of their association with polygamists, not unlike the sexual deviance suggested by Oneida apparel or the free love accusations identified with New Harmony dress.

A Hybrid Reform

Isolated groups and individual reformers who never came together with a shared philosophy or strategy to change the dress of American women made up the pantaloons dress reform movement in the mid-nineteenth century. No single organization or person consolidated the varied reasons for advocating a short dress and pantaloons. This hybrid characteristic of dress reform is important because it is one of the features that differentiated the movement from other antebellum reform movements.

Many of the early dress reform efforts may have hurt the later attempts of woman's rights advocates and made it more difficult for them to introduce their costume. The lifestyles or perceived lifestyles of early reformers prepared a hostile environment for the introduction of the freedom dress. The public mind quickly associated the short dress and pantaloons with "questionable" sexual practices—i.e., polygamy, free love, and prostitution. Some people considered the Oneida costume the dress of free lovers, and hydropathist and health reformer Mary Gove Nichols did not help the cause of dress reform when she proclaimed herself an advocate of free love.

At the heart of these factions were the men who dictated what women were supposed to wear. Men's stated motives usually sounded laudable: providing women with a costume that allowed them to work, serve God, or attain good health certainly seemed a noble objective. Male reformers did not want to change their dominant position in relation to women, which explains why few made major alterations in their own clothing and why change was "good"—so long as it was handed down by a Father Noyes or a King Strang. When men sanctioned women's trousers, women may have gained some authority, but within those closed communities men did not imagine that they lost control or status when they allowed women to wear a garment that had been traditionally allied with masculine strength. Furthermore, women in private spaces did not adopt pantaloons to upset the gendered power structure in place. Instead, these women continued to conform to the societal values that granted men authority over women. Thus pantaloon reform dress symbolized a new form of female exploitation. Either by encouraging women to wear trousers or by discouraging women from wearing them, male leaders made certain that everyone understood that men *really* still "wore the pants." Only when women, without male approval, chose to wear pantaloons in public did they pose a threat to the masculine "right" to govern and command—"What shall we do when women wear the breeches?" In 1851, woman's rights activists shocked society when they put on pantaloons, marched briskly down public streets, and openly challenged the accepted gender system.

Whither have fled the gallant hearts
So famed in many an olden story,
Who felt that woman's smile imparts
The truest sense of earthly glory?
Alas! the men, degenerate cases,
With ladies now have changed their places,
And gentle dames once served so true,
By many courtly squires and knights,
Their own campaigning now must do
To win the cause of Bloomer-rights.

—*Democratic Review,* September 1851

Pantaloons in Public

Woman's Rights and Freedom Dresses

On a brisk spring day in 1851, Elizabeth Smith Miller, Elizabeth Cady Stanton, and Amelia Jenks Bloomer strode through Seneca Falls, New York, in short skirts with "Turkish trousers"—and pantaloons and women's struggle for power came together for the first time in U.S. history.[1] Never before had women used pantaloons to challenge the nineteenth-century gender system. Now woman's rights advocates "made the personal political," taking pantaloons reform dress out of private homes and into the muddy streets. This incident touched off a short-lived but intense debate about several things: the relationships between dress reform and the actions of woman's rights; the influence of the popular press in ridiculing and ultimately helping to suppress "Bloomer-rights"; and the stability of the separate spheres model that shaped white, middle-class society.

The popular press found the story of three respectable, middle-class white women wearing pantaloons irresistible. Several newspapers, including the *New York Tribune,* the *Boston Carpet-Bag,* and the *Chicago Tribune,* reported on the incident and jokingly proposed names for the outfits. Bloomer herself had suggested "Camilia," but woman's rights advocates favored the term

The *Water-Cure Journal* published this engraving of Amelia Jenks Bloomer in the freedom dress but appropriated the costume as its own and identified it as "The American Costume." *The Water-Cure Journal* 12 (October 1851): 96.

"freedom dress." The press, however, rejected all other labels in favor of "Bloomer," and it stuck.[2] Playing with variations on the word, journalists created new adjectives and nouns: "Bloomerism," "Bloomerites," and "Bloomers."[3] Amelia Jenks Bloomer did not invent the garment, and she was not the first to wear or advocate it, but her name quickly became synonymous with the costume.[4]

A Freedom Dress with "Turkish Trousers"

The "true" story behind the origins of the woman's rights dress reform will probably never be known, although contemporary stories and historical accounts purported to record the origins of the bloomer.[5] Conflicting sources and anecdotal evidence call many of these reports into question, however. The press's coverage was insubstantial and inaccurate, and feminists contradicted each other in tales of their decision to change their style of dress. Bloomer contributed to the confusion when she wrote that she first "heard" of the dress being worn at water cures, first "read" about the costume in the *Seneca County Courier,* and first "saw" the outfit on Elizabeth Smith Miller.[6] Looking for the "truth" in history is problematic, and in the case of freedom dresses the anxiety experienced by nineteenth-century observers and participants is much more interesting than who actually wore the costume first.

In all likelihood, a series of coincidences led Miller, Stanton, and Bloomer to cut off their long skirts. A satire on women's dress appeared in a local conservative newspaper and suggested that female readers adopt short skirts and "Turkish trousers." Bloomer used the pages of the *Lily, A Ladies' Journal, Devoted to Temperance and Literature*[7] to respond with humor and corresponding sarcasm. "Really," she admonished, "we are surprised that the cautious editor of the *Seneca County Courier* has so far overcome his opposition to woman's rights as to become himself an advocate of their wearing the pantaloons!"[8] The *Courier*'s editor was not amused by Bloomer's "levity" and reprimanded her for not taking the subject of female dress more seriously. Surprised by the scolding, Bloomer pointed out that if she or Stanton had proposed the change in dress and said "what you did, it would have been set down against us; and no doubt many men would have refused to support the *Lily,* lest our 'politics' should corrupt their wives, and lead them to don the pantaloons." She went on to approve the editor's views on changes in woman's costume, especially thanking him for "breaking the ice" on the topic of pantaloons for women.[9] But as Bloomer bantered with the *Courier,* Elizabeth Smith Miller was already altering her dresses.

Miller had begun experimenting with short skirts and trousers before articles about woman's dress captured readers' attention. How did Miller come to design the costume? Her later explanations often disagreed with her earlier accounts. The *Courier*'s stance on female apparel, the antifashion rhetoric in circulation, the shared disapproval for women's dress that existed in 1851; this atmosphere, no doubt, stimulated Miller's experiment. But her design differed radically from what proper women wore in public and—most shocking—included pantaloons, a man's garment. Evidence suggests that Miller saw women wearing pantaloons or knew about private reform dresses. She may have seen a short dress at a health spa and become so enamored of it that she adapted the costume for her own use.[10] Or Miller could have been inspired by pantaloons reform garments at the Oneida Community close to her father's Peterboro home.[11]

Three years before, Miller may have read of Fanny Kemble's exploits in Lennox, Massachusetts. Kemble, along with several other women, had appeared in public "equipped in coats, vests, and pantaloons."[12] Forty years later, in 1892, Miller offered yet another scenario. "In the spring of 1851, while spending many hours at work in the garden, I became so thoroughly disgusted with the long skirt, that the dissatisfaction, the growth of years, suddenly ripened into the decision that this shackle should no longer be endured. The resolution was at once put into practice. Turkish trousers to the ankle, with a skirt reaching some four inches below the knee, were substituted for the . . . old garment."[13] Miller tried an innovation when she thought that alternative female apparel was less risky. Later accounts suggested that Miller's father "invented" reform apparel. However, had Gerrit Smith been credited with the idea, the history of pantaloons reform dress would have differed greatly. Reform attire introduced by a prominent man might have gained greater acceptance.

Wearing her new short skirt and Turkish trousers, Miller "hastened to Seneca Falls to visit [her] cousin, Mrs. Elizabeth Cady Stanton."[14] Days after Miller's arrival, Stanton copied the garment and appeared in her own freedom dress. Miller and Stanton then showed Bloomer their outfits and persuaded her to give the costume a try. Bloomer later commented that the coincidence of Miller wearing reform costume as she sparred with the *Courier* about "Turkish trousers" convinced her that she "should practise [*sic*] as I preached." Thus the three women took a private reform and made it public. Bloomer also filled the *Lily* with articles on her, Stanton's, and Miller's pantaloons reform garments. The popular press from New York City to San Francisco and other reform periodicals reprinted many of the items published in the *Lily*. These articles, and a flurry of interest in the "bloomer label," spread the news. At the same time the misperception that the costume originated with Amelia Jenks Bloomer continued.[15]

The basis for the design remains a mystery. None of the dress reformers left detailed accounts about the origins of the short dress and pantaloons style, forcing historians to piece together snippets of information buried in diaries, letters, and published works. Two groups that left intriguing hints about the process of creating reform garments are the Oneida Community and the woman's rights movement. Given the political and social differences between the two, it is all the more curious that they shared a belief in their abilities to introduce elements of fashion from "innocent" or "infantile" sources in order to create a new, acceptable, alternative female fashion. How they came to choose Eastern dress and children's wear and how observers reacted to their choices reveal the cultural investment nineteenth-century U.S. society had made in men's pantaloons.

A misconception about pantaloons reform dress that has persisted into the twentieth century is that dress reformers looked solely to men's clothing as the inspiration for their reform garb—observers considered reform dress "a travesty of male attire."[16] Most of nineteenth-century society, including woman advocates of dress reform, thought male clothing superior to female clothing and freely expressed this opinion. Pantaloons dress reformers, however, wanted to reform female dress for comfortable fit, physical well-being, religious beliefs, woman's rights, or work opportunities—not to blur distinctions between the sexes. Whether or not male clothing actually was more comfortable, convenient, or "natural" does not really matter. Trousers represented physical freedom, and some women imagined being freed from societal restraints as well.

Dress reformers wanted to wear pantaloons so, not surprisingly, their arguments stressed that there was nothing inherently male about trousers and that the garment could be adapted and made feminine. Most pantaloons dress reformers, as women of their time, could not have conceived of themselves as dressed in the "true" male garb of pantaloons, jacket, shirt, collar, tie, and hat, and played down references to borrowing clothing from the opposite sex.[17] Different camps tried different versions. The pantaloons component of the costume proved to be problematic, since the majority of women had never worn an exposed bifurcated garment before.[18] Some did turn to men's wear for ideas, but this course was replete with problems.

Mainstream society did not want women to wear men's pantaloons. However, it is difficult to determine if the resistance of the general public to female trousers stemmed more from the fear that women would seize male power or from the fear that pantaloons-clad women would be unabashedly "sexy." Most of the diatribes against reform dress printed for mass circulation stressed the opinion that women would somehow be coarsened, more "male" if they wore bifurcated garments. Less than a year

Man in his Natural Position, and Woman where she ought to be.

This cartoon suggests that pantaloons were so closely identified with masculinity that, if women wore them, the only result could be a complete gender reversal. *Yankee Notions* (September 1852).

after the introduction of the "bloomers," cartoons began to appear which depicted one of the biggest fears about reform clothing—that men would become feminine. Numerous articles and essays charged that if women wore the pantaloons then it would logically follow that men would assume the feminine characteristic of dependence, as this biting poem makes clear:

> Now then, my dear,
> We'll smoke and cheer and drink our lager beer;
> We'll have our latch-keys, stay out late at night;
> And boldly we'll assert our female rights;
> While conquered men, our erewhile tyrant foes,
> Shall stay at home and wear our cast-off clothes,
> Nurse babies, scold the servants, get our dinners;
> 'Tis all that they are fit for, wretched sinners![19]

Most women and men seemed incapable of imagining clothing that was not gender specific. There was also eroticism inherent in the idea of women in pantaloons. The language of dress in the nineteenth century made "men's pants" into charged, even sexualized, words. Ironically, euphemisms—"inexpressibles," "unwhisperables," "don't mentions,"—meant to allow polite society to avoid the suggestion of sex—did just the opposite.[20]

In such a charged atmosphere, at least two groups of dress reformers—feminists and Oneida Perfectionists—turned away from men's trousers, and looked elsewhere for "safer" models. Clothing from Eastern countries was one choice, although the sexual suggestiveness of pantaloons seemed unavoidable. Western travelers to the East showed a great deal of fascination with Eastern clothing and often affected "Oriental" dress while staying in the Middle East. The veil and the *ferace* (a long, loose robe) captivated Western observers more than any other article of Eastern women's clothing. These articles also suggested eroticism because they hid the female face and form behind drapery and hinted at the sexual pleasures that could be found beneath the flowing cloth. Fashion historian Valerie Steele has found that images of the harem were considered both exotic and erotic. Decades after the freedom dress debuted, Steele notes the "notorious *jupe-culotte* (or harem trouser-skirt) of 1911" caused a scandal, in part, because it indicated the legs.[21] Lady Mary Wortley Montague, who lived in the Middle East while her husband served as an ambassador, wrote in 1717 of the freedom she enjoyed when wearing her pantaloons "here, within the closely-guarded chambers of the harem." There is a hint of the erotic in her writings, suggesting that women in trousers could not be seen outside protected walls because they might arouse men. In a letter to her sister, Montague insisted "the first part of my dress is a pair of drawers, very full, that reach to my shoes, and conceal the legs more modestly than your petticoats."[22] Since no flesh could be seen, Montague argued in favor of the modesty of bifurcated garments. But the physical release of the body implied a sensuality that was not possible for a body confined in stays and long skirts and that was stereotypically associated with Eastern cultures.

The decision of woman's rights advocates to wear "Turkish trousers" expands on recent interpretations of nineteenth-century "feminist Orientalist discourse," which charges that nineteenth-century Western feminists defined aspects of Western life they found objectionable as "Eastern" and made them objects of reform. Thus Orientalist discourse was primarily a "strategy (and a form of thought) by which a speaker or writer neutralized the threat inherent in feminist demands and [made] them palatable to an audience that wishe[d] to affirm its occidental superiority."[23]

Mervat Hatem concludes that Orientalism worked against Western women because they considered their situations so much better than Eastern women's oppression that they were unable to articulate or understand a different form of subjugation—the one under which they lived.[24] Suvendrini Perera observes that Western women consciously appropriated Eastern images to use as representations of the oppression of Western women, yet these same women failed to recognize the suffering of Eastern women as significant.[25] Judy Mabro has found that for centuries Europeans were fascinated and repelled by notions of what the veil was and what it hid.[26] These scholars, however, pay little attention to Western women in Eastern clothing or adaptations of Eastern styles. The following 1864 poem is an example of how "Orientalist discourse" theory might be used to understand nineteenth-century antifashion sentiments.

> Talk of Turkish women
>   In their harem-coop,—
> Are we less inhuman,
> Hampering with a hoop?
> All free motion thwarted;
>   Mortals *a la mort;*
> Life's a thing aborted,
>   Through your draggle-skirt.[27]

The poem compares the "inhuman" "Turkish" harem with the "inhuman" Western practice of wearing physically restrictive clothing. The comparison suggests that Western women dressed in the height of fashion are in the same position as oppressed Turkish women. This ploy could potentially set the stage for the introduction of a new garment for women; ironically, and in contrast to Perera's interpretation, the alternative clothing eventually introduced was that already being worn by "imprisoned" Turkish women: "Turkish trousers."

Sociologist and costume historian Jennifer Craik attempts to clarify the complexities of cultural borrowing within fashion by theorizing that, "because fashion systems are built on the interrelationship and tension between exotic and familiar codes, exotic looks are all the more effective as techniques of display." Exoticism could be expressed through "foreign or rare motifs in fashion."[28] Costume historian Shelly Foote points out that borrowing from the East in the nineteenth century was fraught with difficulties. In her own research she has found that some Western clothing included adaptations of "pagan motifs" (Egyptian symbols). Foote concludes that the close connection between the Middle East and the Bible might be the key to the acceptance and appeal of "Eastern" images, because people in the nineteenth century kept looking for cultural survivals to put them closer to Biblical times.[29] Whether this idea motivated nineteenth-century feminists to try Near Eastern trousers is difficult to determine, but it certainly shows the complex threads involved in adopting aspects of one culture into another. Using Craik's theory we can begin to see the feminists' acceptance of "Turkish trousers" as part of the tension between freedom of movement (an exotic element) and the constraint of fashion (the familiar).

Craik's discussion of how non-Western cultures incorporate Western elements into their fashions helps us understand what the nineteenth-century feminists may have ended up doing. Craik is convinced that clothing is important in the "deployment of power and prestige," and she suggests that individuals can strategically use elements of fashion from different cultures to produce a new "dress code." These new codes can be commentaries on "political exigencies as well as practical ways to negotiate the conflicting departments of existence."[30]

Once woman's rights advocates decided to try a combination of short dress and trousers, they needed to decide what their particular costume would look like. At first, the women did not consider a change in clothing to be a political move but an opportunity to enjoy greater freedom of movement. Since much of U.S. society considered pantaloons more hygienic and comfortable than long skirts, it is not too surprising that the feminists would contemplate incorporating trousers into their reform. Designing the dress proved relatively easy; the women simply modified the existing fashion. The description of the original "Bloomer costume" paralleled current styles "except that [the] skirts have been robbed of about a foot of their former length."[31] The pantaloons, however, proved more problematic. Costume historian Stella Mary Newton suggests that the number of "popular engravings of melting beauties in Turkish trousers that followed the cult of Byron and the French conquest of Algeria" influenced the feminists' costume design.[32] Avoiding a direct appropriation

DANCING GIRLS AT THE WEDDING.

This Western interpretation of Middle Eastern female attire has the same basic silhouette of the U.S. pantaloons reform outfit, making it easy to imagine women turning to illustrations such as this for inspiration. *Graham's Illustrated Magazine* 53 (August 1858).

of Western men's wear, they incorporated "Turkish" trousers into their costume. In backing away from male trousers, woman's rights advocates attempted to distance themselves from the image of power conveyed by the garment. They also sought to distance themselves from the sexual implications that society invested in the "unmentionable" male pantaloons. Images of Eastern women, however, particularly Arab and Turkish women, conveyed a highly erotic picture to the West.[33]

The freedom costume's soft, curving pantaloons proved to be the most "feminine" of the pantaloons designs. The woman's rights leaders gathered the hem of their pantaloons "into a band and buttoned round the ankle," or, what they thought prettier, a "gathered or plaited up" hem which had been "trimmed to suit the taste of the wearer."[34] This ankle treatment created a line that began at the hem of the skirt, curved slightly away from the body, and then gently rounded back to the ankle. The gathering or pleats added fullness to each leg and the resulting look was one we commonly associate with "harem" pantaloons and seldom imagine men wearing.[35]

Despite the "femininity" of the costume, however, the connection between the woman's rights agitators and pantaloons reform dress led critics to denounce it as masculine—or to level charges of licentiousness.[36] Bifurcated garments, no matter how "soft" the design, belonged exclusively to men. Stanton, Bloomer, and Miller may initially have tried "Turkish trousers" because they were different and exotic and offered freedom of movement, but at the same time the women created a new "dress code." That is, they made wearing pantaloons with a short dress into a political statement about woman's status in the United States.

Whether the sexually provocative elements of Eastern dress made it undesirable to most dress reformers is not clear. However, the woman's rights advocates appear to be the only dress reformers to wear "Turkish trousers." Some dress reformers may have shunned Turkish trousers because they did not want their costumes associated with Eastern clothing. Others rejected the full pantaloons because they associated the garment with the cause of woman's rights. Ideological reasons kept some women from wearing any modification of the Turkish style. Other reformers simply thought the "pretty and piquant dress—too juvenile in its *tout ensemble* . . . for grown up women."[37] Thus, "Turkish trousers" became one means of identifying the political or ideological orientation of the wearer. Unfortunately, not all woman's rights advocates favored the "harem" pantaloons, which further complicated one's ability to distinguish visually among reform costumes.

Historian Amy Kesselman accepts unequivocally that "the new costume" was "modeled after the dress of Moslem women" and that it "met a particularly warm reception among practitioners and advocates of hydropathy and water cure." In contrast to Kesselman's interpretation, evidence reveals that some water-cure establishments in the United States borrowed techniques and spa outfits from European health resorts. Furthermore, the NDRA, which had a large hydropathic following, implied that they based their American costume on men's wear.[38] Because pantaloons reform garments closely resembled one another, Kesselman's assumption that they all had the same roots is understandable.[39] However, water-cure doctors and the National Dress Reform Association objected to Turkish pantaloons for several reasons including their fullness and their offense to one's sense of Americanism. Similarly, many antifashion commentators objected to fashionable dress because of its French origins. They feared that once French dress entered the country, French ideas and French beliefs would soon follow. The hydropaths and the NDRA concurred with these sentiments and often stated that American women needed to get out from under the control of foreign nations, notably French fashions. Turkish trousers, with their tie to the Near Eastern nations, would have been inappropriate to wearers of the American costume because the American costume "show[ed] the world that in dress, as well as religion, society and government, [Americans] are able to follow [their] own ideas."[40] Wearing Turkish trousers implied that American women were too weak or unsophisticated to create a truly "American costume" and, instead, had to borrow their clothing design from another country.

Years later, the authors of the *History of Woman Suffrage* offered one of several reasons explaining why the feminists gave up wearing the freedom dress: "No sooner did a few brave conscientious women adopt the bifurcated costume, an imitation in part of the Turkish style, that [*sic*] the press at once turned its guns on" the costume. This suggests that perhaps the use of Near Eastern dress may have had something to do with the general disapproval of the short reform dress and pantaloons.[41] According to Marjorie Garber, "despite the rage for artifacts *a la Turque* in style and home decoration," the freedom dress's "'Turkish' connotations" precipitated negative repercussions. Some critics branded the outfits heathenish because of their association with Islam.[42] Mrs. L. G. Abell, for instance, questioned the morality of women who could give up the dress "civilization and Christianity have so kindly given" them. Abell did not limit her criticism to women dressed in "Eastern" dress, but saw women in "male attire" and women wearing "Turkish costume" on the same continuum.[43]

Women in Pantaloons, or the Politics of Clothing

Elizabeth Cady Stanton, Amelia Jenks Bloomer, and Elizabeth Smith Miller initially tried Turkish trousers because they were different, exotic, pretty, and offered freedom of movement. But at the same time, the women made a political statement. Even before she wore her first short dress, Bloomer recognized that a woman's wearing pantaloons had political implications. As a political strategy, the three women initially downplayed any political associations and promoted the physically liberating and healthful aspects of reform clothing. "None of us ever lectured on the dress question, or in any way introduced it into our lectures," recalled Miller. "We only wore it because we found it comfortable, convenient, safe, and tidy—with no thought of introducing a fashion," or, apparently, a political statement, "but with the wish that every woman would throw off the burden of clothes that was dragging her life out."[44] Stanton recalled that in the short dress she "was always ready for a brisk walk through sleet and snow and rain, to climb a mountain, jump over a fence, work in the garden," activities with which a long dress interfered. The overweight Stanton probably did not participate in the exercises she enumerated, but the clothing made her feel as though she could.[45] Worried about her sister's health, Lucy Stone wrote, "Do take care of your health Nettee—and to that end, I wish you would wear a bloomer. . . . IT IS A GREAT DEAL the best for health."[46]

Woman's rights dress reformers also learned that health was political when they used their clothing to champion health issues. Feigning innocence about the potential of their costume to disrupt the nineteenth-century sex/gender system, the women stressed their support of other health dress reformers. Dismayed that dress reform was being linked exclusively to Bloomer and her associates, water-cure doctors moved their message out of private health resorts and into the public realm. A festival held at Glen Haven Water Cure in August 1851 introduced spa reform dress to those in attendance. Stanton and Bloomer, both in short dresses and pantaloons, showed their support by praising the affair.[47] Theodosia Gilbert, perhaps the first hydropathic patient in the United States to wear the costume, attended wearing "a short green tunic not reaching to the knee, and white linen drilling trousers made *a la masculine*," in contrast to Stanton and Bloomer in trousers "*a la Turk*."[48] During the festivities, hydropathist James C. Jackson proposed the formation of an organization designed to educate the public about women's health, strengthen the infant dress reform movement, and support women who wore the new outfit publicly. No one took up his suggestion, including Stanton and Bloomer. The women did not perceive a need for a formal dress reform organization because, they said, knowledge of private informal dress reform activities inspired more women to change their apparel with each passing year. Five years later, as interest in pantaloons dress reform waned, water-cure doctors and patients organized the National Dress Reform Association.

Woman's rights activists joined physicians, physiologists, the press, and others in the belief that some change in fashionable dress was "absolutely necessary for the health of women." Although the stated intention of the freedom dress was to improve women's health (a politically nonthreatening stance), it debuted in the same year that the woman's rights conventions began meeting. The costume seemed part of the demand for equal rights.[49] At first, Stanton ignored the political potential of reform dress, but it was not long before she vocally made the connection between the freedom of movement allowed by the reform dress and women's desperate desire to escape from "everlasting bondage."[50] Thus Stanton also politicized women's fashionable dress; according to her, long skirts symbolized woman's "degradation" in society.[51]

Stanton began to use clothing strategically. The simple sentence, "None of us ever lectured on the dress question," is the key to understanding the sophistication of the feminists' political strategy when it came to reform dress.[52] The women refrained from speaking and lecturing on short dresses; however, they *wore* short skirts and pantaloons. The roots of the woman's rights movement can be traced to the silencing of women in the abolitionist circles. Playing on the conventions that denied women the right to speak, especially to mixed audiences, the woman's rights dress reformers continued the tradition of not speaking—and acted instead. The feminists deserve credit for recognizing that what people saw was as important as what they heard and for knowing that women were judged by their appearance.

Historians have done a grave disservice to the woman's rights activists by relying on the written and spoken word for evidence of their politics. Looking at the pantaloons they chose to wear speaks volumes about their political strategies.

From championing the utilitarian aspects of the short dress and pantaloons, Stanton focused on dress reform as a principle in her feminist philosophy, making woman's rights a rallying point for pantaloons dress reformers.[53] The freedom dress became "a political statement."[54] The short dress and trousers emerged from private homes, closed religious communities, and insulated health resorts and became a "public" and "political" costume linked inextricably to the fight for woman's rights—a dramatic switch. All women who attempted to reform dress after 1851 felt the ramifications. Although woman's rights would not be the only reason women wore short dresses and pantaloons, it became impossible for other dress reformers to separate their rationale for wearing reform clothing from issues of woman's rights. A woman could join any number of popular and unpopular reform movements and no one would be the wiser, except in her immediate circle of acquaintances and friends. The moment a woman put on pantaloons reform dress she was marked. Wherever she went and whatever she did, people who saw her assumed she supported the fight for woman's equal rights. Directly and indirectly, woman's rights issues shaped pantaloons dress reform throughout the second half of the nineteenth century.

Although Elizabeth Cady Stanton was largely responsible for politicizing the freedom dress, she had doubts early on about whether the woman's rights supporters should have taken up the dress reform cause. When the hostile reactions proved greater than anticipated, she realized a retreat would publicly humiliate both them personally and the woman's rights cause. Her doubts probably influenced her decision not to join the hydropathists in creating a dress reform organization in the summer of 1851. She wrote to her cousin Elizabeth Smith Miller, "We are very much like the poor fox in the fable, who having cut off his tail and not being able to restore it, found that nothing remained for him to do but to persuade the other foxes to do likewise."[55] A rueful Stanton would have to persuade other women to take up a dress reform to which she was no longer fully committed.

"Having performed this surgical operation on our entire wardrobe," she said, nothing remained "but to induce as many as possible to follow our example." Although she doubted that short dresses and pantaloons were the answer, Stanton understood the perils of fashionable attire and that women would have no peace "until we cut off the great national petticoat."[56] She ultimately convinced Paulina Wright Davis, Lucy Stone, Sarah and Angelina Grimké, Mrs. William Burleigh, Celia Burleigh, Charlotte Beebe Wilbour, Helen Jarvis, Lydia Jenkins, and Amelia Willard, among others, to wear the freedom dress.[57] But, it took Stanton over six months to persuade Susan B. Anthony to adopt the dress. Reluctantly, Anthony donned the outfit on a trip east in December 1852, and cut her hair short. She insisted, however, that her skirts be a few inches longer than those worn by Stanton and Bloomer. Shortly after making the transition, she wrote to Lucy Stone, "What think you Lucy, I am in short skirts and trousers, and have spoken in Auburn!"[58] What finally seems to have convinced Anthony to shorten her skirts and wear Turkish trousers was her belief that the costume, unlike variations on fashionable dress, did not alienate the "hardworking women of America."[59] Anthony later stated that in her opinion, "I can see no business avocation, in which woman, in her present dress, *can possibly* earn *equal wages* with man—& feel that it is *folly* for us to make the demand until we adapt our dress to our work."[60] Thus, Anthony hoped to be an example for working women in the United States by wearing a costume that owed more to function than to beauty. And she made the link between dress reform and the rhetoric of equal rights explicit—which was what some supporters of the status quo feared most.

The Women Go Still Further: Freedom Dress in the Popular Press

Stanton and Anthony were understandably hesitant: the popular press was having a field day with the new fashion. The editors at *Harper's New Monthly Magazine* outlined the range of reactions to dress reformers: "Some ridicule them; others sneer contemptuously or laugh incredulously, and others commend them for their taste and courage."[61] *Harper's,* in contrast to other general interest publications, featured the "Turkish" costume on its fashion pages and considered the possibility that pantaloons and short dresses could be the next fashion rage. The September 1851 fashion page reported on the growing popularity of "close fitting" garments, reduced volume in skirts, and women's waistcoats, which resembled "those worn by gentlemen." The

TURKISH COSTUME.

Harper's version of "Turkish costume." This hardly seems the answer to dress refomers' quest for a practical and healthful outfit. The "feminine" features would, theoretically, make this dress more acceptable to mainstream society. However, it seems likely that the model is wearing a tightly laced corset and numerous petticoats beneath her shortened skirt. *Harper's New Monthly Magazine* (July 1851).

Harper's fashion editor thought that an important and "radical" alteration in style might occur at any moment. It is more likely, however, that *Harper's* was gently satirizing dress reform. While the magazine reported on "the general favor in which 'Bloomers' are held," it also noted that "neither sneers, caricatures, or serious opposition" would prevent the short dress and pantaloons from gaining popularity.[62] Just as the *Seneca County Courier* supported the idea of women in pantaloons in the abstract, *Harper's* had its own ideas about pantaloons for women, too. In fact, *Harper's* version featured some of the worst aspects of fashionable dress—a tight waist, excessive trim, sloping shoulders, and a full skirt—and it is difficult to imagine woman's rights agitators accepting this fashionable bloomer.[63]

Godey's Lady's Book and Magazine, a popular women's magazine, was more up-front with readers pressuring the periodical to comment on freedom dresses. In September 1851, the editors refused to offer an opinion on the costume; they chose instead "to allow [the dress] to take its natural course without . . . interference." *Godey's* considered the costume less than a fad, a freakish moment in the history of fashion destined to die a quick death. The magazine never directly criticized bloomers, although several articles made *Godey's* disapproval clear.[64] Readers shared *Godey's* and *Harper's* rather benign reactions to reform apparel. In fact, coverage of freedom dresses in popular magazines—good and bad press alike—brought the dress and the campaign for woman's rights to many middle-class women in the United States.

Surprisingly in the midst of all the press coverage—mostly negative—a group of artists rendered flattering portrayals of Amelia Bloomer and the Bloomer costume. Sheet music designed for display on the piano in middle-class drawing rooms featured "bloomer girls" reminiscent of ballerinas. Most of the music was for popular dances and was not significant musically; few pieces had lyrics. The most logical explanation for this phenomenon of flattering visual images of pantaloon-wearing women coexisting with the often vicious denunciations of woman's rights advocates in the press and in cartoons is probably that sheet music artists mistook the bloomer for a fashion craze. One of the few bloomer songs with lyrics, "The Bloomer's Complaint," supports this theory. The bloomer sings, "They [people complaining about her clothes] know very well that their own fashions change; With each little change of the season; . . . 'out of all manner of reason,' If we take a fancy to alter our dress."[65] Most of the bloomer songs were written in 1851, which further suggests that once the association between the costume and women's rights had been forged the music was no longer welcome on middle-class pianos.

Although she lived in California in the early 1850s, far from Seneca Falls and feminists in Turkish trousers, Louise Amelia Knapp Smith Clapp knew about freedom dresses. She may have read about the costume in *Godey's* or *Harper's* or any number of other periodicals. Her thoughts on the outfit and woman's rights mirror those found in publications not openly hostile to the causes: Louise Clapp, like many middle-class white women, was curious and puzzled. She did not understand how women,

It is curious that in the midst of the hostile atmosphere and among the ugly depictions of Bloomer costumes, sheet music was illustrated with some romantic versions of the outfit. This particular piece, produced in 1851, is also dedicated to "Mrs. Bloomer and the Ladies in Favor of the Bloomer Costume." From the author's collection.

"many of whom, I am told, are *really* interesting and intelligent," could "spoil their pretty mouths and ruin their beautiful complexions by demanding with Xanthippian *fervor,* in the presence, often, of a vulgar, irreverent mob, what the gentle creatures are pleased to call their 'rights?'" She wondered about what interested women in presidential elections and other political issues. But above all Clapp could not comprehend how women could "so far forget the sweet, shy coquetries of shrinking womanhood as to don those horrid bloomers?" Clapp recognized the implications of wearing trousers. "As for me," she wrote, "although a *wife,* I never wear the—well, you know what they call them when they wish to quiz henpecked husbands—even in the strictest privacy of life." Within the nuclear family men were supposed to wear the pantaloons, literally and metaphorically. Given the often primitive conditions she lived under, one might expect to find Clapp a proponent of the short dress and pantaloons. Instead, she preferred "trailing drapery," and "sweeping petticoats."[66]

Louise Clapp's reaction to woman's rights campaigns and reform garments was typical. Women like her were content with their lives, their clothing, and their sphere and saw no reason to change any of it.[67] This silent majority was largely responsible for dress reform's failure to win over large numbers of converts. Although they privately objected to the costume, most middle-class women did not actively denounce the garment or work to get rid of it; that activism would have been unseemly. Instead, they simply ignored pantaloons reform dresses in all their permutations. In the end, this passive resistance did more damage to the cause than the hostile actions of aggressive opponents. However, animosity was the more immediate concern.

In February 1851, Miller, Stanton, and Bloomer could not foresee that their opponents, especially men, would expend enormous energy to get the women back in long dresses. The caricature of cigar-smoking, trouser-wearing, "mini-skirted" feminists was a popular attack, and pursued the woman's movement into the twentieth century.[68] The "masculine feminist" became synonymous with the image of the "ugly feminist," and all pantaloons dress reformers, feminist or not, had to contend with these exaggerations. The barrage of printed words and pictures wore away at the woman's rights advocates' resolve to remain true to their principles. Condemnation of feminists in pantaloons penalized women for public acts by going after their private lives and throwing their womanhood into question.

WOMAN'S EMANCIPATION.
(BEING A LETTER ADDRESSED TO MR. PUNCH, WITH A DRAWING, BY A STRONG-MINDED AMERICAN WOMAN.)

The text that accompanied this caricature, "Woman's Emancipation," was a satirical piece written by "Theodosia Eudoxia Bang," "Principal of the Homeopathic and Collegiate Thomsonian Institute for developing the female mind." Thus the artist and writer are making fun not only of bloomers but also some of the other reforms in which women were involved. This joke appeared a month after *Harper's* featured "Turkish costume" on its pages. *Harper's New Monthly Magazine* (August 1851).

Readers could not take their eyes off the trousers, never forgetting that this was exclusively a male garment. A report in an 1852 edition of the *New York Times* summed up what men risked when women wore pantaloons: "These ladies assert their claim to rights, which we of bifurcated raiment are charged with usurping. This claim conflicts with, and if secured, will tend to diminish the rights of masculine mankind.... But the ladies go still further; and he must be blind who does not perceive in these low murmurings, a storm that shall eventually rob manhood of all its grand prerogatives."[69] "Bifurcated raiment," no doubt, counted as one of manhood's "grand prerogatives."

Vicious verbal and physical criticisms were "mechanisms" used to get the women "back into their socially sanctioned places and into the uniform that symbolized that place."[70] The numerous attacks on freedom dresses and the women who wore them reinforced the notion that the sex/gender system was fragile and could easily be toppled by the seemingly simple act of women changing their clothes. Or rather, men who made such attacks revealed the depth of their investment in that system—and a great fear of losing any advantage, or giving over any signs or symbols of gendered authority (pantaloons, cigarettes, public action, etc.). They tried to diminish the threat by belittling it.

Clearly, the press marked the reform costume as subversive. Prior to the introduction of the freedom dress, satirists targeted fashionable dress. However, their humor tended to be "gentle" and playful as they laughed at women's attempts to be more feminine and ladylike. The threat of pantaloons reform dress invited "biting" humor, and even violence and abuse, from critics.[71] Newspapers identified all pantaloons dress reformers with "those who advocated the right of suffrage," and accused feminists and dress reformers of being "strong-minded," "Bloomers," "free lovers," advocates of "easy divorce," and "amalgamations."[72] Linking reform garb to unpopular ideas was another means of discrediting it. Women's appropriating trousers directly challenged a gender system that clearly distinguished femininity and masculinity. Critical observers claimed they saw men, or a "third sex," or even "no sex" when they saw women in pantaloons. The fear that women would lose their gender identity did not equal the corresponding and irrational fear that men would lose their masculine gender identity and become feminine. Attacking reform costumes and reformers, anxious critics encouraged women to dress in the acceptable manner to reproduce and maintain what Jean V. Matthews describes as the "cultural conception of the feminine."[73]

In 1852, *Godey's* headlined an article "Men's Rights Convention." The piece satirized woman's rights conventions and noted how women seized "those garments which, from time immemorial, have been [men's] rightful badge." The members of the fictitious convention reasoned that if women could make "an unblushing claim" on trousers, then they would try to wrest "all our masculine privileges."[74] Beneath the humor lies fear: that women would take more from men than just their *symbols* of power. *Godey's* also noted that dress actually affected a woman's personality. Not only did clothing shape women, but women "were decidedly imitative." If a woman put on a short skirt, trousers, and a jacket, she would probably thrust her hands into the pockets, speak coarsely, and give a loud laugh. Dressed as a male, a woman could not help but behave like one—in all his vulgarity.[75] "Here I am known only as one of the women who ape men—coarse, brutal men!" Susan B. Anthony lamented.[76]

Once dress reform and woman's rights entered the public arena, articles, speeches, and sermons denouncing masculine women or women disrupting the established gender relations persisted to stifle the demands of feminists.[77] Years later, when it looked as if the passage of the nineteenth amendment was imminent, suffragists still faced the charge of "seeking to don their husbands' clothes." One suffragist astutely pointed out that women had always worn men's clothing and that suffragists were "only trying to get women the right to wear their own." (In most states in the nineteenth century, husbands owned their wives' dresses and fathers owned their daughters' frocks.[78])

When women infringed on men's claim to trousers, male opponents launched a counterattack. The jeering laughter of crowds, physical attacks, and satirical poems and articles wore away at the resolve of dress reformers of all kinds. Even though these attacks sparked some women's commitment to reform, others succumbed to the pressure and returned to long dresses and, by implication, their traditional domestic roles.[79] After years of what they called "petty crucifixion," feminists gave up the freedom dress, "with the feeling that the large freedom they gained for their feet bore no comparison to the bondage that beset their spirits."[80]

Back to Long Skirts: The End of Feminist Dress Reform

Opponents succeeded in forcing the woman's rights advocates back into long skirts, allowing feminists to speak about rights but refusing to tolerate action on those convictions. With the exception of Gerrit Smith, even prominent male supporters such as William Lloyd Garrison used every argument available to dissuade the feminists from wearing the freedom dress.

For the sensitive Anthony, wearing the freedom dress was particularly hard. Reports such as one that appeared in the *New York Sun* commented on Anthony's "ungainly form rigged out in the bloomer costume and provoking the thoughtless to laughter and ridicule by her very motions on the platform."[81] Public humiliation must have been difficult for Anthony to bear. On one occasion, while in New York City, Anthony and Lucy Stone set out for the post office. On the crowded streets the two women soon "noticed that we were being encircled." In a matter of moments a "wall of men and boys" shut them in "so that it was impossible to go on or to go back." The crowd "laughed at" the women, "made faces," "said impertinent things," and "would not let us out." Eventually a male acquaintance spotted them and "went for a policeman and a carriage, and [they] escaped, with only a little rough treatment at the last."[82] At one point Anthony wrote to Stone, "Oh, I cannot bear [wearing the dress] any longer."[83] All the women experienced harsh treatment from strangers, but Anthony, who had a higher profile, suffered greatly for a costume that never made her feel entirely comfortable.

Stanton bore public criticism with more humor than Anthony, saying, "Seven vials of wrath have been poured on my devoted head. I think they were bottled by one of my New York sisters. They have a metropolitan odor."[84] Although difficult to endure, the disapproval of Stanton's own family members was another matter. Her son refused to let her visit him at school dressed in the short dress. Henry Stanton, her husband, barely won his second term to the New York Senate because slogans such as "Twenty tailors take the stitches, Mrs. Stanton wears the breeches" plagued his campaign.[85] But as long as woman's rights advocates felt that the principles behind their dress were important, they stoically tolerated the public ridicule along with Stanton and Anthony.

Lucy Stone proved to be the most stalwart. Following the trend established by earlier private dress reformers, Stone wore her first freedom dress exclusively at home. After about a year, she joined the other woman's rights activists in wearing the outfit publicly, and decided to have all of her future dresses made short. People frequently commented that Stone looked more attractive in the freedom dress than most women. Presenting a pleasing appearance, however, did not exempt Stone from laughter, stares, or insults. She bore these with calmness and dignity.[86]

Feminists' interest in dress reform crested during 1851, merely months after they first put the costume on. Some of the women realized that the "dress was drawing attention" away from the issues of employment, education, and suffrage.[87] However, having opened the Pandora's box of dress reform, they insisted on seeing it through, and at times only sheer force of will kept the women in the freedom costume for the next seven years. Stanton summed it up: "Had I counted the cost of the short dress, I would never have put it on; now, however, I'll never take it off, for now it involves a principle of freedom."[88] Notwithstanding her good humor and principles, by the end

LUCY STONE.—FROM A DAGUERREOTYPE BY BRADY.

Lucy Stone in a Bloomer costume of black silk and velvet. *Illustrated News* (May 28, 1853).

of 1853 Elizabeth Cady Stanton was the first woman's rights leader to stop wearing the pantaloons and dress. Before giving up the freedom dress entirely, she experimented with an alternative style. Her new outfit included a "short" dress (though not as short as the freedom dress), but "no pants." Anthony worried that it would be said that the reformers "doffed their pantaloons the better to display their legs." During the brief trial of the new dress, however, Stanton "had stepped on it and torn it twice," although it was shorter than most gowns. The failure of her second effort convinced Stanton to return to conventional long skirts. By the time of the 1854 Woman's Rights Convention in Albany, "her petticoats [had] assumed their former length, and her wardrobe [was] cleared of every short skirt." She implored Lucy Stone to give up her short skirts and pantaloons as well, "for the sake of the cause." "We put the dress on for greater freedom," Stanton continued, "but what is physical freedom compared with mental bondage?"[89]

Stanton also begged Susan B. Anthony to "let down a dress and a petticoat." Anthony, however, continued to wear the freedom dress. Stone disagreed with Stanton and wrote, "it is all fudge for anybody to pretend that any cause that deserves to live is impeded by the length of your skirt. . . . It is all a pretense that the cause will suffer."[90] However, being practical, Stone reversed herself and decided to have some long skirts made. She reasoned that circumstances would determine the appropriate length of a garment. The decision caused her some personal conflict: "Women are in bondage. Their clothes are a great hindrance to . . . mak[ing] them pecuniarily independent; . . . is it not better, even at the expense of a great deal of annoyance, that [we] . . . should give an example by which woman may more easily work out her own emancipation?"[91]

Stone's return to long skirts convinced Anthony (when Stanton's arguments could not) that she should also switch back. Writing to Stone in 1854, Anthony asked, if you "cannot bear the martyrdom of the dress, who, I ask, can?"[92] Several months after the Albany convention, Anthony reluctantly let down the hems of her dress and petticoats, having worn the freedom dress for a little over a year. The change in Anthony's attitude toward the costume—reluctant to put it on, then hesitant to take it off—stemmed from her conviction that in wearing the short dress she embodied the principles of the woman's rights cause. For her, giving up the freedom dress seemed a personal as well as a political defeat.[93]

Anthony wore the freedom dress after most of the woman's rights leaders had given it up. Only Elizabeth Smith Miller and Amelia Jenks Bloomer wore the costume longer. Miller, under pressure from her father, continued to wear the dress for another seven years, even though she thought the dress "awkward" and "uncouth" at times. She eventually fell victim to her "love of beauty," and little by little, lengthened her skirts.[94]

Bloomer wore the dress longer than any of her comrades. When she eventually gave up the costume that bore her name, eight years after she put it on, she claimed "practical reasons." In 1855, Amelia and Dexter Bloomer moved to Council Bluffs, Iowa. Starting life anew in a "land of strangers," Bloomer's short skirts sometimes embarrassed her, but she continued to wear them out of principle. However, the high winds "greatly annoyed and mortified" her when they blew her skirts up over her head. Determined not to give in to nature, Bloomer loaded the hem of her skirt with shot. Unfortunately, the wind continued to whip her skirt about, bruising her legs. At

The Smith-Miller
Family. Elizabeth Smith
Miller, after her return to
long dresses, is the female
figure standing on the
left. Her father, Gerrit
Smith, is seated. Courtesy
of the Madison County
Historical Society.

the same time, the "light-weight" wire hoop skirt began replacing petticoats.
Sometime in 1858 Bloomer decided that the new undergarment embodied
dress reform ideals and laid aside her short skirts and pantaloons, insisting
that she was not compromising her ideals. "I determined that I would not
be frightened from my position," she wrote, "but would stand my ground
and wear the dress when and where I pleased, till all excitement on the subject had died away."[95]

Explanations of why feminists stopped wearing the freedom dress come
from the women themselves, their biographers, and historians. Anthony
characterized dress reform as "intellectual slavery" and "mental crucifixion."
The woman's rights leaders agreed that audiences fixated on their clothing
and failed to listen to their words. At all times dress reformers braved the
scrutiny of observers with "unfriendly eyes."[96] Stanton decided that critiques
on fashion were less important than woman's political rights. Anthony concluded that by urging two reforms, "both are injured, as the average mind

can grasp but one idea at a time." Therefore, in order to keep attention focused on woman's rights, the women returned to long skirts.[97] Another interpretation dismissed the political implications of freedom dress and theorized that the outfit's design flaws contributed to its unpopularity and demise.[98] Other analysts suggested that as a side issue in the struggle for woman's rights, dress reform did not have the activists' full attention.[99]

Political savvy played a large part in their determination to return to long dresses. The women understood that America's reform fervor had changed shape. Dress reformers outside of the woman's rights movement still saw themselves as participants in a crusade to create an ideal society in which women and men lived in equality, in harmony with nature, and blessed by God. The daily life of individuals became their crusade's battleground. But woman's rights leaders turned from individual to collective action, endeavoring to change institutions through the court system and legislation.

The freedom costume, the dress feminists hoped would symbolically and physically liberate women from the strictures of socially defined womanhood, further imprisoned them, alienating the very women to whom they were trying to appeal. Conventional female dress, then, became as much a strategy and a political issue for the supporters of woman's rights as the freedom dress had been. They compromised one ideal to get another they thought of greater value. These women understood that the radicalness of the freedom costume set their cause back; giving up the costume was one of their first overtly political acts.[100] Over a hundred years later, members of the National Organization for Women would employ a similar tactic and wear conventional middle-class dress as they lobbied Congress.

Looking back at the dress reform experiment, Stanton lamented the choice of costume. The "artistic" and "convenient" dress "in which Diana the Huntress is represented," she hypothesized, would have better met their needs, if they had only thought of it earlier.[101] It is unlikely that Greek drapery would have found many champions. Such a costume, though, would not have directly challenged the ideals of femininity and masculinity since it did not include pantaloons and would have been more "feminine," part of a classical ideal, already in place, of female power.

Negative publicity and the controversy the reform garment generated are the most obvious explanations of the decision to abandon the freedom dress. But it is hard for us to fathom the intensity of the public censure. Outcry against the feminists' costume extended from coast to coast and even to England. Women wearing the freedom costume endured laughter, jeers, yells, having sticks and stones thrown at them, and other acts of violence; they also had to deal with pressure from family members.

Oddly enough, there was also pressure to *keep* the pantaloons. "No act [in Stanton's] life ever gave [her] cousin, Gerrit Smith, such deep sorrow" as her decision to give up the freedom dress.[102] To Smith the whole revolution in woman's position turned on her dress. He published an open letter to Stanton on the subject. He raged at Stanton and the other erstwhile dress reformers in the bulletin. He complained that the "woman's rights women—persevere, just as blindly and stubbornly, as do other women, in wearing a dress, that both marks and makes their impotence." After giving up the freedom dress, the feminists not only wore long dresses but often dressed quite fashionably, further fueling Smith's anger. "I am amazed," Smith continued to rave, "that the intelligent women engaged in the 'Woman's rights movement' see not the relation between their dress and the oppressive evils, which they are striving to throw off."[103] Stanton, Anthony, and the other activists did, in fact, comprehend the role of dress in oppressing women, but they decided finally to focus their attention on the overtly political arena of legislation rather than the implicitly political arena of fashion.

Unable to induce his cousin and the other feminists to return to short dresses, Smith persuaded his daughter Elizabeth Smith Miller to continue wearing the costume for years. Gerrit Smith's dogged insistence is striking, bizarre, and even hypocritical. As a strong abolitionist, Smith took little notice of Stanton's earlier campaigns for woman's rights, and after the Civil War he failed to support her efforts to win woman's suffrage.[104] Yet in the 1850s he made himself a vocal supporter of dress reform—why? Smith supported some woman's rights principles, but he blamed women for their subordinate position in society and emphasized women's weakness for fashion as the greatest source of their oppression. By making women's secondary status self-imposed, Smith cleared men of charges that they dominated women, and reinforced the belief that legislative changes would not elevate women who could not overcome their own faults. Gerrit Smith was not the only one to publicly condemn Elizabeth Cady Stanton and her colleagues. Other dress reformers shared his interpretation of the role of beauty and fashion in women's oppression, calling the women "traitors" and "Arnold[s] in the camp," and accusing them of damaging dress reform and the "cause of women generally."[105]

Health, religious, and independent dress reformers in the nineteenth-century United States had their own ideas about woman's status, but the public inevitably linked pantaloons reform dress to the distinctive political demands and style of the woman's rights movement. This connection angered the many dress reformers who did not support woman's rights and did not want to be identified with the cause. In fact, disagreement over the sources of women's oppression and the solution to the problem often led to displays of open hostility among pantaloons dress reformers themselves. Each group had its own definition of "woman's rights," and the only conviction they all shared was that women needed some variation of the short dress and pantaloons. But no matter what purpose their group served or what reasons they gave for wearing shorter skirts and pantaloons, dress reformers continued to be associated with woman's rights and the woman's rights movement. The public also linked woman's rights leaders with the reform costume long after they had given it up. In 1866, for example, a *New York Times* reporter writing about a woman's rights convention scanned the crowds but saw no woman "in attendance wearing the bloomer or 'short' dress," unaware that most female activists had given it up ten years earlier.[106]

Public dress reform, although a political failure, exposed the precarious, gendered foundations of society. Dr. J. C. Jackson's assertion that the reform dress "sprung up simultaneously" raises an interesting question. Why did dress reform surface in so many contexts in 1851? Perhaps the incapacitating aspects of fashionable dress—heavy skirts and tight corsets—had reached such an annoying level that women could no longer ignore them. It seems more likely, however, that the excitement and agitation generated by the freedom costume awakened other dress reformers to the possibilities promised by a change in clothing. Before 1851, reformers did not see the broader applications for their dress and pantaloons, only what the costume could achieve within their communities, such as renewed health or spiritual enlightenment. But when reform dress and woman's rights came together, it seemed that clothing could indeed signal a change in something as basic and imbedded as separate spheres, and the guiding principles of the "masculine" and "feminine." And as hard as pantaloons dress reformers tried to distance themselves from the notorious woman's rights leaders, the more firmly the two were joined in the public mind.

Traditionally defined fashion, dependency, and femininity were portrayed as the province of "real true women," and the conviction that "masculine" attire would lead to "masculine" behavior convinced critics that society was at risk. As innocuous as it may look today, the reform costume threatened women and men secure in conformity and the status quo, and pushed the boundaries of nineteenth-century womanhood. When men thought women infringed on exclusively male rights and privileges, they struck back in the public forum of newspapers and magazines, belittling their targets with satire and ridicule. Others, afraid of losing what they had, joined male detractors and actively condemned pantaloons reform dress. Sometimes the attempts proved successful, and potential reformers decided dress reform was not worth the struggle. At other times, the resistance sharpened a woman's commitment. No organized campaign against pantaloons dress reform ever arose, but scattered opposition effectively preserved sex-distinctive clothing, charging that reform would alter the "fundamental laws of nature." The result would be dangerous both to women and society, since dress reformers coveted male roles and devalued traditional womanhood. A primary concern was that dress reform would blur the differences between the sexes and "unsex" women or men.

The short dress and pantaloons became a symbol of major change for women. To opponents it represented a dangerous readjustment in the relationship between the sexes. Some adversaries saw the reform costume as only the beginning. If dress reform succeeded, they feared, it would lead to a vastly different society, without comfortable traditions and values, and even, perhaps, without social or class distinctions. Moral criticism of female apparel was a sort of desperate measure to disqualify women's move toward increased equality, and by implication, their right to political participation. Pantaloons meant actual ruling power, and both still belonged to men—for the time being.

To breathe, or not to breathe; that's the question
Whether 'tis nobler in the mind to suffer
The slings and arrows of outrageous fashion,
Or to bear the scoffs and ridicule of those
Who despise the Bloomer dresses.
In agony,
No more?—and, by a dress to say we end
The side-ache, and the thousand self-made aches,
Which those are heir to, who, for mere fashion,
Will dress so waspish.

—*Water-Cure Journal,* June 1853

Out of the Closet

Health and Religious Dress Reform
after Freedom Dresses

Efforts to reform dress did not die with the freedom suit, nor did the scoffing, sneering, and ridiculing of trouser-wearing women. The entrance of pantaloons dress reform onto the public stage changed the nature of private dress reform, and the human body became a site at which doctrines of health reform and religion came together. Nineteenth-century journalists had devoted considerable time to reporting on the political freedom dress and in doing so misstated, perverted, and misrepresented dress reform as a whole. The general public, unaware of the variety among dress reformers, asked, "What is a Bloomer?" "One who *pants* for notoriety," laughed the *Dollar Newspaper*.[1] For some women the prospect of being the center of attention and standing out prompted them to try reform dresses and pantaloons. A writer for the *New Yorker* recalled the pleasure his grandmother experienced when as "a girl on a farm near Penn Yan, [she] secretly made herself a bloomer dress and flaunted it before her shouting menfolk."[2] For other dress reformers, being singled out by the "unpleasant remarks" and "occasional titters" made them "more decided in the good cause of Dress Reform."[3] Some believed that to complete their mission they would have to learn to ignore the remarks of the "foolish and fastidious," the "do-nothings," the "street-loafers," the "gentleman-fop," and the "snickerers."⁴ Not all devoted reformers were able to make such positive use of the insults. Instead, they surrendered or hid from the crowds, and many more women stayed away from the outfit and never considered wearing it. Despite hostility, however, dress reform continued to find support among popular health reform movements and emerging alternative religions.

Long Dresses, Again

Strong belief in their spiritual mission, and the role of short dresses and pantalettes in attaining it, did not sustain Oneida Perfectionists when they met with antagonism. Hostile public opinion forced Oneida women to wear long dresses when they appeared in public. Resigned to living with petty name-calling and slurs, Oneidans were not prepared for the acceleration of the hostility and violence directed at them. In New York's Grand Central Station, a few Oneida women openly wore Community short dresses, "perhaps in an attempt to bring a message of deliverance to the fashion-bound women of the outer world." The women soon found themselves held up by the ridicule of an "insensate public"; the police had to rescue them from the angry mob. After that trying episode, "common sense was deemed the 'better part of valor' and worldly garments were provided for traveling females."⁵ Occasionally an Oneida woman appeared publicly in the short dress, but it was not wise to do so too often, as several Community women discovered. Dressed in short skirts and pantalettes, they walked the streets of Hartford, Connecticut, and attracted so much "unpleasant attention" that they were forced to find their way home through back streets.⁶ Ultimately, such angry bands forced Oneida women to wear their reform garments only in private, and Oneida Community members feared the animosity of mobs enough to sanction anonymity when they ventured out of their cloistered environment. The Community, however, refused to give up the costume entirely, and some Community members even "felt that the way outsiders always looked at them and talked about them" helped to strengthen their faith and bound the Community more closely together.⁷

Residents of country communes had an easier time wearing the short dress, "but in the city or village, we are quite imprisoned." In the house at New Haven, Perfectionist women wore their costumes, "but to go out into the street involved a troublesome change." Venturing outside without changing their clothing was a sort of "martyrdom" the city communitarians chose not to face.[8] Wearing "worldly" long dresses assured the women that they would not have to worry about being accosted in public. "The Public," a closet housing "a suitable wardrobe of women's long dresses, coats and hats of assorted sizes," provided an alternative to the short dresses when Community women "were obliged to travel in the outside world."[9]

The reactions of the public discouraged many women from wearing a costume they might otherwise have endorsed. Similar circumstances affected other women interested in pantaloons reform dress. Adela Orpen recalled Olive, a young and fashionable "Bostonian" who visited Kansas in the early 1860s, and her experiences with reform costume. Olive "took to the reform dress" and vowed that she would continue to wear "bloomers" when she returned to the East—"sometimes at least." Although in Kansas Olive felt committed to her new outfit, she never wore it back home. The first sign of an observer's contempt for her garments "scorched the bloomers off her, as if they had been subjected to real flames." Olive enjoyed the short dress and pantaloons and the freedom of movement they gave her, but she did not hold to a larger ideology or community that might have sustained her through the ridicule—although as the Oneida Community demonstrated, an ideology did not always compensate for the pain and humiliation brought about by overwhelming disapproval.[10]

Mrs. M. M. Jones, a strong supporter of reform dress, would have sympathized with the young Olive. Jones considered the American costume and its many variations to be "the most sensible, tasteful, and convenient dress" available to American women.[11] However, by 1865 she no longer wore the dress herself, because, she said, "public opinion, in a city like this [New York City], is a thing that not one woman, nor twenty women, nor a hundred women, can alter or change; and public opinion *will not* allow a lady to wear a short dress in our streets without subjecting her to one continual martyrdom." Jones went on to say that the nature of the city, the mix of classes and the anonymity, allowed people to behave in ways they might not if they knew their victim. Remembering her own experiences, Jones lamented, "I never believed in total depravity until I wore the reform dress in New York," but after her experiences with "*little imps of Satan* ... [she was] prepared to credit almost anything!" Responding to dress reformers who claimed to visit the city without experiencing harassment, Jones acknowledged that days would pass when nothing happened except some staring. But visitors did not stay in the city long enough, she said, to see their complacency and beliefs in the acceptability of their costumes destroyed by surprise attacks.[12]

APPEARANCE OF A LADY IN THE NEW BLOOMER COSTUME.

A variety of publications featured pantaloons outfits on their pages, providing an opportunity to see the range of costume styles in circulation. Since most of the illustrations are line drawings such as the one pictured here, they are artists' interpretations of the pantaloons reform dress and not necessarily based on actual garments. *Peterson's Magazine* 20 (October 1851).

Thus, Jones put away her pantaloons costume. The controversial politics of the woman's rights movement alone do not account for the attacks on other dress reformers. However, bringing reform dress to the attention of the public encouraged observers to take a closer look at all pantaloons dress reformers—and they did not like what they saw.

Healthy Reform Dresses: The NDRA

Like high fashion, which reformers repudiated, pantaloons reform dress immediately focused attention on the wearer. The reading public knew about Bloomers and woman's rights agitators, and women adopting the costume to improve their health—the most socially acceptable reason for advocating pantaloons dress reform—looked no different. Although society found the ambitions of health-conscious dress reformers commendable, their short dress and trouser ensembles remained unacceptable, and in lumping health reform dress reformers together with woman's rights

BLOOMERISM—AN AMERICAN CUSTOM.

All pantaloons dress reformers had a difficult time overcoming the negative associations that images such as this one of cigar-smoking dress reformers generated. *Harper's New Monthly Magazine* 3 (August 1851).

advocates public scrutiny and disapproval politicized the actions of women who preferred personal reform to formal politics. At the same time, the health reform message was often lost as the dress reformers found themselves in a defensive position—arguing against the woman's rights movement rather than for better health for women through dress.

Dress reformers who considered themselves health reformers struggled to legitimize what they thought of as a more rational way of dressing. To this end, numerous women testified that reform dress improved their health and saved their lives. The newly cured often reacted with the enthusiasm of the religious convert and fervently embraced pantaloons dress reform. Many early dress reformers adopted the costume because they became convinced of its "physiological, pathological, or hygienic advantages" over long dresses.[13] The ideal of good health bridged some of the ideological differences among dress reformers; however, different definitions of what constituted a "healthy woman" and how she was to achieve good health prevented the reformers from joining forces and creating a mass reform organization. The closest they managed to come was the National Dress Reform Association.[14]

Curiously, after 1851, when a shift might be expected with women gaining control of dress reform, the evidence shows that a man continued to have a major role in the management and organization of the only successful institutionalized national dress reform movement in the period. Almost five years after he first proposed it, Dr. James C. Jackson presided over the establishment of the NDRA, which started accepting members in February 1856 and met for the first time at the Glen Haven Water Cure in New York state. The NDRA could only have come about after dress reform went public: although most of the press on pantaloons dress reform was negative, many women first learned about dress reform from popular printed accounts. They were then able to use the information they gleaned from these sources for their own purposes. Using the strategy of the woman's rights activists, the NDRA initially promoted the healthful attributes of their costume. The organization's constitution stated that, "especially in regard to long skirts, tight waists, and all other styles and modes which are incompatible with good health, refined taste, simplicity, economy and beauty," women should reform their dress.[15]

At the first annual convention, members elected Amelia Jenks Bloomer one of ten vice presidents. Bloomer accepted the honorary position, although she never attended any of the meetings. Expressing lukewarm support for the fledgling organization, she suggested that the NDRA "learn wisdom from the experience of the past" and not champion any particular style of dress, but lop "off all excrescences" from fashionable dress.[16] The association did not take her advice and advocated the "American Costume."[17]

From year to year, speeches on the health aspects of reform costume accounted for a substantial portion of the conference programs. In her opening address at the first NDRA meeting, president Charlotte Austin Joy stated that the convention had been called "for the purpose of modifying the style of the dress of woman so as to improve and benefit her health."[18] Among the resolutions passed were several stressing health concerns, such as: "Resolved, that our efforts in this direction are founded strictly upon motives of duty; that we feel as much bound to insist upon proper, safe and beneficial modes of dressing, as upon temperance in eating and drinking. We urge the Dress Reform as a philanthropic measure—as a measure to promote public health."[19] Subsequent lectures focused on poor health and fashionable dress, and the following year, Dr. Harriet N. Austin elaborated on the health issue—"Women CANNOT be what human beings should be till they have better bodies"—and foreshadowed the association's later commitment to woman's rights.[20]

The American Costume

The American costume's pantaloons were "about the length of gentlemen's," cut "at the bottom like gentlemen's," and "made like men's."[21] If we accept nineteenth-century and current standards for what "masculine" looks like, then the American costume looked more masculine than any other reform outfit. The impression is borne out by Seventh-day Adventist Ellen G. White's forceful comment that "we shall never imitate Miss Dr. Austin or Mrs. Dr. York. They dress very much like men."[22] James C. Jackson maintained that his wife and adopted daughter patterned the American costume after male apparel.[23] Descriptions give an ambiguous picture of the dress's masculine and feminine features. Sometimes the short dress seemed to resemble a man's frock coat and the pantaloons like a man's trousers. But, like most dress reformers, the NDRA members still wanted to maintain a distinction between male and female dress. They wanted female apparel to become more healthful, but the organization always believed that the categories, female and male, needed to be preserved. It was even suggested that if the clothing of the sexes became identical, then women and men should wear badges that announced their sex or all men should cultivate facial hair.[24]

Written descriptions and instructions on how to make the American costume left many readers confused and with the wrong impression—that the American costume was a single style. The "basic" American costume consisted of short skirt and pantaloons and was arranged to "secure sufficient warmth to every part of the body" and to leave "every muscle and organ free from restraint." Once these conditions had been met, the wearer had a great deal of freedom in choosing "material, color, shape, etc."[25] The dress usually corresponded to simplified fashionable gowns with the exception of the length and underpinnings. Harriet N. Austin insisted that the *"whole garment* should be of the same material."[26] *The Laws of Life* assured its readers that "the style as at present worn by Miss Austin, is far removed from that which Mrs. Bloomer wore." Since in the minds of NDRA members, the pantaloons dresses differed dramatically, they considered it inappropriate to call their reform garment the "Bloomer."[27] It is difficult to tell whether dress reformers followed Austin's instructions closely. At least one woman thought the costume had been standardized and referred to herself as a "regular Bloomer," one who wore the established garments.[28] There were no authorized dressmakers or pattern manufacturers certified to sell official patterns, so it is not surprising that personal taste influenced individual garments.

The length of the dress proved to be a big source of concern for reformers. A reformer suggested that the ambiguous term "short dresses" be replaced with "sensible dresses," because in the public mind short skirts conjured up images of dresses worn well above the knee.[29] The skirt of the American costume supposedly fell to the knees, a length that prevented "it being stepped upon while descending stairs," but women wore the dress at almost all possible lengths.[30] Some reformers wore their skirts longer in the hope that detractors would not notice their pantaloons and would leave them alone. Nevertheless, shortening the skirt enough to allow the pantaloons to be visible incited criticism of the reformers.

The NDRA convened annually until 1865, giving dress reformers opportunities to see other reformers in costume and to share ideas and stories. Conventions usually drew crowds ranging from two hundred to four hundred people, although the number of members versus the number of curious onlookers is impossible to determine. The negligible membership requirements encouraged people to join: members had to be over twelve years of age, sign the constitution, and declare themselves in agreement with its objects. White, middle-class, married women made up the largest portion of the membership roster. Female members frequently had suffered an illness at some point in their lives before joining the organization and had worn some version of the American costume during their convalescence. The association failed to keep precise membership records but estimated that between six thousand and eight thousand women joined.[31] By 1864, the NDRA's membership included representatives from nineteen states. Of these, New York, Wisconsin, Ohio, Michigan, and Illinois had the most members; California, Indiana, and Missouri had the fewest.[32]

The Sibyl: A Review of the Tastes, Errors and Fashions of Society helped to connect geographically distant reformers and became a valuable tool for recruiting members to the cause of dress reform and to the NDRA. In 1856, Lydia Sayer, a future NDRA president, established the paper in Middletown, New York, with the help of John Hasbrouck, editor of the *Whig Press* and her future husband. Lydia Sayer Hasbrouck had her own agenda when she

Dr. Lydia Sayer Hasbrouck, water-cure physician, editor of the *Sibyl*, and officer of the NDRA, is shown here wearing one of her American costumes. Courtesy of the Historical Society of Middletown and the Wallkill Precinct, Incorporated, Middletown, New York.

began the reform journal. She saw publicizing dress reform as the *Sibyl*'s primary mission, but she also believed a reform in clothing was part of the broader health reform movement. To encourage people to live in harmony with nature, the editor included articles on temperance, diet, and other health-related issues.[33] Hasbrouck also wanted to advance the cause of women, and to this end she featured women performing traditionally male tasks on the *Sibyl*'s masthead.[34] At first she wrote almost everything printed in the *Sibyl*, but the journal soon became the main, if unofficial, voice of the NDRA.[35] Eager to share their experiences, dress reformers from around the country ordered subscriptions and wrote to the paper.

Directly and indirectly, husbands and fathers "consent[ed], approv[ed] and up[held] their wives and daughters in dressing" fashionably and irrationally. The NDRA thus wanted husbands, fathers, and brothers brought into the organization to encourage their wives, daughters, and sisters to

The *Sibyl*'s nameplate.

dress in a more rational way, and on occasion women reformers were slighted in the desire to cater to male supporters.[36] At one of the earliest conventions, an advertisement declared that "Gerrit Smith, Rev. Samuel J. May, and several other *gentlemen*" had been invited to speak at the convention—no women were mentioned. The omission did not go unnoticed by the female members of the association.[37] As an organization of its time, the NDRA and its leadership had a difficult time dissociating from the common belief that the presence of men legitimized their reform. Several women awakened to the knowledge that placing men in the foreground diminished women.

Regardless of the NDRA's policy of promoting male membership, at no time during the organization's existence did a man serve as president, although men continued to wield varying degrees of influence behind the scenes. J. C. Jackson, in fact, retained a great deal of power over NDRA management.[38] Women presided over most meetings and usually made up the majority of the speakers. Like woman's rights conventions, the NDRA meetings offered many women their first public speaking experiences. Leaders of the national organization counseled a local branch when they learned that it did not permit women to speak at meetings, insisting that this implied "ladies were incapable of doing their own talking."[39] The leadership of the NDRA wanted women to accept responsibility for dress reform, and this meant not only wearing reform clothing but also taking charge of meetings and speaking in public if necessary. Although the association pushed women into new, sometimes uncomfortable, positions, it continued to stress the importance of the two sexes working together for dress reform—regardless of the numerous problems that arose from this commitment. Eventually, the female members realized that the male members could not understand what women went through when they dressed fashionably or endured when attired "rationally." This realization caused a schism between female and male members of the Association and hastened its demise in 1865.

The Laws of Health and Freedom

An 1857 resolution asserted the NDRA's conviction that women had "RIGHTS to be secured and wrongs to be abolished." The resolution elaborated on the "TRUE way" to work out the desired result—begin at the "lowest point of [women's] depression" and build up their health. Convinced that the route to political and legal rights lay in the improvement of a woman's health, pantaloons dress reformers argued that they needed to awaken the consciousness of the public to the inferior "bodily growth, bodily health, and bodily beauty" of women.[40] The NDRA expected healthful reform garments to make it possible for women to fulfill their important positions as citizens of the country. The association even passed a resolution to this effect: "Resolved, That we shall never have a truly republican government until woman's rights are acknowledged to be equal and identical with those of man, and until they are protected as fully as those of man."[41]

As early as 1851, water-cure dress reformers had stressed the connection between the American costume and a commitment to republican citizenship and individualism, and Mary Gove Nichols challenged women to wear the short costume by asking if they made up "a nation of cowards, or whether they [were] the true daughters of the men of '76?"[42] By putting on the dress, women made "their Declaration of Independence."[43] Given the NDRA's water-cure legacy, it is not surprising that the organization chose the name "American Costume" as a symbol of its nationalism. The name also reflected the group's search for a "traditional" costume that represented America just as ethnic, peasant dress was associated with particular countries in Europe. At the same time, members did not want their dress confused with the fashionable clothing "devised by the dissolute capitals of Europe."[44] Although women organized within the association to work together to reform dress, the NDRA did not push for legislative reforms because members believed individual reform, not institutional reform, would have the greatest effect on American society.

Some dress reformers saw implications for the lives of healthy women that went beyond having healthy babies or living free of disease. They directly connected woman's rights with woman's health. As a result, the NDRA voted in 1859 to expand its constitutional objectives to include woman's rights objectives, directly correlating fashion's excesses to women's oppression. The association seemed to have awakened to the realization that fashion robbed women of their health *and* their rights. The amendment read, "The objects of this Association are to induce a reform in dress—that of woman in particular, especially in regard to long skirts, tight waists, and all styles and modes which are incompatible with good health, refined taste, simplicity, economy and beauty: also to promote a better observance of the laws of health and the freedom and elevation of woman generally." The female members welcomed the amendment and reasoned that once women attained "the highest possible degree of physical development" they would become "genuine women, and re-create society"—their opponents' biggest fear.[45]

While we might expect the NDRA to be sympathetic to woman's rights campaigners, the association, in fact, campaigned to discredit Elizabeth Cady Stanton and other woman's rights advocates. They mockingly blamed Lucy Stone's desire "to get and please a husband" for her return to long skirts, and pressure from the church for Elizabeth Cady Stanton's "defection" to fashionable dress. NDRA members discounted the strain caused by harassment as a legitimate reason for abandoning dress reform because they were convinced that all "true" reformers had to bear unfavorable public opinion.[46] Dress reformers committed to changing woman's position in society (such as those who joined the NDRA) differed from the woman's rights movement in their interpretation of the role of beauty and fashion in woman's oppression. Feminist activists did not see dress as the major site of women's oppression. They focused on the role of government and laws in maintaining women's subordination. Working for the passage of legislation thus seemed the most expedient means to woman's rights. In contrast, the NDRA argued that fashionable dress caused women's oppression. Members expected the reform in dress and in woman's rights to work concurrently—as individual women changed how they dressed, the vote, economic opportunities, and political offices would open up.

According to the resolutions passed by the National Dress Reform Association in 1860, woman could never be expected "to be recognized the equal of man, until she emancipates herself from a dress which is both cause and the sign of her vassalage."[47] Members of the NDRA adamantly believed dress to be the most important reform facing antebellum society, and they were the only group to place this much stress on dress reform. All of the other pantaloons dress reformers regarded dress reform as an important component in a larger platform, not the primary feature of their ideologies. In 1867, Mrs. O. P. M'Cune declared, "The greatest reform the world is in need of is a reform in the dress of its women."[48] This stubborn, narrow commitment to dress reform as the only reform that could change women's status also contributed to the association's demise.

The year 1859 saw this significant change in the NDRA's purpose, but it also proved to be a tumultuous year in the United States, as conflicts over slavery increased. Borrowing ideas from abolitionists and the woman's rights movement, the NDRA incorporated slave images into their official rhetoric. But with their awakened sensitivity to women's issues came insensitivity to the plight of enslaved African Americans in the South, as the NDRA opportunistically compared the "negro slavery crisis" to women's "slavery" to fashion. Before 1859 references to women's enslavement to fashion were not uncommon, but during that year they exploded and became more explicitly related to slavery in the South.[49] The appropriation of slave images demonstrates an ambiguity in antebellum health dress reform. The idea of being enslaved to "passion, appetite, [or] fashion" suggested the condition was beyond the control of the individual. Yet women were told to cast away their "chains," or, in other words, give up their enslavement by practicing self-control. This sentiment blamed women for their own enslavement, but the words borrowed from slavery also conjured up disturbing images of fashion's control over women and provided women with emotionally stirring images of the freedom that could be bought with rational dress and pantaloons.

The NDRA insisted that the personal was political when they compared fashion "slavery" to southern slavery and when they maintained that only a strong, healthy woman could strive for her "rightful" place in society. NDRA members believed that women died because they practiced an unhealthy way of life—especially in their choice of clothing. To the health dress reformers who filled the ranks of the association, physical emancipation equaled political emancipation: physical vitality would free women's bodies, thereby allowing women to turn their attention away from themselves and toward political issues. Because women had not reached the perfected state of a healthy body, the NDRA did not often concern itself with the formal political issues of the day.

Once Civil War broke out in 1861, the members of the NDRA interested in working for the war effort agreed to suspend their annual conventions; other members continued meeting. Small crowds attended the 1860 and 1861 conventions, and no convention met in 1862. But in 1863, although the war continued, the NDRA's executive committee called a meeting to let the "public . . . understand that the Association is still alive" and that the "friends" of dress reform continued in their devotion to its principles. With the 1863 convention members hoped to show "both by percept and example, their faith in the nobility and worthiness" of the dress reform cause.[50] An estimated six hundred to eight hundred people attended, the majority being women in the pantaloons reform dress. Many of these women had spent time in hospitals near their homes, sewn uniforms, and cooked for soldiers, all the while maintaining their allegiance to dress reform. They insisted that the "movement for a Reform in Woman's Dress [was] an important item in this great warfare."[51]

The NDRA's executive committee ignored any ramifications the war had on dress reform. At the convention they discouraged women from discussing the war and asked them to speak exclusively about the American costume. Not everyone agreed to follow the directives of the committee and when their chances to speak came, unmindful of possible rebukes, some spoke about women and the war. This forthrightness could have grown from the women's involvement in the NDRA activity plus their assistance during the war—becoming more "political" despite themselves and the NDRA. Overall, few lectures dealt with the war, and at the conclusion of the convention, those in attendance agreed it had been successful. Annual meetings continued to be held throughout the remainder of the Civil War. Writing to encourage Gerrit Smith to attend the 1865 meeting, Jackson noted that the "reform in the last two years of the war has made the most satisfactory progress." He wrote of whole townships and counties where women wore the American costume, albeit exclusively as a working dress. The letter concluded with Jackson's hopes for the future of dress reform: "we mean to labor on, hoping that, by and by, the public eye will become accustomed to a new style of dress for woman, and therefore the public mind will be led to consent to its adoption."[52] But approximately three months after Lee surrendered to Grant, the NDRA met for the last time, in Rochester, New York, on June 21, 1865. In May, the optimistic Jackson did not foresee his role in the power struggle that would break up the NDRA.

Seventh-day Adventists: The Reform Visions of Ellen G. White

As the NDRA met for the last time, the Seventh-day Adventists (SDA) were just beginning to experiment with short dresses, bringing together religious fervor and the doctrine of good health. The Adventists' decision to move in the direction of dress reform was a logical outgrowth of their apprehensions about fashion, their knowledge of other antebellum health reform activities, and Ellen White's visions of physical and mental health. From the beginning, the Adventist church concerned itself with questions of dress. Historian Ronald L. Numbers, who has studied White's relationship with clothing from her childhood to the early years of Adventism until her support of pantaloons dress reform around 1867, argues that at first modesty in dress was "a matter of . . . religion" for White but that after 1863 she started preaching her health message.[53] In the years prior to 1863, Adventist doctrine focused on moderation in clothing, not a new style of dress. After 1867, White encouraged her female followers to wear reform garments.

Many Christian religions emphasized a need for modesty in female dress—this was not new or unique to the Adventists. Few religions, however, ever moved beyond these arguments and suggested a radical alternative. The Adventists not only proposed alternative apparel, but also seemed to transgress gender lines with their proposal that women wear pantaloons. A closer look at the Adventists shows that by the time the SDA supported reform dress, their ideas about religion and health had become intertwined.[54] From their earliest days, Adventists considered decorative ornamentation sinful and believed that fashionable, "immodest" dresses had the potential to seduce a woman into assuming the role of sexual temptress and would lead to other sexual transgressions. Until the 1860s, the SDAs found that plain durable dress satisfied God's desires for his "human angels."[55] The Adventists also believed worldly dress distracted women from their holy pursuits. "None can serve God and fashion," was a popular sentiment of early SDA followers.[56] In 1858, Adventist Ann E. Gurney reminded her spiritual sisters and brothers that dressing like people of the world meant "holiness" departed "from the heart and the Spirit of God is grieved." A sister from Allegan, Michigan, agreed that worldly fashions did not become women "professing godliness." "The outside is an index to the heart," R. S. observed; therefore it "becomes us to adorn ourselves in modest apparel, and with a meek and quiet spirit."[57]

In 1867, James White concluded that fashionable dress "must partake largely of the Satanic."[58] It is likely that if Ellen White had not had her spiritual visions, then Adventist sisters would have continued to wear modest, simple dresses and would never have given serious consideration to pantaloons and short reform styles.

Over her lifetime, Ellen Gould White received five spiritual visions that dealt with the topic of dress reform, and she interpreted her visions in a series of "testimonies" published by the Adventist Church. Seventh-day Adventists believed the "Spirit of God" gave Sister White her visions, and they used her testimonies to complement the "Holy Scriptures."[59] White's first views on dress reform were conservative and disapproving. Her 1863 vision condemned "the so-called reform dress" for immodesty.[60] In 1864, her "Testimony 10" explained why Adventists could not wear the American costume, saying that wearing the controversial attire "would cripple our [SDA] influence among unbelievers." She reasoned that this injury was greater than any health benefits that could come from wearing short dresses and pantaloons. Instead of pantaloons reform dresses, she continued to promote the simplified dress already being worn. This stand against the American costume later caused White many problems because detractors and critics questioned the reliability of her visions.[61]

SDAs, Woman's Rights, and Reform Apparel

Ellen G. White's writings on women stressed the need for women to resist the enslavement of domestic drudgery and cultivate their minds, but she did not encourage women to take up the cause of woman's political rights. Letters from Adventist missionaries in the field also often remarked on woman's rights as a positive goal. SDA dress reformers focused on dress as a cause of woman's oppression, just as NDRA dress reformers had. For example, missionary S. W. Dodds pointed out that Kansas led in the fight for woman's rights, and that it could be shown "that the dress question lies at the bottom of [woman's rights], even; and in fact, of all reforms for women."[62] Suffrage seemed a ridiculous goal while women dressed "in a costume that unfits them for equal health, equal duty, equal usefulness, and equal intelligence."[63] However, once woman realized the error and dressed sensibly, she would not only become healthy, but "self-reliant, independent, and [able to] determine for herself her political privileges and social status."[64]

Thus, like other dress reformers who placed greater emphasis on health or religion, the SDA dress reformers could be supportive of woman's rights even though they did not consider it the most important problem facing nineteenth-century women.[65]

Given their stance on the primacy of dress as a cause of woman's oppression, it is not surprising that the SDAS criticized woman's rights leaders, "attired in . . . fantastic rig, overloaded with skirts, dragging a long trail, and furbelowed with frills and flounces."[66] Gail Hamilton, "in a vein of sarcastic humor," described women's fate as long as fashion reigned: "May the women's rights women [who relinquished their short suits] be forever forced to see men legislate and women sit still!"[67] Pantaloons dress reformers, especially those with feminist tendencies, had a difficult time accepting the advocates for woman's enfranchisement and woman's rights as "butterflies of fashion."[68] To them, fashionable dress seemed at odds with woman's independence of mind, spirit, and body.

Before the turn of the century, Adventists wrote little publicly about the ideals of womanhood or woman's rights, instead focusing on whether women should preach in a mixed-sex congregation. Although supportive of reform wear, as long as it appeared conservative, and even though she held a position of power in the church, Ellen Gould White cannot be called an early feminist, nor did she actively support woman's rights.[69] A letter she wrote to Mary Loughborough in 1861 made White's personal position on gender relations clear. "We women must remember that God has placed us subject to the husband," she wrote. "He is the head, and our judgment and views and reasonings must agree with his if possible. If not, the preference in God's Word is given to the husband where it is not a matter of conscience. We must yield to the head."[70]

But dress reform had piqued her interest, and E. G. White became determined to find and adopt a style that avoided the "extreme and unfavorable aspects" of the Oneida short dress and the American costume and remained in harmony with her visions. The fact that "not one in twenty of the sisters who profess to believe the *Testimonies* has taken the first step in the dress reform" compelled her to elaborate specifically on her dress reform visions.[71] In "Testimony 11," in addition to expanding on her visions, she interpreted more clearly the style of clothing that had been revealed to her.

The 1864 vision was the first time a specific style recommended itself to White. In the vision were "three companies of females." The first dressed in "fashionable length." The second "had gone to the extreme in the short dress," wearing the American costume. The third wore gowns in a "proper, modest and healthful" length.[72] Soon after her vision, White visited Jackson's retreat, "Our Home on the Hillside," and benefited from water-cure dress reform ideas. Upon her return to Battle Creek, White worked on her version of reform dress, but adamantly insisted that the Seventh-day Adventist reform apparel would not closely resemble the water curists' attire. The apparent discrepancy between her 1863 and 1864 visions caused White a great deal of trouble. The earlier vision had condemned the use of the American costume because it seemed to destroy the visual distinctions between women and men, and Deuteronomy 22:5 clearly stated that women should not wear "that which pertaineth unto man." And despite her visit to Jackson's "Home," White denied earthly influences on the design ultimately adopted by the Adventist sisters—instead attributing sda outfits to divine inspiration.[73] The reform apparel developed for the Adventists, according to White's assessment, was economical and healthy, but did not appear "mannish." Her disclaimer to the contrary, sda attire closely resembled outfits such as the American costume and the freedom dress.[74]

To encourage her female followers to change their dress, White explicitly outlined her expectations, gave a detailed description of the costume, and put on the garments herself. In September 1865, she wore her reform dress for the first time. For the next two years, she cautiously dressed in the short skirt and pantaloons—wearing a long dress (without hoops) until certain the response to her reform apparel would be favorable.[75] By 1866, the doctors at the Adventist health reform institute advocated the short, loose-pantalooned costumes for their female patients. The following year, the Fifth Annual Session of the General Conference of Seventh-day Adventists resolved to recommend the reform dress described in "Testimony 11" and "in use at the Health Institute" to Adventist women.[76]

White took careful note of the length of the hydropathists' and ndra's American costume, which differed from the sda reform dress in the length of the skirts. The Adventist gown, as described by White, reached "to about the top of a ladies' boot," in contrast to the American costume, which did "not reach to the knee."[77] White misrepresented the length of the American costume, and her comments about the garment angered Dr. Austin and other wearers with what appeared to be attacks on their modesty. Adventist D. M. Canright declared, "the [sda] reform dress and the

American costume are two very different things. All could readily see this." But not everyone could, even though at "nine inches from the floor," the SDAS wore perhaps the longest reform dress.[78]

More than any other dress reform leader, Ellen G. White concerned herself with uniformity of appearance. Rather than giving detailed sewing instructions in Adventist newsletters and papers, Sister White sold dress patterns. She begged her "sisters, not to form your patterns after your own particular ideas," and she asserted that "correct patterns and good tastes" made for acceptable reform dresses, while "incorrect patterns and bad tastes" did not. When the disobedient did not follow the patterns, they were scolded. "Pants cut after their own fashioning, not after 'the pattern,' without starch or stiffening to give them form, and clinging close to the limbs" were unacceptable, reprimanded White, and costumes that did not follow the pattern could only be described as "deformed dress" not reform dress.[79] Unlike other reformers, who allowed for variation in short dress and pantaloons ensembles, White did not: "Anything eight or nine inches from the floor is not the reform dress. It should be cut by an approved pattern, and fitted and made by directions from one who has experience in this style of dress."[80] The Seventh-day Adventist reliance on patterns for purchase differed from Oneida and the National Dress Reform Association, which encouraged women to devise their own styles. However, making the pantaloons and dress the same color and in the same material became a "look" favored by many dress reformers, including the SDAS. Having the dress and bifurcated garments fashioned from the same fabric made it less obvious that the wearer wore trousers.

White's pamphlet "The Dress Reform," which succinctly outlined the Adventists' stance, began with a statement dispelling any notion that as Christian women the Seventh-day Adventist sisters wore pantaloons reform dress to "attract notice." This contrasts directly with how other religions and some communal societies sometimes used clothing to declare their separation from the world.[81] However wrong it might be for Adventist women to differ from others, she wrote, sometimes "it [was] necessary to differ in order to be right." Although White expected the "grace of God" to guide the dress reform mission, the reasons she delineated for promoting reform dress dealt more with the secular than with the religious. She objected to fashionable dress because it was "not convenient," "not healthful," and "under certain circumstances, it is, to say the least, not the most modest, on account of exposures of the female form."[82] After 1867, the Adventist publications included many letters in favor of the short dress, and some SDA members took up the cause of dress reform with great enthusiasm.

On the sixth of October 1869, Seventh-day Adventist missionaries and doctors, Dodds and Brice, "officiated in the organization of the first Dress Reform Association" in Kansas—the "Tonganoxie Dress Reform Association." The missionaries reported on dress reform's progress in Kansas and felt convinced that it would spread if they could only organize a large-scale, all-encompassing movement.[83] In 1870, Dr. Dodds reported that the Tonganoxie association continued to thrive and that some of the dress reformers wore the costume "abroad, into other States; and the girls are wearing it to school." She also noted that neither a proliferation of smaller dress reform associations nor a large mass organization had occurred.[84]

For some Adventist sisters, the dress proved an indirect answer to their prayers. "How often have we prayed for humility?" asked M. J. Cottrell. Answering her own question, she pointed out that "the dress reform is calculated to humble us." Sister Cottrell, who shirked her duty and failed to wear reform dress, compared wearing the short dress and pantaloons to the suffering of Christ at Calvary. Daily she found some excuse not to put on the dress, "but there stood the cross," reminding her of her weakness. Eventually Cottrell donned the distasteful garment and prayed for the strength to be true to her convictions.[85] Although Sister Cottrell used reform dress as a test of her faith and the faith of her sisters, Ellen Gould White clearly stated in "Testimony 30," "I did not make the dress a test question." Looking back over the Adventist dress reform experiences in 1881, she realized they had not been successful. "Extremists" had used the costume as the "sum and substance of their religion"; they reveled in the burden, and as a result "were diverted from God and the truth." Others zealously adopted and created their own versions of reform dress. Ironically, in the end, White did make reform apparel a test. By not speaking or writing about the dress for several years, she tested the sisters to see if they would wear simple, reform dress or dress in worldly fashions. Most of the Adventist sisters failed the test. White blamed the entire church, not just the women. "There is a terrible sin upon us as a people," she wrote. The sin, allowing women to dress in a style inconsistent with their faith, had to be eliminated or the church risked demoralization.[86] The point had been reached, however, when this reform could no longer triumph over the numerous obstacles placed in its path.

White and her few supporters pointed out the merits of short dresses and pantaloons from health and religious standpoints. They saw the body as a temple for Christ; as such, it needed to be healthy and strong to do God's work. "Diseased bodies and enfeebled minds" offended God because they demonstrated that his followers did not respect the body or "temple" God had given them. Although the Seventh-day Adventists were successful in combining health and religion in their theology, allowing and even encouraging women to wear trousers was one of their least productive experiments.

The Effect of Public Reform on Private Reform

Clothes—especially women's—were regularly connected with notions of sin and pride. The Reverend T. DeWitt Talmage reasoned that, since God thought "womanly attire of enough importance to have it discussed in the Bible," it must be significant.[87] In late 1852, Lucy Stone noted Reverend Sunderland's sermon from the text, "A Woman shall not wear any thing that pertaineth unto a man," and voiced surprise that bloomers had been "attacked by the pulpit."[88] Anxiety about female sexuality influenced many decisions about how women should dress, what was said about their apparel, and how their look was ultimately judged.

The woman's rights freedom dress had brought nationwide and worldwide publicity to the cause of pantaloons dress reform, but after 1855, woman's rights activists no longer led the movement to reform dress. They kept in touch with its activities, however, and frequently reported on them in their publications. In practical terms, by trying to disconnect short dresses and pantaloons from the movement for woman's rights, dress reformers attempted to depoliticize the terms of the debate and make it appear that pantaloons were just one clothing choice among many for women—but a choice that could benefit both men and women. James C. Jackson urged men to encourage women to wear reform garments in order to give them access to "ease, comfort, grace, fitness"—and a kind of limited power to which fashionably attired women did not have access.[89]

But dress reformers were being drawn from a larger pool than health reform advocates and religious communities. The publicity that attended the reform costume's 1851 entrance into the public arena acquainted a number of women with dress reform, and they had their own reasons for adopting the costume.

The "Bloomer" dress's the dress for me—
    I own I love it dearly;
And every season, light and free,
    I'll wear it all so cheerily.
'Tis good for work, 'tis good for play,
    'Tis good to walk the street, sir,
It gives us comfort, grace, and speed,
    For it fetters not our feet, sir,
Oh, what a harassed life they lead
    Who follow after fashions;
She is a vain and fickle thing,
    And gives no satisfaction.

—*Sibyl*, June 1, 1858

"I'm Coming Out as a Bloomer"

Eccentric and Independent Dress Reformers

After reform dress entered the public arena, some women—independent of organized movements—took the opportunity to wear pantaloons. Their reasons varied almost as much as the population of North America, and a few were eccentrics. Yet there were apparently a number of women who adopted versions of pantaloons reformed dress out of necessity and convenience—because it allowed them to work with ease. This part of dress reform belongs very much to women of the middle and lower classes, and those who headed west as settlers.

The numerous articles, cartoons, and poems in print gave the impression that pantaloons-wearing women were a common sight—they received a disproportionate amount of press coverage. But in the mid-nineteenth century, few people ever actually saw a dress reformer. Even after the freedom dress made headlines, dress reform continued to be practiced predominately in private. "For more than two years I did not even have the pleasure of seeing an individual that wore the Dress. I was all alone," lamented Merab Hotchkiss Dresser.[1] Hiram A. Reid recalled the thrill of seeing a "Bloomer" for the first time. A workman first noticed the woman and shouted, "A Bloomer! a Bloomer! come and see a Bloomer!" Naturally "all hands ran to the front window" and Reid "had the pleasure of seeing a live 'Bloomer,'" in the company of "three fashionably dressed ladies." Although Reid was quite thrilled with the excitement of seeing a costume he had only read about, his offended co-workers "began a tirade of scurrilous and obscene remarks fit for a bar-room discussion of woman's right to vote."[2] The publicity that began with the woman's rights foray into dress reform became the medium through which much of the information about reform garments reached the average woman. Still, a few individual voices give clues to the impulses that led individual women throughout the United States to experiment with their dress.

The negative fanfare that attended dress reform stories begs elaboration on the questions of who wore reform dress and why. The decision rested with each woman, but shared experiences and personality traits help explain dress reform's appeal to women who were not otherwise interested in reform causes. The typical woman who put on a short dress and pantaloons was not a feminist, a member of the Oneida Community, or any other alternative religion, nor did she belong to the NDRA or follow the regime of health reform. She did not identify herself as a dress reformer. Instead, she stated that she wore pantaloons for "practical" reasons and seldom in public. Work—paid and unpaid—and health concerns were the strongest personal motivations. Women often attributed their private decisions to wear reform dress to the way it eased the burden of household work, especially the day-to-day tasks that required freedom of movement. This may explain, in part, the class and rural bias; most of these women did not occupy prominent positions in society. A larger number lived in rural areas or small towns than sizable urban areas. The number of middle- and lower-middle-class women suggests that they had a greater interest in reforming fashions than members of the upper classes or working classes did. More married women altered their wardrobes than never-married women, and while some married women had the emotional support of their husbands, an almost equal number did not. Not surprisingly, women characterized as "outsiders," women who did not "fit in" to their communities, and women who held unconventional views elected to wear short dresses and pantaloons more often than women who held on to traditional ideas.[3] Yet beyond this speculative description, most of the individual women who reformed dress are lost to the historical record.

Life on the Farm and the Trail

Henry Ward Beecher remarked that reform dress as "every-day working dress" lacked "adaptativeness" to the city, where fashionable dress connoted a life of leisure.[4] Once Lucy Stone began wearing reform dress exclusively in the country, she realized that there was not much "good to be derived from wearing it in the city."[5] Most middle-class women, including urban dwellers, did not live a life of leisure, but worked within the home. However, the majority of these women did not wear reform garments, instead adapting fashionable dress to accommodate their lifestyles. Some designated certain dresses for working around the house and kept others in reserve for meeting company, Sunday church, and social occasions. Modified fashionable dress as a housedress did not carry the same connotations as work clothing; reform outfits were associated with "hard work" or manual labor.

On the other hand, "farmers' wives" were frequently used to document the comfort and convenience of work costume. In 1864 Margaret E. Bennett wrote to the *Sibyl,* expressing her hope that "the example of … women farmers" would encourage the spread of dress reform. Most interpretations of why women in agricultural areas wore reform garments turned on the acknowledgement of the costume's superiority as a "working-dress."[6] However, others feared something subversive might be afoot when farmwomen started wearing "britches." The reform costume struck Professor William M. Nevin "as being only one of the many manifestations of that wild spirit of socialism or agrarian radicalism which is at present so rife in our land."[7] There is no evidence, however, that rural women dressed in pantaloons for subversive or political reasons. Bennett enumerated the chores improved by wearing the dress, "washing, cleaning house, making butter and cheese, taking care of children, & c."[8] Mrs. Whittlesy also had a difficult time containing her excitement over short dresses and pantaloons: "I can do the work for 16 cows, and 18 persons in the family; can walk 7 miles and be none the worse for it." All of this she attributed to wearing reform garments.[9] "Country women were particularly grateful" for the costume, reported the *New Yorker* decades later, because "it was wonderful for milking."[10] H. W. Beecher pointed out that a rural woman in a "long dress and multitudinous petticoats" could not cross brooks, scale fences, navigate through bushes and weeds, or climb rocks.[11] Yet even in rural America, women who wore pantaloons did not have an easy time. One wrote to the *Sibyl* about her husband's

Could this have been a typical reform outfit? If so, it is easy to see why most women wore it only in private. More than any other reform dress illustrated thus far, this garment is obviously used for work. "Stereopticon View, ca. 1867." Courtesy of the State Historical Society of Wisconsin (WHi [X3] 37029).

opposition: "The first short dress I made last summer my husband hid away in a box of bran, and threatened to set fire to it if I ever put it on."[12] The husband of an Illinois dress reformer received an anonymous letter, in which he was told that he "must be a perfect fool to let his wife make herself a laughingstock for the whole town."[13] The association of farm work and rural and small town life with the short dress and pantaloons also worked against its greater acceptance and use. Purchasing or sewing provincial work outfits did not appeal to most women who preferred to spend their money on stylish, new dresses and keep worn, outmoded gowns for housework.[14]

The testimony of women who wore freedom suits on the westward trail reinforces the primacy of work as a motivation for wearing such clothing.

The rough terrain proved important in encouraging women in the West or moving to the territories to adopt short dresses and trousers. The landscape to the west of the Mississippi influenced female mountaineers' decisions to wear similar costumes. In 1858, wearing the American costume, Julia Archibald Holmes became the first woman to climb a Colorado mountain—Pikes Peak. A witness to the memorable ascent, J. D. Miller, acknowledged that Holmes showed "good sense in wearing bloomers for the climb, since there was no trail and the route went through rocks and brush." Holmes's own assessment of her dress focused on the freedom of movement it allowed her. But she also knew that she made a statement about her independence and did not shrink from stating her belief "in the right of woman to equal privileges with man." The mountain-climbing women who followed Holmes also challenged traditional ideas about women's dress, many of them wearing a variation of freedom dress. Isabella Bird, for example, wore reform dress when she climbed Longs Peak and rode alone through the Colorado wilderness.[15]

Yet the usual portrayal of "the West" or "the Frontier" conjured up images of masculine achievements: explorers conquering unknown terrain, miners finding buried gold, and homesteaders building ranches and farms where none existed before. The picture of unlimited possibilities and opportunities was in many ways limited to men, and although women accompanied men on their travels and survived the hardships of settlement, some historians are examining whether women shared male ambitions to head West or had visions of their own they wished to fulfill.[16] On the surface, it would seem that pantaloons reform dress had a better chance of being accepted in the West and on the trail than in other parts of the country, due to the general upheaval of traditional living patterns.

Yet some women tried to replicate aspects of their former lives on the trail and in their homesteads in an attempt to cope with their sense of isolation and their fears of leaving "civilization."[17] Reform garb had no place in the lives of such women. Dress and appearance were an opportunity to maintain a sense of their identity as "feminine" women; efforts to preserve the sexual division of labor also worked toward this goal. Thus these women used dress to exert personal control over their identities—unlike the impositions of father figures such as Owen, Noyes, and Strang. However, the harsh conditions on the trip west thwarted even the most valiant efforts on the part of some women to maintain their traditional notions of feminine appearance. After the freedom dress appeared in 1851, some women discovered its adaptability to life on the move. Other women "lacked the courage" to try the outfit, those with paltry funds could ill afford to make a "special" traveling outfit, and still others vowed never to wear such garments as long as they had a "real" dress to wear. One opponent of short dresses claimed that she had never found her long dress to be the least inconvenient. Furthermore, she questioned the propriety of wearing a short dress and trousers costume, especially *"for a woman* among so many men." Her reaction may have less to do with the notion of women wearing pantaloons than with the very practical way in which women used their long skirts to shield one another when they needed to relieve themselves. A short skirt simply could not provide sufficient cover under such conditions.[18]

The rules of etiquette on the frontier often proved more rigid than those in the East, as many newly transplanted women clung to their notions of "civilization." For example, Kate Stephens recalled the formal correctness with which frontier women paid their social calls: "In those early summers of our farm-life near Laurel Town, the ladies calling on Mater commonly came in strict formality . . . clad in light-colored silks, soft greys, blues, greens and lavenders, the skirts full, reaching the ground and giving an affect of the wearers floating. . . . Light colored kid gloved their hands, and in the left they almost always carried, together with a lace-edged handkerchief, a card-case of mother-of-pearl, or ivory, or silver."[19] An Oregon pioneer who had "been absent from civilization—otherwise Ohio—for more than a year," nevertheless became the fashion authority for her entire neighborhood.[20] Women resisted "practical" clothing especially articles such as pantaloons that were considered masculine garments, they preferred their "domestic uniform" of long skirt and white apron no matter how difficult the upkeep. In the unfamiliar and exotic frontier, familiar gendered dress helped some women retain their sense of personal identity.[21]

Although large numbers of women rejected or did not even consider the possibility of wearing pantaloons on their journey west, other women extolled the virtues of wearing reform costume. Numerous testimonials contributed to reform costume's popularity as traveling garb.[22] Albert D. Richardson recalled passing a woman in reform dress "who apparently weighed about two hundred and fifty [pounds], and who, while her better half was soundly sleeping in the wagon, was walking and driving the oxen."[23] Presumably her dress facilitated her performance of these tasks. Bradford Ripley Alden also reminisced about the practice of women wearing short skirts and trousers; according to a fellow traveler, "Bloomerism has done wonders for Oregon—all the women emigrants, who cross the plains, dress in that style."[24] He credited the reform costume with enabling women to join the movement west. Miriam Davis Colt also noted that wearing a practical reform outfit suited the "wild life" on the trail. She felt able to "bound over the prairies like an antelope" and did not worry about "setting her clothes on fire while cooking when these prairie winds blow."[25] In 1854, Maj. Edwin A. Sherman took note of "two ladies dressed in brown linen 'bloomers'" preparing to journey to California. Throughout the trip, the women endured a great deal of criticism until conditions forced the travelers to ride mules for a while: "The two women in 'bloomers,' who never had ridden on horseback, were now in proper attire; for like all the rest they had to ride astride."[26]

In contrast to the often nasty remarks directed at women in freedom dresses, women who crossed the plains in reform costume occasionally received praise. For the "excursion [west] it [was] just the thing," however "frightful" it might appear on all other occasions.[27] Emigrant Frances Sawyer did not wear the outfit, but thought it "a very appropriate dress for a trip like this."[28] Apparently, though, after living out of covered wagons for months at a time, women and men eagerly returned upon arrival to a state of middle-class respectability, which included long dresses for women.[29] A practical application for short dresses and trousers encouraged toleration and even approval. However, women who chose to wear pantaloons costumes for other than utilitarian purposes faced difficulties in justifying their choice. Major Sherman, longtime resident of California and occasional supporter of the freedom dress, advised Mary Atkins, "If you want to succeed in California, discard at once your 'bloomer' garb. You will find it difficult to succeed otherwise."[30] The young woman followed his advice, and the school she opened proved to be very successful, both academically and financially.

Women wearing pantaloons did not have an easier time gaining favor in frontier settlements than their counterparts in the eastern regions. Frontier responses to the reform costume ranged from enthusiastic acceptance to horrified ridicule, not unlike the reactions elsewhere. Ten years after the introduction of the "notorious" freedom dress, Adela Orpen recalled that little boys often took stones and hurled them with "violence and a most disconcerting accuracy" at women in Kansas who appeared in pantaloons. To be the first dress reformer to enter a frontier town or village required a great deal of courage or "a very obviously strong man as escort."[31] To be the only woman in town to wear the "innovative" costume had its dangers and inconveniences. In Laurel Town, Kansas, after the only pantaloons wearer passed the "town-wit" lounging in front of a store, he burst out angrily, "They ought to catch that woman, and cut off her legs to match her skirts."[32] Sir Richard Burton reacted with appalled horror when he saw a trouser-clad woman at Horseshoe Station during his tour of the American West in 1860, characterizing "the Bloomer" as "an uncouth being" and comparing her to various animals.[33]

Ignorance about life in the West twisted both negative and positive responses to the costume by those in the East. The *Water-Cure Journal* hinted that western women had a special need for the costume as an aid when they had "to flee from those savages who abound in those regions, and who have already murdered and made prisoners of numberless women." Properly attired, in "Rocky Mountain Bloomers," women increased their chances of a successful escape and survival, reported the periodical.[34]

If greater numbers of women were able to wear pantaloons in the West this trend could be attributed, in part, to the isolation and the need for a more durable and practical work outfit. Theoretically, because long stretches of time passed between visits or encounters with other people, more women might feel comfortable wearing an alternative to traditional work dresses since few other people would see them.[35] Frontierswomen worked in their homes, but their definition of what encompassed their sphere of domestic responsibilities expanded to include "yards, barns, fields, and forests." Some women found long skirts unsuitable hindrances to the performance of their duties, so they donned the more "convenient" pantaloons outfit with little thought given to the social or political implications of wearing an article of men's wear. Yet indirectly, pantaloons-wearing female homesteaders forged new roles and muddied the distinctions between male and female spheres.[36]

Knowledge of the freedom dress style quickly made its way across the continent because improved communications promptly relayed the information, the coverage in a variety of periodicals was quite extensive, and some women openly wore the attire on the trip west. By July 1851, months after Elizabeth Smith Miller and her cousin stepped out of their long skirts, the *Alta California* reported on "bloomers" in San Francisco. Mrs. Cole, a local dress store proprietor, had patterns, displayed a sample of the costume in the window, and wore a dress of "green merino, fitting well to the figure above the waist and reaching below the knee some 3 or 4 inches . . . [and] loose, flowing trowsers [*sic*] of pink satin, fastened below the ankle." The dressmaker received a few orders for the costume but most women "scarcely dare[d] adopt it" because of its "distinctiveness."[37] The lack of orders may also have had something to do with the misperception that "bloomers" were the latest in fashionable trends. Women with small clothing allowances would have been more likely to purchase dresses they perceived as having long lives than to buy the latest "fad."[38] Resistance to the costume might also have come from racial prejudices stimulated by the "prevalence of the Chinese women's bifurcated costume" commonly seen on the streets of San Francisco.[39]

Although supporters of reform costume as a "working-outfit" focused their attention on physical or manual labor, some reformers speculated that the professions would also open up for women. Hydropathists had consistently argued, even before they supported pantaloons dress reform, that women should be doctors, especially to other women. Later, they included such occupations as "Ornithologist, Geologist, or Botanist" on their list of career opportunities for women.[40] A change in clothing did not open up male-dominated professions, although working-class women may have worn reform attire in textile mills and mines. A writer in the *Oneida Circular* mentioned having seen a "statement too that [the short dress] has been adopted by some of the factory girls in New England."[41] It appears that the mill girls adopted short dresses but not the trousers. Instead they wore stockings and boots beneath their shortened skirts. Other equally casual references imply that the costume had some following among the working classes, although no "hard" evidence supports the suggestion about mill workers. A factory setting seems a logical place to find a garment that made it easier for women to work, and some working-class women probably adopted the reform dress, but the experience is unlikely to have been widespread given the attendant controversy. Work (paid and unpaid, manual and professional) as a reason for changing women's dress suggests an awakening of ideas about female and male positions in society. However, in situations where women needed to do the work of men on the frontier, survival was often at stake and women's condition as an equal considered temporary. Such circumstances did not lead to a revolution in dress or social status.

Curiously, writing in 1863, Harriet Beecher Stowe reported on a conversation she purportedly had with Sojourner Truth. Stowe asked Truth about her thoughts on woman's rights, and Truth commented on bloomers. "Some of 'em [woman's rights advocates] cam round me, an' asked why I did n't wear Bloomers," she said. Truth replied to the query, "I had Bloomers enough when I was in bondage. You see … dey used to weave what dey called nigger-cloth, an' each one of us got jes' sech a strip, an' had to wear it widthwise. Them that was short got along pretty well, but as for me …" She concluded, "Tell *you,* I had enough Bloomers in them days."[42] Truth, like the mill girls, focused on the short skirts associated with bloomers, not the trousers that most of American society seemed fixated on. Although short skirts suggest physical liberation for most women, they do not hint at usurping male power or privilege. For Truth, however, a short skirt reminded her of an embarrassing and humbling aspect of slavery—having her legs exposed against her will. Again, it is the cultural context in which a garment is worn that determines its status as radical, liberating, or binding.

Part-time Dress Reformers

The average dress reformer recognized and believed in the superiority of reform dress but could not bring herself to wear it all the time. Name-calling, harassment, and the overall appearance of the outfit made it impossible for most women to choose reform garments as their daily wear. Generally, part-timers donned trousers when they worked around the house, garden, or farm, but did not wear them when out in public or when company called. This partial commitment drew fire from women who braved public scorn by wearing the pantaloons outside the home. Dress reformers could ill afford to play into the hands of observers who eagerly noted and wrote about the dissension within their ranks; nevertheless, they seemed unable to stop their public bickering. Because pantaloons dress reformers did not present a united or at least a supportive front to the public, they made themselves easier targets for insults.

"Is not our first work in reform that of reforming ourselves?" demanded M. A. Hunter, as she questioned part-timers' commitment to the cause of dress reform. She called them weak cowards who were unable to follow their principles, and other pantaloons dress reformers also felt this way about their less-committed sisters. Fatima B. Cheney noted that where she lived, "a score or more" women wore the pantaloons for working. However, Cheney decided that she would only send the names of "those who appear in public with it on, as well as at home" for inclusion in the list of dress reformers published in the *Sibyl*. The periodical printed intermittently an informal directory enabling dress reformers to contact one another and to gain courage from their numbers.[43] Although their concerns varied depending on the "camp" with which they were allied, many full-time dress reformers worried about the image part-timers projected and that part-timers diluted the political potential of reform clothing.[44]

Some committed dress reformers had a difficult time accepting women who could see the superiority of reform costume, but did not dare "adopt it, for fear of ridicule." One disgusted reformer spat out, "Afraid to do right for fear of ridicule! Pshaw!"[45] This type of response angered M. M. Jones, who accused the leading reform advocates of insisting it "[was] woman's duty to wear [reform dress] everywhere, and under all circumstances," and, if need be, to become a martyr to the cause.[46] Jones did not believe dress reform to be a crusade important enough to ask women to endure "the slow torturing fires" of humiliation. At least one Seventh-day Adventist had less tolerance for "dress reformers who are ashamed to wear the reform dress on all occasions." M. L. Perry insisted these "half-way, compromising reformers" did more harm than good.[47]

Full-time reformers who berated the half-time activities of other reformers probably hurt their cause as much, if not more, than the part-timers. Their scolding could not have been well received by a general public already critical of dress reformers. But full-timers were not satisfied with the piecemeal breakdown of the old fashion system and expected more from dress reform than personal, individual conversions.

Part-timers actively participating in the cause (as opposed to those women who wore the outfit but were not interested in dress reform per se) resented the criticism. R. C. Alexander wondered why members of the NDRA should consider her a "clog instead of help" or why her name could not be included among the names of other dress reformers.[48] In fact, part-timers probably accounted for a larger proportion of pantaloons-wearing women than the full-time reformers wanted to admit. As Alexander and others argued, part-timers shared a belief in reforming woman's dress, and they contributed to spreading the word about the costume even if personal reasons prevented them from wearing it all the time.

Dr. Dio Lewis and Gymnastic Costume

Part-time dress reformers could also be found among the groups of women and men actively trying to prevent disease through healthful living. Many of these women wore loose-fitting costumes during an illness and then gave them up once their health returned. Clara Barton, the founder of the American Red Cross, was just such a "temporary" dress reformer. Barton became a patient at Dr. Jackson's sanatorium in 1876, and once she began to feel rejuvenated, Barton adopted the American costume used by the spa. She quickly gave up the costume when a visitor made fun of it.[49] Many water-cure patients, no doubt, could be categorized as temporary dress reformers. Although health spas recommended that their female patients wear loose gowns and full trousers while in residence, they did not insist on the practice if the water-cure "uniform" made a woman feel uncomfortable. Even at a health resort committed to pantaloons dress reform, the decision to wear the American costume rested with each woman.

Dr. Dio Lewis, an advocate of improved female health, education, and exercise, approved of reform dress as an exercise outfit.[50] Physical education and exercise should not be confused with sports. Clothing for sports developed along a different line than women's exercise dress.[51] Women and men often participated together in sports (horseback riding, croquet, tennis, and such), and women generally wore everyday clothing or some adaptation of it.[52] Fashion historians Phillis Cunnington and Alan Mansfield argue that maintaining the skirt and feminine artifacts in such clothing reflected a conciliatory spirit on the part of women; to make their entrance into the traditional domain of male sports acceptable, women continued to wear "feminine" apparel.[53] Exercise or physical education, on the other hand, was usually a single-sex activity that took place in a private gymnasium or house. Because men did not see women while they exercised, women found it possible to wear a costume that would have been unacceptable in mixed company.

Women's colleges began to institute physical training programs in the 1860s, and in 1861 Lewis established the Normal Institute for Physical Education, which promoted gymnastics for men, women, and children. Colleges, including Vassar, adopted Dr. Lewis's system of "light gymnastics." Lewis also emphasized proper dress, which allowed freedom of movement while women exercised, and several schools adapted his gymnastic dress for their own programs.[54] Women at Vassar were required to have a "light fitting dress adapted to . ... exercises" in 1865. The next year, they wore a "uniform gymnasium dress of gray flannel, high necked, long sleeved, and ankle length skirts, with bloomers under the skirt." The women of Elmira College in Elmira, New York, wore a black alpaca ensemble with Turkish drawers under a skirt finished ten inches from the floor.[55] "Dr Dio Lewis's gymnastic costume," according to one enthusiast, "[was] an artistic costume" and "much prettier than the 'Reform Dress.'" However, the only significant difference between this dress and other reform dresses seemed to be that "the stocking" showed with the gymnastic dress. Although gymnastic costume was generally worn indoors only in the presence of other women, some enthusiasts envisioned it venturing out-of-doors and taking its place among other reform costumes. As a result, some women "ligature[d] the leg tightly in order to keep it smooth," and to keep attention away from the exposed stocking; doing so made the gymnastic costume less of a health reform than other reform costumes. A proponent of the gymnastic dress suggested that the public would eventually become accustomed to seeing a bit of stocking "if their ideas are not outraged at first."[56]

More and more women followed the advice of health reformers and put on comfortable dress to exercise. But, like many dress reformers before them, they wore their "unusual" costumes only in the company of other women or in closed environments. While they took advantage of physically liberating, healthfully invigorating, and "bodily emancipating" gymnastics and calisthenics, women did not necessarily translate these experiences into any form of feminism. Using the issue of dress and public display, Dio Lewis made a scathing analysis of women's secondary status in society. Men established standards of female body size and fashion, Lewis argued, in order to control women, literally and figuratively. Corsets and small shoes, he pointed out, limit women's ability to breathe and walk and, by inference, their ability to function fully in society.[57] Again, a prominent male figure asserted his authority on the question of female dress and claimed many women among his enthusiasts.

While dress for physical education held the promise of other freedoms for women, its only being worn in private (usually at expensive and exclusive educational facilities) prevented it from gathering a large following. Historians are beginning to question whether such early costumes inspired later reform dresses.[58] Costume historian Shelly Foote suggests that "further research into the initial use of [exposed trousers in sports costume]" will uncover a connection with freedom dress.[59] However, the current work being done on exercise costume hints that it developed independent of reform costume, or that short reform dress and pantaloons may have influenced exercise clothing, rather than the reverse.

Individual women proposed their own healthful apparel—which most closely resembled reform dresses already in circulation, but never settled on a single short dress with pantaloons design.[60] They believed a need existed for an improved style of woman's dress, and having no other model to work from, reformers altered the design of the short dress and pantaloons. Numerous women and men concerned themselves with finding an acceptable and attractive alternative to women's fashionable dress.[61] But throughout the course of pantaloons dress reform no one design ever suited or appealed to all.

M. Angeline Merritt's book, *Dress Reform,* gave a basic dress pattern and guidelines to be followed in making reform apparel. She began with the length of the "saque" or dress, which Merritt insisted "must be determined by the good taste and judgment" of the wearer. However, she strictly forbade the use of lacings, stays, whalebones, buckram, or any other stiffening or tightening agents in the dress. Merritt termed the trousers "pettiloons," a hybrid of petticoat and pantaloons, and fashioned them after "the *whole drawers* worn by misses." She suggested a number of ways women might make the pettiloons visually interesting and attractive. For example, women could follow the "Turkish model" with gathering at the ankle, or allowing for excess fullness and letting the pettiloons "sag" at the ankle.[62] Merritt's instructions offered a framework within which women could develop their own variant of reform costume.

Ellen Beard Harman, M.D., also had ideas about what a reform costume should look like. She decided the "Premium Dress" embraced all the principles of dress reform and appeared more attractive "than any other costume yet before the public." The oversized pantaloons buttoned to an underdress and tapered to the ankle. The dress followed the line of a man's sack coat, extended "a little below the knee," opened in front with buttons, and had pockets on the side. Harman disliked reform dresses that looked like "long dress[es] cut short" and designed the Premium Dress, in part, to "correct" this flaw.[63] Another reform style, worn with some frequency, was "the Weber dress," which looked "purely masculine," although supporters suggested "feminizing" modifications.[64]

The perfect reform dress that combined both healthful and aesthetically pleasing characteristics eluded dress reformers for over fifty years. However, Gerrit Smith, among others, found it easy to say, "I would add, however, that deficient as I am in skill and taste in these respects, I nevertheless think that I could devise a better than the 'Bloomer dress.'" He did not propose a superior dress, despite his belief that it would take little effort to do so.[65] Countless other critics of reform costume also neglected to present viable alternatives. "We ridicule the fashionable woman's costume," ranted the *Circular,* "and call it awkward and ugly looking; we see that it disguises and shackles her form, making her a totally different looking being from what nature made her. But we could ridicule the short dress as well as the other for its misrepresentation of her form; though an improvement on the ordinary fashion, it is still a disguise, and as a reform it is in reality but an approximate one."[66]

Cross-Dressing?

Dr. Mary Edwards Walker—classified by one historian as "the most famous American cross-dresser"—offers a useful case study for researchers interested in the historical construction of gender and sexuality and the role clothing has played in that construction.[67] Anecdotal evidence suggests that the nineteenth-century United States teemed with women who dressed "outside their sex." One-eyed Charley Parkhurst, a stagecoach driver, "smoked, chewed tobacco, drank moderately, played a social game of cards or dice for the drinks," voted, and was "one of the boys." Death claimed Parkhurst in 1879 and revealed that "he" was really a "she." "Mountain Charley," a legendary trapper in the western territories in the 1850s, was really a woman or, possibly a figure derived from the stories of several women. Memoirs published by different women claiming to be the mountain man make it difficult to determine the "true" story. "Murray

Hall" associated with politicians, drank to excess, smoked and chewed tobacco, and sang vulgar songs; only after her death from breast cancer was her real identity as Mary Anderson discovered. When authorities learned that Jennie F. Westbrook lived as Frank De Nyce, she was charged with "vagrancy in assuming a disguise for an improper purpose." Fifteen-year-old Emma Barnes signed on a whaler as George Stewart; she succeeded in her disguise until in an unguarded moment her natural voice gave her away. Sisters-in-law Grace and Rachel Martin, masked in their husbands' garments, armed themselves and ambushed an enemy patrol. During the Civil War, more than four hundred women managed to masquerade as soldiers, the most famous being Confederate Loreta Janet Velazquez ("Harry T. Buford") and Union soldier Sarah Emma Edmonds Seelye ("Franklin Thomson").[68] Entrenched ideas about gender roles often aided women in their charades—few in nineteenth-century society even considered the possibility that a woman could be a soldier, the common presumption being that women could not meet the physical demands of combat. All of the women in the above accounts cross-dressed and all, at least for a time, passed as men. Their adventures make for fascinating reading—their lives take on the elements of escapist fiction, and, perhaps, some of these characters *are* fabrications. We will never know how many women in nineteenth-century America cross-dressed, but these tales suggest that more than a few women passed as men.

Dr. Mary Edwards Walker differs from the typical image of the cross-dressing woman. What set this maverick apart was her refusal to hide her biological sex and live as a man. In some ways, women who cross-dressed and passed as men accepted prevailing nineteenth-century notions about gender, for only as "men" were they able to stretch the boundaries that circumscribed their roles. Walker refused to be constrained. Instead, she challenged traditional gender categories.

Born in Oswego, New York, in 1832, Mary Walker was only nineteen when woman's rights leaders introduced the freedom dress. As the fifth daughter born to farmers, she often had to perform chores traditionally assigned to male family members or workers. Her "somewhat unorthodox" parents believed in abolition and healthy clothing and made sure their girls were educated for careers. All five of the daughters taught school prior to marriage. When Mary Walker was sixteen, her father is supposed to have said to her, "Now, Mary, I don't want you to ever wear corsets. It is a shame that women encase their bodies in those steel torture instruments."[69] While she was a schoolteacher, she tried her first bloomer dress and experimented with several variations. A Walker biographer has suggested that she started wearing trousers so that her father could have a "son."[70] After only a few years, the unorthodox Walker gave up teaching to pursue a career in medicine. She and her future husband, Albert E. Miller, received their medical degrees in 1855 from the short-lived Syracuse Medical College, an Eclectic school. While in medical school, Walker continued to wear short dresses with trousers. Her classmates, female and male, accused her of being too lazy to wash her clothes, of wanting to show off her legs, and of seeking notoriety. They refused to believe that Walker genuinely preferred bloomers to long dresses.[71]

Walker's commitment to dress reform included wearing a short dress and pantaloons at her wedding, much to her bridegroom's dismay. The wedding defied tradition on several other points, including Walker's refusal to allow the word "obey" in her vows and her insistence on retaining her maiden name—although she agreed to place the initial "M" before Walker. The couple immediately set up a medical practice in Rome, New York, but within two years marital and professional difficulties resulted in a separation. Walker eventually moved to Iowa, where she secured a divorce from Miller in 1860.[72]

With the onset of the Civil War, Walker requested a position as an army surgeon. Although repeatedly denied a commission, Walker volunteered her medical services and continued to make requests for an appointment. In 1864 the U.S. government designated her a contract-surgeon, a position at the bottom of the scale of medical professionals. She was sent to Chattanooga, Tennessee, but shortly thereafter the army's medical director revoked her orders and position.[73] While serving in Tennessee, Walker said she recognized more than ever the burden of women's clothing and started wearing a military uniform similar to that worn by the male officers. Dressed in gold-striped trousers, felt hat, and jacket, for the first time Walker donned predominantly male garments. She never attempted to disguise her sex with the uniform.[74] It has been implied that Walker wanted to disassociate herself from Civil War nurses by wearing a uniform that proclaimed her professional standing—a reasonable assertion given her ego[75]—yet this does not

Although titled "Mary E. Walker in Bloomer costume," this photograph may show the pantaloons reform outfit that Walker wore during her military service. Courtesy of Oswego County Historical Society, Oswego, New York.

sufficiently explain her continued use of pantaloons after the war. After he first saw her, Gen. William Tecumseh Sherman supposedly demanded, "Why don't you wear proper clothing? That toggery is neither one thing nor the other!"[76] At the close of the war, however, President Andrew Johnson awarded Walker the Congressional Medal of Honor for Meritorious Service on November 11, 1865.[77]

An 1866 arrest brought Mary Walker and the reform costume (she was then wearing) to national public attention. The *New York Times* reported that "a few rowdies, who were anxious to get a glimpse of her peculiar attire," followed Dr. Walker through the streets of Manhattan. Instead of dispersing the "rabble" that surrounded the dress reformer, a police officer arrested Walker, charging her with "disorderly conduct and pearing [sic] in male costume." Justice Mansfield honored the complaint and set Walker's bail at $300. She spent several hours in jail before her attorney found funds and posted the bond. A week prior to this incident, another zealous officer had detained Walker as she strolled through lower Manhattan. However, the sergeant at the station house immediately released her, "announcing the complaint trivial." Upon her release Walker entered a grievance against that arresting officer. The subsequent trial and her second arrest within a week drew a great deal of press coverage. Throughout the trial, Walker insisted that the officer had arrested her for wearing masculine clothing and not for drawing a crowd and disturbing the peace. No one conceded that this had been the case, and the arresting officer maintained that he had charged her for creating a public nuisance.[78]

The myth that Congress passed legislation permitting Walker to wear men's clothing began around this time, and the idea that she would ask a male institution for permission to wear her preferred style of clothing angered Walker. Although the myth persists, Walker did not ask for or receive congressional sanction to wear trousers. Since it was not illegal for women to wear male clothing unless disturbing the peace or committing some other crime, it would not have been necessary for Walker to petition Congress. In 1881 Walker did petition the New York State Legislature to run for the office of U.S. Senator, and this may have contributed to the later confusion.[79] Another issue in which Walker dealt with Congress makes the legend even more far-fetched. Walker insisted that the Constitution had, in fact, granted women the right to vote, and that they did not need the authorization of an organization of men—Congress—to practice that Constitutional right.[80]

Within the next few years, Walker's clothing evolved until it was indistinguishable from an average middle-class gentleman's apparel. Sometime in the 1870s, her costume stabilized, and she wore a variation of male trousers, coat, vest, and top hat for the rest of her life. Walker, however, said, "I don't wear men's clothes, I wear my own clothes."[81] The press continued to persecute Walker because of her clothing, and painted the picture of her as eccentric and bizarre. Walker seemed to irritate almost everyone with whom she came in contact, including woman's rights leaders and

Dr. Mary E. Walker in full menswear. The high collar, top hat, and carefully knotted tie suggest that male clothing could be as "inconvenient" as female attire. However, as a woman dressed unapologetically in men's clothing, Walker made observers uneasy and suggested the possibility of female power. Courtesy of the George Arents Library, Syracuse University.

suffragists. Even among this group of women, many of whom had shared the humiliation of being scorned because of their dress, Walker found herself the object of derision.

In many instances, Walker's choice of dress inspired hostile attacks—including being pelted by rotten eggs and set upon by dogs.[82] *Hit,* Walker's 1871 text, suggests that the daily barrage of harassment hurt her: "If men were *really* what they *profess* to be, 'the protectors of women,' they would never arrest one for dressing herself in a comfortable and health and life saving manner." She continued, "But *until* the 'good time coming' comes, when women can dress hygienically without being *martyrized,* thousands of wrongs and sorrows must result every year, that are perfectly needless, aye, *agonizing!*"[83]

Walker appeared to be a living contradiction—both feminine and masculine—in a world that clung to the visual distinctions of clothing to help distinguish women from men. Walker certainly shows that for women to reap any of the benefits of cross-dressing— safety from sexual assaults, opportunities to make money, and access to a man's world of camaraderie and acceptance—they had to hide their biological sex. Women who "became" men could find acceptance. Women who remained women but borrowed the clothing of their fathers and brothers had a different experience—one that rated disapproval at the very least.

Walker asserted that women had "the inherent *right*" to dress as they "please[d]," and added, "the idea that 'women cannot be distinguished from men,' is a piece of *bosh*."[84] She also insisted that she wore male apparel because it was more comfortable than female dress. In fact, a quick look at nineteenth-century masculine styles, some of which Walker wore, reveals high collars, neckties, form-fitting jackets, and tight pantaloons that could be as restrictive and bothersome as a woman's outfit. Comfort hardly seems a strong motive for wearing male attire. Still, male clothing seemed superior to "outlandish and extravagant" female dress, as well as sensible, comfortable, and convenient. When Walker and others spoke of comfort, they did not only refer to freedom of movement, but to the comfort of being able to forget one's body and the clothing that adorned it, and the comfort of being able to choose one's clothing from all available possibilities.

Male garments were not only about comfort. As reformer Mary Tillotson observed, in the public mind, "Pants are allied to Power."[85] Other commentators in the nineteenth century agreed. Educator Horace Mann wrote that "cunning tailors and [dress]-makers" made the only "noteworthy" differences between the sexes because "by the cut of his shears" the tailor also made women. Thus, reasoned Mann, the tailor "can turn a man into a woman or a woman into a man," simply by making "the nether portion of their garments bifurcated or cylindrical."[86] With a snip of the scissors a tailor makes the man—or woman. The cutting and lopping and snipping are *dis*empowering for men but empowering for women. When a woman's hair is cut or her skirts are lopped, it is a *man*'s loss and a woman's (purported) gain.[87] Many critics feared this gain and attacked women who used apparel to step outside their gender. One author, quoting the Bible, insisted that women and men had "to distinguish themselves in their outward dress," and that any attempt to remove "the true and proper boundary between" the sexes was a serious crime against society.[88] In 1889, the French author John Grand-Carteret noted that trousers were "the living expression of authority," and that women "would dearly love to get a better grasp on this god [pants]!"[89]

Additionally, choosing to wear a man's suit for practical reasons can be seen as a symbolic demand for freedom from the traditions that marked women as inferior and limited their life choices—an indication that women wanted change not simply to cross over into men's roles. Over the course of her life, Walker's choice of dress seemed to impede her more often than it empowered her.

After the war and her divorce, Walker needed to make a living. She tried to repeat her successful European lecture tour in the United States; however, she never drew large enough audiences to support herself. She moved to Washington, D.C., and lobbied Congress for several causes, including a war pension for herself.[90] For a time she allied herself with the woman's suffrage movement, but she soon became convinced that the Constitution already guaranteed women the right to vote. All women needed to do, she argued, was show up at the polls in large enough numbers and exercise that right. To supplement her income and to give voice to her opinions on women and dress, Walker published two books, *Hit* (1871) and *Unmasked; or the Science of Immorality* (1878). In the 1880s and 1890s, when she was in her late fifties and early sixties, with a declining medical practice and fewer lecture opportunities and ways to earn her living, Walker agreed to appear on stage in Dime Museums throughout the country, and people paid to see the woman dressed as a man. Even as it advertised Walker's appearance at "Wonderland," in 1893, a Buffalo, New York, newspaper acknowledged that there was "something grotesque in her appearance on a stage built for freaks." At the end of her life, the impoverished Walker labored to eke out a living.[91] She became a sideshow freak, creating an odd parallel to biographical interpretations that characterized her as eccentric from the start.[92]

Physical comfort hardly seems a strong enough motive to sustain anyone through the torment that Walker endured for her clothing choices. To many observers, she seemed literally to "embody" the predictions that women would take on male attitudes, mannerisms, and prerogatives if they wore any article of men's clothing. Although Walker insisted that her femininity was apparent despite the garments she wore, pictures of her make it clear that this was not always true. When she first started wearing trousers, Walker kept her hair long, which made her more easily recognizable as a woman. Later in life, however, she kept her hair short. Her experiences suggest that more than simple "fashion" and comfort were at stake. By stepping into men's pantaloons, Walker and pantaloons dress reformers threatened the boundaries of male territory. Newspapers in Wyoming asked, "Will the [voting] woman smoke?"—as if men feared losing their stogies and cigarettes along with their claim to masculine citizenship and trousers.[93]

Gender distinctions were extremely rigid in the nineteenth century, and when those distinctions were blurred, observers usually found the experience very upsetting. They still do. For example, the artist who painted Dr. Walker's portrait for a 1982 commemorative stamp chose to "emphasize the femininity of her subject rather than her *addiction* to male attire" (emphasis mine). To that end, she painted Walker in a "Victorian dress" with a "jabot of frilly lace," items Walker would never have chosen for herself. The use of the word "addiction" implies that Walker's choice of dress is somehow sick—and this was in 1982, not 1882.[94]

When women appropriated pantaloons and other articles of male apparel, they directly challenged the binary gender system that required gender-distinctive dress. Many critics dealt with their anxiety over changing gender roles by attacking cross-dressers. One editorial writer fumed, "Clad in the majesty of trousers and the splendor of a frock coat. . . . Dr. Walker represents herself outwardly to be a man, she claims to be a woman . . . . What must be demanded by all who have the interests of the Republic at heart is the refeminization of Dr. Walker. Her trousers must be taken from her—where and how is, of course, a matter of detail."[95] The assaults on women dressed entirely, or in part, in masculine apparel were attempts to preserve the existing gender system by forcing women back into long dresses and by implication into their feminine roles.

Make-Believe Women

In a culture that increasingly used clothing to signify class, if women of all classes dressed in the same garment, they could obliterate one of the most powerful visual markers of status—fashion. This potential made the Bloomer costume undesirable to many women, including those of the upper class, "fashionable women" who never adopted reform dress. Pantaloons reform dress departed from current aesthetic standards to such an extent that it could not be considered, even briefly, a fashionable style, and many assumed that the garb originated among the lower classes. A few fashion magazines featured the costume on their fashion pages while it was still a novelty, but stressed that their interest in it related to their hopes that the costume might be the first sign of an "original" American fashion.[96] When rumors spread that women of questionable morals—"make-believe women"[97]— appropriated short dresses and pantaloons, it became more important for "respectable" upper-class women not to be seen in the costume. Baggy bloomers became a popular visual gag in minstrel shows and, in yet another gender reversal, male comedians dressed as women dressed as "men" or in reform garb.[98] As one woman explained, both prostitutes and dress reformers, "as a class, are such a set of people as I should not like to be associated with."[99] One magazine editor worried that Europeans would be conned into believing that all American women in the "respectable" classes wore reform garb: "A female, probably a cheap dress maker, named Dexter, has been lecturing in London on the 'Bloomer costume'; and it appears to have been assumed by her, as well as in many English journals, that this ridiculous and indecent dress is common in American cities, where, as of course our readers know, if it is ever seen, it is on the persons of an abandoned class, or on those of vulgar women whose inordinate love of notoriety is apt to display itself in ways that induce their exclusion from respectable society."[100]

Popular characterizations of trouser-wearing women as "ladies who [wore] a feeble imitation of male attire in the streets" or as "indecent women who [wore] satin breeches in the theatre" further explain what discouraged "proper" women from trying reform attire.[101] So few women dressed in pantaloons that those who did found themselves singled out and held up as bad examples. When a theatrical production required it, actresses and dance hall performers appeared on stage in trousers, and the act of wearing pantaloons confirmed the already low opinion most people held about women in theater.

The supposed number of prostitutes in reform dress upset the public more than actresses in pantaloons. The editor of the *International Magazine* noted that, with the exception of "persons who walk our St. Giles's at late hours," few wearers of reform garments could be found in New York City.[102] Numerous essays addressed the charge that prostitutes attired themselves in the costume. No one posited an explanation of why prostitutes would choose to wear short skirts and trousers. The most obvious one would be that prostitutes traditionally signaled their profession and availability by revealing their drawers—until the middle of the nineteenth century, most respectable women did not wear drawers. Thus, the exposed bifurcated undergarments of prostitutes and the trousers visible beneath reform dresses may have been linked, resulting in speculation that streetwalkers wore reform breeches. Realistically, the "good-time girls" who wore fashionable dress or imitations of fashionable dress probably far outnumbered those who dressed in reform costumes.[103] But as early as August 1851, rumors circulated that "our outcast sisters wear [reform dress]." Hydropathist Mary Gove Nichols asked, if "these poor fallen ones wear clothing—is that a reason for its disuse?" She recognized this line of attack as an attempt by "bad and foolish men [who] want to frighten us."[104] The evidence, in fact, does not support a broad generalization that prostitutes wore the reform costume. No doubt the rumors proved effective in keeping some women away from it.

Passive Resistance

Most women in the United States and its territories passively resisted the reform simply by not wearing any of its variations. Few women in the southern states (the number is almost negligible) ever took up the cause of dress reform or wore a costume of pantaloons and short skirt. And the evidence strongly suggests that only white women (although few from the upper classes) became involved in the reform.[105] Perhaps most damning to the cause of dress reform was the opposition of women to the reform outfit. Had the majority of women chosen to wear short skirts and pantaloons, the history of pantaloons dress reform would have been vastly different. Antoinette Brown Blackwell noticed immediately that there was "much more prejudice against it among the ladies than the gentlemen."[106] Around 1854, most of the woman's rights advocates and leaders joined the ranks of those women who did not wear pantaloons reform dress. The writings of the reformers often leave the impression that thousands and thousands of women converted to the short dress and pantaloons.[107] Although scattered throughout the country, the ranks of the pantaloons dress reformers were a distinct minority of U.S. women.

It has been hypothesized that pantaloons reform dress led some women to feminism. While the casual observer might have interpreted a pantaloons-wearing woman as a feminist, she did not necessarily see herself as such. All women who wore trousers flouted male authority; however, many ignored or pretended that they did not recognize the threat their clothing posed to the established gender system. Reformers who wore the garb in groups or in supportive surroundings often found it a tool that led them to feminism or spiritual enlightenment or a healthful lifestyle, but most women who put on pantaloons for comfort while working did not come to a feminist awakening.

Mary Edwards Walker's choice of dress may have originated as a statement of sexual identity or sexual preference—we will never know for sure. But her choice was also, fundamentally a statement of a divorced, educated, and ambitious woman of the nineteenth century. Walker's insistence that she wore her own clothes, her personal redefinition of female apparel, alters interpretations of cross-dressing. In refusing to recognize her garb as "male"—although everyone else in nineteenth-century America clearly thought it was—Walker did not consider herself a cross-dresser. Asserting her right to her own garments, she in a sense broke away from the bondage of gender and the visual symbols of gender such as long skirts. Studying women such as Walker, who "cross-dressed" but did not attempt to pass as men will make it apparent that cross-dressing and dress reform were more than a matter of wardrobe.

Women's paid and unpaid work, the feminization of fashion, the emergence of a woman's movement, health reform, and religious Perfectionism all influenced pantaloons dress reform yet did not bring about a single dress reform agenda. Although pantaloons dress reform drew on ideas from a number of popular sources, among the crusades attempted by antebellum Americans, pantaloons dress reform had perhaps the narrowest appeal. For many adherents, even after pantaloons dress reform came to the attention of the public, the reform continued to be private, almost secret. Furthermore, the reform focused on the reformers themselves—dress reformers needed to change their own attire before they could induce others to change theirs. Unlike other antebellum reforms, the pantaloons dress found greater acceptance in rural areas rather than in cities. But perhaps the most important feature that distinguished pantaloons dress reform from other reforms was its visual nature. Short dress and pantaloons costume made the reformer highly visible; it was not simply an abstract philosophy or set of beliefs. Yet, despite its notoriety, pantaloons dress reform would fade from view.

A Suggested Epitaph
Here lies
(Quite safe at last from reckless rumors)
The erst well-known
and
Well-abused
Miss Bloomer
Living too long,
She saw her once bold coup
Rendered old-fashioned by the Woman New.
By noisy imitators vexed and piqued,
Her fads out-fadded
and
Her freaks out-freaked,
She did not die till she had seen and heard
All her absurdities made more absurd.
In short,
She found Dame Fortune but ill-humored,
And passed away
In every point out-Bloomered.

—*New York Truth,* January 17, 1895

What Happened
to Dress Reform?

On Sunday, December 30, 1894, Amelia Jenks Bloomer's "brave and noble spirit passed away." Her Council Bluffs obituary mentioned many of her reform activities but made no allusion to her most obvious legacy—the reform costume that bore her name. As indicated by the poem from the *New York Truth,* her passing did not go unnoticed by the satirical press, which could not pass up an opportunity to display its wit.[1] But while Amelia Jenks Bloomer's death saddened many, it did not signify the end of an era in pantaloons dress reform—that had already occurred.

After 1879, few dress reformers had continued to crusade for or wear short dress and pantaloons ensembles. The National Dress Reform Association had disbanded sometime in 1865 or 1866, and with its demise the most active and vocal group of the mid-nineteenth-century dress reformers drifted away from the cause. The Seventh-day Adventists, who began to wear reform dresses around the time the NDRA ended, also let their interest in the reform lapse after only a few years. And with the breakup of the utopian Oneida community, the last sizable organized group of women to adopt short dresses and pantaloons dispersed. Some women continued to wear pantaloons reform costumes, but as isolated individuals they never gathered enough support to make reform dress the sensation or threat it had once been. Dress reform continued to capture the attention of women and men, but from the 1870s forward it was transformed into strikingly different movements.

The National Dress Reform Association Falls

The last recorded meeting of the National Dress Reform Association took place in Rochester, New York, on June 21, 1865.[2] According to the local paper, nearly eight hundred women— many wearing the American costume—and men attended the convention. Association President Lydia Sayer Hasbrouck called the gathering to order and the conference followed the established program, with various committees giving their reports— the nominating committee proposed that Dr. Mary Walker serve as the next president. After taking care of the routine business on the agenda, the president opened the floor to anyone wanting to address the assembly. Hydropathist James C. Jackson, "father" of the NDRA, took advantage of the opportunity to deliver a "forcible" speech on short dress and pantaloons. At the conclusion of his remarks, the business committee read eighteen of the twenty-eight resolutions presented for the association's consideration. Thus ended a typical NDRA convention morning.[3]

The afternoon session began innocuously enough with a discussion of the resolutions introduced at the morning meeting. However, a group of young men made rude remarks and noises throughout the session, provoking Jackson to threaten to have them arrested. Apparently the threats frightened the wrongdoers and the disturbance quieted down. Hasbrouck then asked for opinions on the proposed resolutions. Jackson again volunteered to speak. Hasbrouck, rather annoyed, suggested that Jackson might be in danger of monopolizing the meeting and called upon others to take a more active role in the proceedings. The outspoken Hasbrouck made it clear that she did not want the meeting under Jackson's total control, but he did not take kindly to the reprimand and responded that although he had "styled" the convention in Rochester two years before, he had come to this meeting determined to let it run itself, if possible. The strain between Hasbrouck and Jackson exacerbated the already tense atmosphere created by the presence of hecklers. The troublemakers apparently attended the meeting for the sole purpose of creating a ruckus and frequently interrupted the afternoon's last two speakers, who ignored the outbursts. Surprisingly, the NDRA members had never before faced the problem of verbal harassment at their meetings.[4]

The convention gathered again in the evening for the final session and to listen to another address by Jackson. This time commotions in the audience constantly interrupted his attempts to speak. The culprits, several young men, cheered and clapped boisterously. The mayor of Rochester politely asked the audience to keep still. This plea might have been effective if it had not been for the remarks of a "gentleman" who audibly joked that, while the mayor had announced that Dr. Jackson's speech would be brief, it was not. The wisecrack produced a round of applause, cheers, and laughter. Jackson refused to continue, and the meeting adjourned amid confusion and unresolved business, thereby marking the last formal gathering and the beginning of the end of the National Dress Reform Association.[5]

For several weeks after the convention, the Rochester newspapers printed editorials and letters to the editor that tried to make sense of the fiasco. The letters did not focus on the young men or the disturbance they created, but dealt with the way Jackson handled the incidents. The female members of the NDRA were well acquainted with taunting and ridicule from strangers, and the Rochester episode did not touch them in the way it seemed to affect Jackson. President Hasbrouck even seemed to relish the attention, negative or positive, that wearing the dress invited.[6] In view of this attitude, it is not surprising that she and seventeen other female members wrote to the local papers, acquitting the citizens of Rochester of the "charge of discourtesy." Instead the women severely criticized Jackson, who made a "bitter, malignant and wholly unjust and uncalled for" attack on the mayor's efforts to control the situation.[7] Although they included praise for all the work Jackson had done for the NDRA and dress reform, they were critical of his behavior at the 1865 meeting. His actions made them realize that there were inherent problems with the presence of men in an organization concerned with women.

The eighteen women stated that since Jackson did not wear the pantaloons reform dress and had not been subjected to "vulgar slurs and base insinuations," he did not understand how to handle potentially volatile situations. Nor did he fully comprehend the necessity of creating good relations with possible supporters of pantaloons dress reform. These female NDRA members concluded that while men could sympathize with women, they could never empathize with their dress reform experiences—an argument that has persisted into the modern women's movement. This was a key element of the problematic relationships between male leaders of women's reforms and the women themselves.[8]

The quarrel between Dr. Jackson and Dr. Hasbrouck was not their first. In many ways, these two "strong-minded" individuals held the NDRA together, and the rift between them had broad repercussions within the association. Hasbrouck championed woman's rights issues and the association increasingly showed this influence. Jackson also supported woman's rights, but he preferred the NDRA to stress health concerns. By 1865 the objectives of the association were no longer as clearly defined as they had been, which confused potential members and discouraged them from joining. Infighting and squabbling, together with other problems, led to the NDRA's demise. Although the last few conventions drew large audiences, the number of women who wore the pantaloons ensemble seemed to be decreasing along with general interest in the reform.

After the Civil War, the country busied itself with Reconstruction and the election of a new president. Under these circumstances, dress reform no longer seemed as important. In 1864 the *Sibyl* closed down due to loss of subscriptions and the increasing cost of production. Additionally, Hasbrouck suffered from exhaustion; she could no longer continue her high level of involvement in several reforms and be responsible for the *Sibyl* as well. The journal had been important in relaying dress reform and NDRA information. The *Laws of Life* attempted to fill the void, but as a hydropathic journal it did not possess the almost single-minded devotion to dress reform that characterized the *Sibyl*.[9] In the absence of the *Sibyl* and the presence of tension between Hasbrouck and Jackson, and with the decline in pantaloons dress reform interest, the National Dress Reform Association faded away.

Seventh-day Adventists Give Up Reform Dress

In 1865, Seventh-day Adventist Ellen G. White had cautiously experimented with reform dress. Approximately one decade later, the costume disappeared from Adventist doctrine. White's first efforts at dress reform were hesitant: she wore the short dress when she felt comfortable and asked the SDA sisters to do the same. The pantaloons costume never became a compulsory step for Adventist women on the road to spirituality. It had been a part of White's plan for healthful living. However, the dress never proved to be popular among the Adventists. A short time after its introduction, Sister White stopped speaking on the subject of pantaloons reform dress and then ceased wearing the costume herself. Within ten years, most Seventh-day Adventist women no longer wore reform dress. In 1877, White reinterpreted appropriate Adventist apparel and recommended that Christian women dress simply, in a manner pleasing to God. In doing so, she reintroduced early pre-reform dress arguments. "Pride of dress is not a small matter but a serious evil. It causes time, thought, and money to be spent in the decoration of the body, while the culture of the heavenly graces is neglected. Precious hours that our Saviour has exhorted us to devote to prayer and the study of the Scriptures are given to an unnecessary preparation of apparel for outward display. By and by there will be a sad reckoning of the waste of our Lord's goods in needless display."[10] In the span of a few years, the topic of pantaloons dress reform, which had been the focus of a great deal of Adventist attention, simply dwindled away.

The subject of pantaloons dress reform, however, had not completely disappeared from the Adventist legacy. In the winter of 1897, White "received urgent letters from two leaders in educational institutions in the United States, Joseph Haughty, principal of South Lancaster Academy, and E. A. Sutherland, president of Battle Creek College." Several Adventist women had approached these male leaders, believing that their profession of faith and "their loyalty to the Spirit of Prophecy" demanded they return to the pantaloons reform dress of the 1860s. These women also convinced other Adventist sisters, including Haughty's wife, of the necessity of changing their apparel. In desperation Haughty and Sutherland wrote to White, "in hope that God would reveal to them what they should do."[11] The men managed to persuade those interested in reforming dress "to wait until word could come from Ellen White on the matter." Sutherland saw that if the sisters pressed the issue, it could cause "quite a disturbance to the church." He wrote White on May 12, "there are many good sisters here who would put the dress on cheerfully and wear it if the time has come to put it on." Although Sutherland and Haughty had confidence in their ability to deal with most of the spiritual questions brought to their attention, they believed the question of dress required White's counsel, and they implored her to reply at her earliest convenience.[12]

White's response stopped the dress reform agitation before it became anything more than a discussion of possibilities. She wrote, "In answer to the questions that have recently come to me in regard to resuming the reform dress, I would say that those who have been agitating this subject may be assured that they have not been inspired by the Spirit of God."[13] The letter continued for several pages, with White reassuring the SDA sisters that the Lord had not indicated that it was their duty to return to the reform dress. White then went on to explain, matter-of-factly, why Adventists no longer wore or championed the reform dress, an issue that she had let slide in the 1870s. She now took the opportunity to clear up decades of misinformation so that all Seventh-day Adventists could understand their dress reform heritage: "The reform dress, which was once advocated, proved a battle at every step. Members of the church, refusing to adopt this healthful style of dress caused dissension and discord. With some there was no uniformity and taste in the preparation of the dress as it had been plainly set before them. This was food for talk. The result was that the objectionable features, the pants were left off. The burden of advocating the reform dress was removed because that which was given as a blessing was turned into a curse."[14]

White concluded by assessing current turn-of-the-century fashions, which she considered "sensible" and lacking the "objectionable features" of mid-nineteenth-century fashionable dress. She also speculated that enemies of the Seventh-day Adventist religion would like to see SDA followers "diverted" and involved in a "controversy over the subject of dress." White approved of the style of clothing SDA women currently wore and encouraged them to continue to "dress plainly." In closing, White begged her "people to walk carefully and circumspectly before God. Follow the custom of dress in health reform, but do not again introduce the short dress and pants unless you have the word of the Lord for it."[15] Dress reform quietly departed as an issue for Seventh-day Adventists, in contrast to the controversy and difficulties it had generated when introduced to the religion thirty years earlier.

The Last Short Dress

In the 1870s the Oneida Community took what turned out to be a disastrous shift in orientation: John Humphrey Noyes began to focus more on secular affairs, to the neglect of religious matters. Stirpiculture (Noyes's personal experiment in eugenics) seemed to take a great deal of his time—not just the theory, but the practice. "God willing," wrote one young woman, "he intends to have a child by Helen, Constance, and me."[16] It is estimated that Noyes had ten children during the stirpiculture experiment. In 1877 he resigned, and the Community could come to no shared conclusion on a successor to take his place. The Community struggled to find a way to integrate the apathetic young people into Oneida's religious and social life. Finally, with Noyes gone, the question of who would introduce the young female virgins into Oneida's sexual practices rose in importance. Ultimately Noyes fled Oneida in 1879 to avoid arrest on charges of statutory rape and could thereafter provide guidance only from a distance.[17] In the end, the disagreeing factions decided to disband the utopian experiment and form a joint-stock company. As a company, they provided employment for members who wanted to work and paid regular dividends on stock apportioned to all members. On January 1, 1881, the Oneida Community was legally transformed into the Oneida Community, Limited.[18]

In August 1879, John Humphrey Noyes sent word from his new home in Canada to the Community recommending that they abandon the practice of complex marriage, one of the first major changes in the Oneida lifestyle. Shortly after receiving Noyes's recommendation, a number of monogamous marriages took place within the Community. Corrina Ackley Noyes remembered the excitement of one of the first marriages celebrated on Oneida grounds: "in from the wings came the contracting parties, two middle-aged men, Mr. Erastus Hamilton and Mr. Otis Kellogg, dressed in dark business suits, and the two women they were to marry, Miss Elizabeth Hutchins and Miss Olive Nash. The women were wearing dark, short dresses. Their hair was short and straight and they had apparently made no effort to beautify for the occasion. That would have been deemed vain and insincere."[19] While the Misses Hutchins and Nash continued to conform to Oneida's doctrine on dress even at their weddings, "Miss Lily," whose marriage ceremony immediately followed the other, felt no such compulsion. Lily attempted to "beautify" herself and wore "a long dress of a beautiful jade green cotton with a slight train," which she had made herself.[20]

Lily's departure from Community standards of female dress presaged a larger rebellion against short dresses, which followed Noyes's flight from Oneida. Francis Wayland-Smith kept the distant Noyes apprised of the conditions within the Community. In a letter dated July 19, 1879, Wayland-Smith outlined the criminal charges made against Noyes of "sexual impurity and harmful and demoralizing practices in your dealings with the young

Father Noyes (bearded and dressed in coat, vest, and tie, arms crossed at his waist) with his female and male followers gathered around him. Courtesy of the Oneida Community Mansion House.

women and girls." After getting that distasteful business out of the way, Wayland-Smith reported on the changes he noted in the Community, including those occurring with women's dress. "I may mention that since you left there has been a noticeable leaning towards long dresses and long hair, among the young ladies," he wrote. Curious about what was happening, he asked one of the female members what the change in apparel meant. Her reply surprised Wayland-Smith, as no doubt it would have surprised the numerous readers of the *Oneida Circular*. The young woman responded that "the desire for long dresses and long hair had always existed, and that the late outcropping was merely on account of the supposed greater liberty secured."[21] Taking advantage of the disruptions in community life, some women donned the long dresses they had apparently coveted for years.

At the time of Wayland-Smith's letter to Noyes, few women actually "appeared outdoors on the grounds in long dresses," and those that did wear long dress publicly did not do so regularly. Some women used the hot weather to explain their return to long dresses, which suggests that the short dress may not have been as comfortable as arguments asserted.[22] However, what began with a few isolated incidents became a serious trend in the Community as Oneida moved further and further away from its religious and utopian roots. The next year, 1880, when some Community women ran into a former female member, she was forced to remark "that they looked much more 'worldly'" in their long dresses "than *she* did" in hers. The former Oneidan wondered why so many of the Community's young women wanted to wear "*long dresses* when she would give *everything* to get on *short* ones again."[23] By 1881 almost no short dresses and pantaloons could be found on the grounds of the former Oneida Perfectionist Community. The costume once heralded as a means to spiritual salvation and lauded as an instrument in the destruction of visual gender distinctions disappeared from the Oneida Community without much resistance from either women or men.

Dress Reform Changing before 1879

Even before female Oneida Perfectionists hung up their short dresses and pantaloons for the last time, a change in dress reform was already taking place. The short dress and pantaloons style had found its greatest following in rural areas and small cities or towns, but between 1870 and 1880 the center of dress reform shifted to larger cities. In addition, around this time several women's clubs, such as the New England Women's Club in Boston and Sorosis in New York, became interested in dress reform—but not in the short pantaloons reform dress.[24] Several historians have identified the changes taking place in dress reform as the beginning of the moderate "second American wave" of dress reform, which emphasized undergarments instead of attempting to redesign women's fashionable dress by introducing a controversial outer garment.[25]

The new breed of dress reformers wanted to sever any connections in the public's mind between their reform and the earlier pantaloons dress reform movements, especially the ties to the woman's rights freedom dress. The new reformers altered garments that were not immediately visible to the eye and that did not visually challenge the sex/gender system. According to Deborah Jean Warner, their tempering of the reform dress and dress reform rhetoric resulted in a movement that "caught on as never before." Unlike earlier dress reform efforts, the reform of undergarments became a profitable commercial venture as well as a reform, and the sale of healthful and rational undergarments continued to rise over time in both retail stores and through mail-order.[26] While earlier reformers had preached an almost "millennial" dress reform, those toward the end of the century spoke of "fitness and efficiency," rhetoric that signaled a more scientific age.

Interest in scientific principles also influenced the emerging dress reform movement in the 1870s. "Health, comfort, and freedom," qualities the earlier pantaloons dress reformers sought, also became a scientific challenge to the new reformers, who believed that they could use science to create clothing representative of these qualities.[27] Mary E. Tillotson, former NDRA member, organized the American Free Dress League in the early 1870s to promote the "science costume," but the organization lasted only three years and was plagued by internal dissension. Around the same time, the journalist Marietta Stow established the National Social Science Sisterhood to encourage the wearing of a "Triple S" costume with "functional skirtage at knee length." (The name for Stow's costume came from the "memory of the three capital S's in the title of the Sisterhood."[28]) Popular novelist Elizabeth Stuart Phelps addressed the New England Women's Club in 1873 and spoke on the relationship between woman's health and her dress. Although she attempted to base her arguments on scientific and rational ideas about health, Phelps repeated ideas already expressed in the literature of the water-cure and other health dress reformers.[29] The "scientific" dress reform that emerged in the 1870s succeeded commercially for a time, and many women wore their rational underwear (rumor had it that some women tight-laced their health corsets, thus negating any health benefits), but the notion persisted that women's outer clothing, especially fashionable dress, suffered from many problems.

Dress Reform after 1879

Contrary to rumors that dress reform collapsed in the late 1890s, numerous references suggest that a variety of dress reforms took place after 1879 and continued into the first decades of the twentieth century. Unlike the disparate groups of mid-nineteenth-century reformers, who shared no ideology but did have the short dress and pantaloons ensemble in common, the late-nineteenth-century and early-twentieth-century dress reformers did not even share a similar costume. Some post-1879 dress reform was tied to the bicycle, physical education, or sports. Other reforms had roots in the Arts and Crafts movement. Others combined interests in health and aesthetics to develop alternative female attire; while still others concentrated exclusively on the corset. In addition, American women gained further exposure to reform dress during the Columbian Exposition in Chicago in 1892.

In the 1890s observers commented a great deal on the subject of dress for the bicycle. To many minds, the "wheelwoman of the 1890s" was synonymous with the "Bloomer Girl." Just as it had forty years earlier, the popular press reported on society's shocked reactions to seeing women on bicycles in "bifurcated" or "rational" garments, and printed humorous cartoons, songs, and poems satirizing the female cyclist. The notion of women clad in "Bloomers" astride their bicycles suggested the possibility of vigorous campaigns for rights and renewed efforts to introduce bifurcated garments to women. The bloomered cyclist also revealed a distinctly *mobile* person— doubly free to move. The bicycle costume was not a dress reform, but a quest for a "uniform" that women could wear comfortably while cycling. Thus "bicycling played a related, but indirect, part in" turn-of-the-century dress reform. Judith Elaine Leslie suggested that female cyclists contributed to changing styles for women with the shortened skirt, which became an acceptable part of cycling wear—unlike the bloomers, which disappeared. However, the idea of bifurcated garments for women had also taken hold.[30]

Another reform garment, very different from cycling costumes, became popular at the end of the nineteenth century—the "artistic dress" of the Arts and Crafts movement, which had roots in the first half of the century. The aesthetes, as the later followers of pre-Raphaelites William Morris and Dante Gabriel Rossetti were known, attempted to combine beauty and utility in their dress designs by basing their clothing on their concept of "nature." The flowing robes of the ladies in pre-Raphaelite paintings and "the elegance and simplicity of the thirteenth century and the classical Greek garments" inspired the aesthetic ideal. The aesthetes, who did not actually see themselves as dress reformers, considered beautiful dress their ultimate goal and even based their arguments against "unhealthy" corsets on the way the garment created ugly silhouettes and debased the natural beauty of the human form. Given the amount of negative press the "ugly" short dress and pantaloons received, it is not surprising that the aesthetes worked in the opposite direction of most mid-nineteenth-century dress reformers, first designing something beautiful, and then adjusting the garment to meet standards of health and comfort.[31] Oscar Wilde helped popularize an aesthetic dress, the "cut-in-one" tea gown, when he brought his reform message to over ninety cities throughout North America in 1882. Aesthetic reform dress, with its long trailing skirts and tight sleeves, could be quite appealing visually, but just as physically "burdensome" as contemporary fashionable dress.[32]

There were other, less notorious, proponents of late-century reform. Frances E. Russell of Saint Paul, Minnesota, led such a dress reform movement.[33] Russell and a special "Committee on Dress Reform" planned to persuade "women of influence," especially women's clubs and societies, to sponsor public events and entertainments where women might appear in reform dress.[34] For the most part, the committee advocated styles similar to prevailing women's fashions, but with a looser fit and shorter skirt. The dresses, however, deviated enough from accepted fashion to cause controversy, and they failed to gain widespread acceptance.

Annie J. Miller and her sister, Mabel Jenness, had some connection with Frances E. Russell's movement. Like the aesthetes, they too disliked the phrase "dress reform." Miller and Jenness propounded a combination of "physical culture, artistic dress and rational (common-sense) undergarments." Through the publication of a magazine devoted to "correct dress," as well as through books and lectures, they spread the message that women could achieve greater freedom in dress and enhance their beauty by exercising and by applying the principles of art to their clothing. The Jenness sisters' imaginative promotions reached many women who desired a change in their dress but who might have been reluctant to accept more radical garments that included trousers. What the Jenness sisters advocated included rational undergarments and outer garments that "were subtle and artistic and meant to be close in design to acceptable fashions of the day."[35]

So, as the nineteenth century came to a close, women and men continued to contend that female apparel needed to change, and well into the twentieth century, women experimented with various ideas to improve fashion and make women's dresses more comfortable, more convenient, and healthier. There was in fact no clear end to dress reform agitation, but after the 1920s the phrase "dress reform" seemed to disappear from public discourse, even though many of its principles lived on in various forms and in continued dissatisfaction with female attire.[36]

Perhaps one of the most difficult things for us to do is to choose a notable and joyous dress for men.

—Oscar Wilde, *Lecture in America,* 1882

Epilogue

Women Wear the Pants

Fashion continued to evolve in the twentieth century, and in a relatively short time would include trousers for women. In 1911, French designers Drecoll and Bechoff-David daringly presented the harem skirt (or *jupe culotte*) as fashionable attire. Belying its label, the harem "skirt" was a bifurcated garment that shared a look not unlike the freedom dress. It shared a level of notoriety with the earlier garment as well. Variations of the harem skirt were still around in 1914, but World War I interrupted the fashion, and instead of appearing in flowing trousers at chic parties, some women found themselves in overalls at munitions factories.[1] Although some people recalled the origins of bloomers, by 1920 the style was more generally associated with the first swimming suits and bicycling and the uniforms women wore as students in gym class. Twenties fashions exposed bare arms and legs—seldom the knees—and seemed to allow women greater freedom of movement. This period also saw the introduction of "specialized" dress for such pursuits as golf, tennis, and motoring. Thus by the end of the decade, many young women would have experienced physically liberating gym uniforms and dress—setting the stage for pants in public.[2]

Beginning in the late 1920s, some women wore trousers for informal day-time activities. It was not until well after the World War II, however, that the fashion became very widespread. Despite earlier generations' growing acceptance of the idea of trousered women, and many women's wartime clothing experiences, it was Andre Courreges's introduction of the pantsuit in the 1960s that prefigured the greater acceptability of trousers for women today.[3] The ready-to-wear fashion industry followed the lead and made pantsuits for day and evening wear available straightaway. By the late sixties, many young women had begun to wear their brother's and boyfriend's jeans; the young men, in turn, started to wear their hair longer. Parents and authority figures became confused and worried as two of the most important gender symbols—hair and pants—lost meaning. Jeans soon lost their tie to revolution and men, as retail stores stocked their shelves with designer jeans and jeans "made to fit women." Despite the growth in the styles of pants available to women, in 1976 Mary Ann Powell made an overstatement when she said, "bifurcation is a totally acceptable facet of feminine life and given no more emphasis than the choice of color in one's apparel."[4]

Gender-distinctive dress continues to play a large role in people's lives today, although not as obvious a role as the one it had in the nineteenth century. Throughout the United States, women at all levels of society can freely wear pants. The "unisex" clothing sold to both sexes follows a "masculine" style line and sizing chart. Heterosexual men are still restricted from donning dresses except as a masquerade or a farcical costume. Some rock groups have played with skirts and fashion magazines ran layouts of American men in kilts (the only masculine skirt) after *Braveheart* hit the theaters; yet the average, middle-class businessman would probably feel uncomfortable in such attire. Imagining a straight-laced male discomfited by a dress and, it is implied, high-heels, signals laughter and smirks (hence the popularity of such films as *Mrs. Doubtfire, Tootsie,* and *I Was a Male War Bride*), but the balance of gender power is not threatened by men in skirts. The rules that determine what a woman should look like and what a man should look like continue to operate.

Today many women wear pants without raising eyebrows, but society has not given up the belief that on some level pants must belong to men. Informal (and formal) rules about when trousers are appropriate for women still circulate. In twentieth-century society, "who wears the pants" resonates in popular culture: the one who wears the pants has the power and is in control. On a recent television talk show, the audience harangued "controlling" women with the accusation that they were wearing the pants in the family. The popular press repeatedly asks, "who wears the pants in the Clinton family?" And when the answer is First Lady Hillary Rodham Clinton, then President Bill Clinton is seen as being less of a *man*.[5] Women such as Rodham Clinton are seen as shrews, nags, harpies, and women who do not know their place. A judge in Columbia, South Carolina, refused to let a female lawyer enter a plea for her client because the attorney was wearing slacks.[6] In 1994, the governor of California signed Senate Bill 1288, which makes discriminatory the practice of prohibiting an employee from wearing trousers at work because of the employee's sex.[7] Few female office managers, politicians, or administrators wear pants to work.[8] Although late-twentieth-century pants did not evolve directly from reform costumes, mid-nineteenth-century dress reformers questioned the validity of gendered garments and opened a dialogue that continues today.

Notes

INTRODUCTION

1. Ronald G. Walters suggests that failure is a characteristic of American reform movements. *American Reformers, 1815–1860* (New York: Hill and Wang, 1978).

2. Robert H. Abzug, *Cosmos Crumbling: American Reform and the Religious Imagination* (New York: Oxford University Press, 1994); Karen Halttunen, *Confidence Men and Painted Women: A Study of Middle-Class Culture in America, 1830–1870* (New Haven, Conn.: Yale University Press, 1982); Sylvia D. Hoffert, *When Hens Crow: The Woman's Rights Movement in Antebellum America* (Bloomington: Indiana University Press, 1995); Steven Mintz, *Moralists and Modernizers: America's Pre-Civil War Reformers* (Baltimore: Johns Hopkins University Press, 1995); Robert E. Riegel, *American Feminists* (Lawrence: University Press of Kansas, 1963); Walters, *American Reformers;* Charles M. Wiltse, *Expansion and Reform, 1815–1850* (New York: Free Press, 1967).

3. *Sibyl* (Sept. 15, 1856).

4. Elizabeth Wilson, *Adorned in Dreams: Fashion and Modernity* (Berkeley: University of California Press, 1985); J. C. Flugel, *The Psychology of Clothes* (London: Hogarth Press, 1930).

5. Lois Banner, "The Fashionable Sex, 1100–1600," *History Today* 42 (Apr. 1992): 37–44; Efrat Tseelon, *The Masque of Femininity: The Presentation of Woman in Everyday Life* (London: Sage Publications, 1995); Valerie R. Hotchkiss, *Clothes Make the Man: Female Cross Dressing in Medieval Europe* (New York: Garland Publishing, 1996).

6. Barbara Clark Smith and Kathy Peiss explore this point in *Men and Women: A History of Costume, Gender, and Power* (Washington, D.C.: National Museum of American History, 1989).

7. Mintz, *Moralists and Modernizers,* 3.

8. Valerie Steele, *Fashion and Eroticism:Ideals of Feminine Beauty from the Victorian Era to the Jazz Age* (New York: Oxford University Press, 1985), 8–9, 16–17, 83–84.

9. I referred to the Oxford English Dictionary to clarify the terms used in this book.

1. PERFECTING AMERICA

1. Abzug, *Cosmos Crumbling;* Barbara J. Berg, *The Remembered Gate: Origins of American Feminism* (New York: Oxford University Press, 1978); Whitney R. Cross, *The Burned-over District: The Social and Intellectual History of Enthusiastic Religion in Western New York, 1800–1850* (New York: Harper & Row, 1950); David Brion Davis, *Ante-bellum Reform* (New York: Harper & Row, 1967); Ann Douglas, *The Feminization of American Culture* (New York: Alfred A. Knopf, 1977); Lori D. Ginzberg, *Women and the Work of Benevolence: Morality, Politics, and Class in the Nineteeth-Century United States* (New Haven, Conn.: Yale University Press, 1990); William Leach, *True Love and Perfect Union: The Feminist Reform of Sex and Society* (New York: Basic Books, 1982), 244–47; Donald Meyer, *The Positive Thinkers: A Study of the American Quest for Health, Wealth and Personal Power from Mary Baker Eddy to Norman Vincent Peale* (Garden City, N.Y.: Doubleday & Co., 1965), 48–55; Mary P. Ryan, *Cradle of the Middle Class: The Family in Oneida County, New York, 1790–1865* (Cambridge: Cambridge University Press, 1981); and Walters, *American Reformers.*

2. There are many studies on communal societies in the United States. For more information on this phenomenon, see Lawrence Foster, *Religion and Sexuality: The Shakers, the Mormons, and the Oneida Community* (Urbana: University of Illinois Press, 1984); Foster, *Women, Family, and Utopia: Communal Experiments of the Shakers, the Oneida Community, and the Mormons* (Syracuse, N.Y.: Syracuse University Press, 1991); William Alfred Hinds, *American Communities and Co-operative Colonies* (Chicago: Charles H. Kerr & Co., 1908); William M. Kephart, *Extraordinary Groups: The Sociology of Unconventional Lifestyles* (New York: St. Martin's Press, 1976); Louis J. Kern, *An Ordered Love: Sex Roles and Sexuality in Victorian Utopias—the Shakers, the Mormons, and the Oneida Community* (Chapel Hill: University of North Carolina Press, 1981); Ira L. Mandelker, *Religion, Society, and Utopia in Nineteenth Century America* (Amherst: University of Massachusetts Press, 1984); Yaacov Oved, *Two Hundred Years of American Communes* (New Brunswick, N.J.: Transaction Books, 1988); Everett Webber, *Escape to Utopia: The Communal Movement in America* (New York: Hastings House, 1959); Arthur Weinberg and Lila Weinberg, *Passport to Utopia: Great Panaceas in American History* (Chicago: Quadrangle Books, 1968); Ruby Rohrlich and Elaine Hoffman

Baruch, eds., *Women in Search of Utopia: Mavericks and Mythmakers* (New York: Schocken Books, 1984); Wendy E. Chmielewski, Louis J. Kern, and Marlyn Klee-Hartzell, eds., *Women in Spiritual and Communitarian Societies in the United States* (Syracuse, N.Y.: Syracuse University Press, 1993); Ernest S. Wooster, *Communities of the Past and Present* (Newllano, La.: Llano Colonist, 1924).

3. For a thorough discussion on the connection between natural laws and religion, see Catherine L. Albanese's *Nature Religion in America: From the Algonkian Indians to the New Age* (Chicago: University of Chicago Press, 1990). Also see George W. Reid, *A Sound of Trumpets: Americans, Adventists, and Health Reform* (Washington, D.C.: Review and Herald Publishing Association, 1982), 22.

4. P. D. Thomson, "A True Sister in the Cause," *Sibyl* (Nov. 15, 1858): 463; "Letter From Mrs. Gove Nichols," *Water-Cure Journal* 14 (Nov. 1852): 112.

5. Catherine L. Albanese, "Physic and Metaphysic in Nineteenth-Century America: Medical Sectarians and Religious Healing," *Church History* 55 (Dec. 1986): 489–502.

6. Harriet N. Austin, "A Response to Fannie's Letter in the February No.," *Water-Cure Journal* 19 (Apr. 1855): 80.

7. "Dress Reform," *Water-Cure Journal* 16 (Dec. 1853): 129.

8. Stephen Nissenbaum, *Sex, Diet, and Debility in Jacksonian America: Sylvester Graham and Health Reform* (Westport, Conn: Greenwood Press, 1980); Jayme A. Sokolow, *Eros and Modernization: Sylvester Graham, Health Reform, and the Origins of Victorian Sexuality in America* (Rutherford, N.J.: Farleigh Dickinson University Press, 1983); Richard Harrison Shryock, "Sylvester Graham and the Popular Health Movement, 1830–1870," *Mississippi Valley Historical Review* 18 (Sept. 1931): 172–83.

9. Late in her life, Susan B. Anthony answered questions about her health and attributed her long life to her "alternative" lifestyle. Mabel A. Potter, "How Susan B. Anthony Keeps Young," *Woman's Home Companion* (Sept. 1904): 46–47.

10. James Strang, *The Book of the Law of the Lord* (Saint James, A.R.I.: The Royal Press, n.d.; rpt., Burlington, Wis.: Voree Press, 1949), 288–89.

11. Spencer Klaw narrates several incidents of illness at Oneida and how they were dealt with by Noyes and the Community. The Oneida Community's first annual report included testimonials from members claiming that faith in Christ had cured them of asthma, sick headaches, weak lungs, kidney disease, and inflammation of the liver (*Without Sin: The Life and Death of the Oneida Community* [New York: Penguin Press, 1993], 122–27). Also see "Table-Talk by J.H.N.—No. 11," *Circular* 1 (Apr. 18, 1852): 92; "Table-Talk by J.H.N.—No. 32," *Circular* 1 (Sept. 26, 1852): 188.

12. Thomsonianism, the major organized medical alternative in the early nineteenth century, stressed the use of botanic medicine. The Eclectics absorbed

most of the Thomsonian physicians when Thomsonianism faded away. The Eclectics were botanic doctors, but also incorporated medical practices from various medical sects. Homeopaths urged the use of drugs in minute amounts to displace a patient's natural disease. Phrenologists related physiology to phrenology and devised methods to tie the brain to the body. Phrenology was later associated with fortune telling. Paul Starr, *The Social Transformation of American Medicine* (New York: Basic Books, 1982), 51–54, 96–99; James C. Whorton, *Crusaders for Fitness: The History of American Health Reformers* (Princeton, N.J.: Princeton University Press, 1982), 124–26; Susan E. Cayleff, *Wash and Be Healed: The Water-Cure Movement and Women's Health* (Philadelphia: Temple University Press, 1987).

13. Lois Banner, *American Beauty* (Chicago: University of Chicago Press, 1983); Linda J. Borish, "The Robust Woman and the Muscular Christian: Catharine Beecher, Thomas Higginson, and Their Vision of American Society, Health and Physical Activities," *International Journal of the History of Sport* 4 (Sept. 1987): 139–54; Linda J. Borish, "Farm Females, Fitness, and the Ideology of Physical Health in Antebellum New England," *Agricultural History* 64.3 (1990): 17–30; Frances B. Cogan, *All-American Girl: The Ideal of Real Womanhood in Mid-Nineteenth-Century America* (Athens: University of Georgia Press, 1989); Ann Douglas [Wood], "'The Fashionable Diseases': Women's Complaints and Their Treatment in Nineteenth-Century America," *Journal of Interdisciplinary History* 4 (Summer 1973): 25–52.

14. Cayleff, *Wash and Be Healed*.

15. For more information on water cures, see Gerald Carson, *Cornflake Crusade* (New York: Rinehart & Co., 1957); Cayleff, *Wash and Be Healed;* William D. Conklin, comp., *The Jackson Health Resort: Pioneer in Its Field: As Seen by Those Who Knew It Well* (Dansville, N.Y.: 1971); Jane B. Donegan, *"Hydropathic Highway to Health": Women and the Water-Cure in Antebellum America* (New York: Greenwood Press, 1986); Amy Kesselman, "Lydia Sayer Hasbrouck and *The Sibyl:* Bloomers, Feminism and the Laws of Life," *OCHS Journal* 14 (Nov. 1985): 39–44; Marshall Scott Legan, "Hydropathy in America: A Nineteenth Century Panacea," *Bulletin of the History of Medicine* 45 (1971): 267–80; Kathryn Kish Sklar, "All Hail to Pure Cold Water!" *American Heritage* 26 (Dec. 1974): 64–69, 100–101; and Harry B. Weiss and Howard R. Kemble, *The Great American Water-Cure Craze* (Trenton: Post Times Press, 1967).

16. Martha H. Verbrugge, *Able-Bodied Womanhood: Personal Health and Social Change in Nineteenth-Century Boston* (New York: Oxford University Press, 1988).

17. Ronald L. Numbers and David R. Larson, "The Adventist Tradition," in *Caring and Curing: Health and Medicine in the Western Religious Traditions* (New

York: Macmillan,1986), 447–67; Ingemar Linden, *The Last Trump: An Historico-genetical Study of Some Important Chapters in the Making and Development of the Seventh-Day Adventist Church* (Las Vegas, Nev.: Peter Lang, 1978); Jonathon M. Butler, "Prophecy, Gender, and Culture: Ellen Gould Harmon [White] and the Roots of Seventh-day Adventism," *Religion and American Culture* 1 (Winter 1991): 3–29; Roy E. Graham, *Ellen G. White: Co-Founder of the Seventh-day Adventist Church* (New York: Peter Lang, 1985).

18. The acceptance of Ellen White as a leader did not mean that Adventists believed in woman's rights. For an interesting analysis of the feminism of Ellen White and the SDA church, see Ronald D. Graybill, "The Power of Prophecy: Ellen G. White and the Women Religious Founders of the Nineteenth Century" (Ph.D. dissertation, Johns Hopkins University, 1983).

19. Numbers, and Larson, "The Adventist Tradition," 447–67; Linden, *The Last Trump;* Butler, "Prophecy, Gender, and Culture," 3–29; Graham, *Ellen G. White;* Dores Eugene Robinson, *The Story of Our Health Message* (1943; rpt., Nashville: Southern Publishing Association, 1955); Reid, *A Sound of Trumpets;* Arthur Whitefield Spalding, *Origin and History of Seventh-day Adventists,* vol. 1 (Washington, D.C.: Review and Herald Publishing Association, 1961).

20. Berg, *The Remembered Gate;* Cogan, *All-American Girl,* Nancy F. Cott, *The Bonds of Womanhood* (New Haven, Conn.: Yale University Press, 1977); Kathryn Kish Sklar, *Catharine Beecher: A Study in American Domesticity* (New York: W. W. Norton, 1976); Barbara Welter, "The Cult of True Womanhood, 1820–1860," *American Quarterly* 18 (Summer 1966): 151–74.

21. Elizabeth Cady Stanton's Declaration of Sentiments has been reprinted in numerous publications. It is also available at a number of web sites, including Women's Rights National Historic Park, Seneca Falls, N.Y.: http://www.nps.gov/wori/declaration.htm.

22. William Leach discusses the connection between the woman's rights movement and health reform in some detail in *True Love and Perfect Union,* 64–80. Also see Regina Morantz-Sanchez, *Sympathy and Science: Women Physicians in American Medicine* (New York: Oxford University Press, 1985), 32.

23. Potter, "How Susan B. Anthony Keeps Young," 46–47.

24. *Hand-Book of the Oneida Community; with a Sketch of Its Founder, and an Outline of Its Constitution and Doctrine* (Wallingford, Conn.: Office of the *Circular,* 1867), 21.

25. Andrea Moore Kerr, *Lucy Stone: Speaking Out for Equality* (New Brunswick, N.J.: Rutgers University Press, 1992), 32–33; Katharine Du Pre Lumpkin, *The Emancipation of Angelina Grimké* (Chapel Hill: University of North Carolina Press, 1974).

26. Conklin, *The Jackson Health Resort,* 149.

27. Letter to Gerrit Smith from James C. Jackson, Mar. 3, 1865, Gerrit Smith Collection, George Arents Research Library at Syracuse University (hereafter SUL).

28. Letter from Helen C. Noyes to Mrs. Smith, July 10, 1877, Gerrit Smith Collection.

29. Scott also notes that the woman's rights women joined and participated in moral reform, abolition, temperance, and other major voluntary associations. In addition, other members of voluntary associations typically belonged to more than one group (Anne Firor Scott, *Natural Allies: Women's Associations in American History* [Urbana: University of Illinois Press, 1992], 56–57).

30. *Godey's Lady's Book,* the periodical most associated with fashion plates in America, began publication in Philadelphia in 1830 with one water-colored fashion plate. (In 1849 Godey printed twenty such plates.) *Godey's Magazine and Lady's Book* (1844–48) was also known as *Godey's Lady's Book* (1848–54, 1883–92) and *Godey's Lady's Book and Magazine* (1854–83). Sarah Josepha Hale became an editor and an important force behind *Godey's* when she joined the magazine in 1837. Frank Luther Mott, *A History of American Magazines, 1741–1850* (Cambridge, Mass.: Harvard University Press, 1957), 580–94; and Ruth E. Finley, *The Lady of Godey's: Sarah Josepha Hale* (Philadelphia: J. B. Lippincott, 1931), 41–63.

31. A number of studies have compared the extant dresses of middle-class women to the illustrations found in "fashion" magazines and discovered that women followed the fashions as closely as they could, but made alterations to meet their needs. See Sally I. Helvenston, "Ornament or Instrument? Proper Roles for Women on the Kansas Frontier," *Kansas Quarterly* 18.3 (1986): 35–49; Sally I. Helvenston, "Fashion and Function in Women's Dress in Rural New England: 1840–1900," *Dress* 18 (1991): 26–38; Joyce Marie Larson, "Clothing of Pioneer Women of Dakota Territory, 1861–1889" (Master's thesis, South Dakota State University, 1978); Fairfax Proudfit Walkup, "The Sunbonnet Woman: Fashions in Utah Pioneer Costume," *Utah Humanities Review* 1 (July 1947): 201–22; Joan Severa, *Dressed for the Photographer: Ordinary Americans and Fashion, 1840–1900* (Kent, Ohio: Kent State University Press, 1995).

32. Douglas A. Russell, *Costume History and Style* (Englewood Cliffs, N.J.: Prentice-Hall, 1983), 308–26; Lucy Barton, *Historic Costume for the Stage* (1935; rpt., Boston: Walter H. Baker, 1963), 358–87; Vanda Foster, *A Visual History of Costume: The Nineteenth Century* (London: B. T. Batsford, 1992), 20–32; J. Anderson Black and Madge Garland, *A History of Fashion* (New York: William Morrow & Co., 1980), 161–73.

33. Banner, *American Beauty,* 61; James Laver, *Clothes* (London: Burke Publishing Co., 1952), 128.

34. Jennifer Craik discusses the tension between the exotic and the familiar in *Face of Fashion: Cultural Studies in Fashion* (New York: Routledge, 1994), 17–43. For an examination of earlier Eastern influence on Western dress see Charlotte Jirousek, "More than Oriental Splendor: European and Ottoman Headgear, 1380–1580," *Dress* 22 (1995): 22–33.

35. Carl Sferrazza Anthony, *First Ladies: The Saga of the Presidents' Wives and Their Power, 1789–1961* (New York: Quill, 1990), 84–85.

36. Harriet Beecher Stowe writing as Christopher Crowfield, *The Chimney Corner* (Boston: Ticknor and Fields, 1868), 131 as quoted and cited in Banner, *American Beauty,* 47, 303.

37. Frances B. Cogan argues in *All-American Girl* that more than one ideal of womanhood existed at this time, including a healthy, athletic female ideal. While I agree that no single ideal existed for all women, I would argue that the fragile, sickly woman was the dominant fashionable female ideal in circulation at this time.

38. John Murray, "Art of Dress," *Quarterly Review* 79 (1847): 380.

39. How and why fashion changes are the subject of many books, and it is not my intention to offer another theory. Instead I will refer the reader to several books that focus on this topic; there are many more not cited here. There seems to be an inescapable fascination with clothing and fashion that crosses all cultures and fields of study (Hollander, *Seeing through Clothes;* Valerie Steele, *Paris Fashion: A Cultural History* [New York: Oxford University Press, 1988]); Wilson, *Adorned in Dreams;* and Naomi Wolf, *The Beauty Myth: How Images of Beauty Are Used against Women* [New York: William Morrow, 1991]).

40. Economist Thorstein Veblen developed a theory of conspicuous consumption to explain the relationship between fashion and economics. His theory continues to be used to explain the complexity of fashion, but numerous others also exist (Veblen, "The Economic Theory of Woman's Dress," *Popular Science Monthly* 46 [Dec. 1894]: 198–205).

41. Costume historian Claudia Brush Kidwell discusses the complexity of the process of fashionable change and the factors that act on it. She describes the process of changing fashions as "an interrelated series of choices"; there are restrictions on the available choices, the most obvious of which is economics. Kidwell clearly shows how complex the phenomenon of fashionable change is. Any suggestion that the 1837 depression directly affected clothing that does not take into account any other factors is a gross oversimplification of the complexities of changing fashion (Kidwell, "Gender Symbols or Fashionable Details?" in *Men and Women: Dressing the Part,* ed. Claudia Brush Kidwell and Valerie Steele [Washington, D.C.: Smithsonian Institution Press, 1989], 124–43). For a dated but interesting account of how feminists influenced fashion see Bonnie Veazey Boynton,

"The Relationship between Women's Rights Movements and Fashion Changes," (Master's thesis, Florida State University, 1974).

42. Norah Waugh, *The Cut of Women's Clothes, 1600–1930* (New York: Theatre Arts Books, 1968), 141.

43. For more information on the sewing machine and its effect on fashionable styles and mass production see Grace Rogers Cooper, *The Sewing Machine: Its Invention and Development* (Washington, D.C.: Smithsonian Institution Press, 1976); and Ruth Brandon, *Singer and the Sewing Machine: A Capitalist Romance* (London: Barrie & Jenkins, 1977).

44. Laver, *A Concise History of Costume,* 172.

45. Barton, *Historic Costume,* 424.

46. Notes to the author from Patricia Campbell Warner. A quick perusal of dress patterns from this period make it clear that skirt width was not exaggerated. Easily accessible patterns can be found in Waugh, *The Cut of Women's Clothes;* and Janet Arnold, *Patterns of Fashion: Englishwomen's Dresses and Their Construction, c. 1660–1860* (New York: Drama Book Publishers, 1964).

47. Norah Waugh, *Corsets and Crinolines* (New York: Theatre Arts Books, 1981), 93; Frank Alvah Parsons, *The Art of Dress* (New York: Doubleday, Doran & Co., 1928), 306–8; Elisabeth McClellan, *Historic Dress in America* (1904; rpt., New York: Arno Press, 1977), 213–84.

48. There is some controversy about how erotic a glimpse of a woman's feet was in the mid-nineteenth century. Some commentators and historians argued that a woman's reputation was at stake if she revealed her legs and feet. Others maintained that women had worn long gowns for centuries, and their legs and feet were not suddenly eroticized because of Victorian prudishness. See Steele, *Fashion and Eroticism,* 112–16; Pearl Binder, *Muffs and Morals* (New York: William Morrow, n.d.), 22–23; and James Laver, *Modesty in Dress* (London: William Heinemann, 1969), 114–15, for different perspectives on the argument.

49. Elizabeth Ewing, *Underwear: A History* (New York: Theatre Arts Books, 1972), 54–67; Karin Calvert, *Children in the House: The Material Culture of Early Childhood, 1600–1900* (Boston: Northeastern University Press, 1992); Laver, *Modesty in Dress,* 134–36; and Robert Kunciov, ed., *Mr. Godey's Ladies: Being a Mosaic of Fashions & Fancies* (Princeton, N.J.: Pyne Press, 1971), 12.

50. Alison Lurie suggested that the increased size and bulk of women's dress in the crinoline and bustle periods showed "the increased importance of women in the domestic and social sphere" and "also allowed them to display their father's or husband's wealth."—an interesting interpretation that does not take into account that the tight bodice and small waist helped women to appear delicate (*The Language of Clothes* [New York: Random House, 1981], 68–70).

51. Parsons, *The Art of Dress,* 306–8; McClellan, *Historic Dress in America.*

52. Jo B. Paoletti and Carol L. Kregloh, "The Children's Department," in *Men and Women: Dressing the Part,* 32–33; Phillis Cunnington and Anne Buck, *Children's Costume in England: From the Fourteenth to the End of the Nineteenth Century* (London: Adam & Charles Black, 1978); Elizabeth Ewing, *History of Children's Costume* (London: B. T. Batsford, 1977); and Clare Rose, *Children's Clothes since 1750* (London: B. T. Batsford, 1989).

53. "Description of Uncolored Fashions" *Godey's Magazine and Lady's Book* (Sept. 1849): 228, is but one example. A six- or seven-year-old-boy's garment included "a short basque or skirt at the waist," and "loose trowsers of nankin." A four- or five-year-old girl might wear a "skirt very full" with "loose trowsers of cambric muslin, edged at the bottom by a bordering of needlework."

54. Smith and Peiss, *Men and Women,* 13–22; Norah Waugh, *The Cut of Men's Clothes 1600–1900* (New York: Theatre Arts Books, 1964); David M. Kuchta, "'Graceful, Virile, and Useful:' The Origins of the Three-Piece Suit," *Dress* 17 (1990): 118–26.

55. The institutionalization of the dark three-piece suit for men has often been linked to the rise of professionalization. For more information on professionalism, see Burton J. Bledstein, *The Culture of Professionalism: The Middle Class and the Development of Higher Education in America* (New York: W. W. Norton, 1978).

56. Aileen Ribeiro and Valerie Cumming, *The Visual History of Costume* (London: B. T. Batsford, 1989), 32; Smith and Peiss, *Men and Women,* 14–21; Aileen Ribeiro, *Dress and Morality* (New York: Holmes & Meier Publishers, 1986), 124–27; Beverly Gordon, "Meanings in Mid-Nineteenth Century Dress: Images from New England Women's Writings," *Clothing and Textiles Research Journal* 10 (Spring 1992): 44–53; Jennifer Craik discusses the phenomenon of fashion becoming a feminine occupation in *The Face of Fashion,* 44, 176–85.

57. Olive M. Hall, "Fashion," *Sibyl* (Nov. 15, 1858): 463; Mrs. M. M. Jones, *Woman's Dress; Its Moral and Physical Principles, Being an Essay Delivered before the World's Health Convention, New York City, Nov., 1864* (New York: Miller, Wood & Co., 1865), 6.

58. Steele, *Paris Fashion;* Black and Garland, *A History of Fashion,* 191–204.

59. The eleventh century is usually designated as the period in which Western-style and gender-based critiques of clothing began. To find examples of negative assessments of dress that extend from the Bible to the 1950s see Laver, *Clothes.*

60. "An Old Doctor's Opinion on Woman's Dress," *Circular* (Apr. 18, 1852): 91, reprinted from the New York *Home Journal.* "The Horrors of Wearing a Hoop. Complaint of Mr. John Smith," *Frank Leslie's Illustrated Newspaper* (June 27, 1857): 64; *Sybil* 4 (Apr. 1, 1860): 721.

61. Halttunen, *Confidence Men and Painted Women,* 62–63, 56–91. William Leach in *True Love and Perfect Union* also takes up this theme in his chapter "The Bee and the Butterfly" (213–59).

62. *Behind a Mask: The Unknown Thrillers of Louisa May Alcott,* ed. Madeleine Stern (New York: Bantam Books, 1978), 6, 13.

63. Emphasis mine. Many of the statements were reprinted in "The Woman's Dress Movement," *Circular* (May 23, 1864): 73–74. It is not uncommon in times of war for appeals to be made to women to give up their love of dress. See Valerie Twelves, "An Investigation of the Impact of the Dress Reform Movement: A Case Study of Reform Movements in the Years 1890 to 1920," (Master's thesis, Cornell University, 1969), 55–56; Beverly Gordon, "Textiles and Clothing in the Civil War: A Portrait for Contemporary Understanding," *Clothing and Textiles Research Journal* 5 (Spring 1987): 41–47; and Linda K. Kerber, *Women of the Republic: Intellect and Ideology in Revolutionary America* (Chapel Hill: University of North Carolina Press, 1980), 38, 44–45.

64. One of the leading authorities on water cure, Dr. R. T. Trall, specifically outlined the damage fashion could do to the female body, mentioning female reproductive organs in his observations. "The fashionable dress diminishes her capacity to breathe; even when she is not laced so tightly around the chest as the fashion is, the heavy skirts, and their being supported around the hips, weaken the abdominal muscles, compress the viscera, depress the uterus and pelvic organs, interrupt locomotion, and thus indirectly render the respiratory function feeble and imperfect" (Trall, *Sexual Physiology: A Scientific and Popular Exposition, twenty-eighth edition* [1881; rpt., New York, Arno Press, 1974], 262).

65. "Woman's Dress and Her Diseases," *Health Reformer* 10 (Dec. 1875): 359, reprinted from *The Doctor,* London.

66. James C. Jackson, *The Sexual Organism and Its Healthful Management* (1861; rpt., New York: Arno Press, 1974), 244–45.

67. James C. Jackson, *American Womanhood: Its Peculiarities and Necessities* (Dansville, N.Y.: Austin, Jackson & Co., 1870), 38. In "'All Hail to Pure Cold Water,'" Kathryn Kish Sklar argues that water curists tended to be more sympathetic to women's special medical problems than were other nineteenth-century physicians. Seen in this context, the hydropathists' concern over the connection between women's reproductive capacity and their dress might be merely another manifestation of that sympathy. However, water-cure doctors' arguments were no different than those used by other physicians when arguing the health costs of women's fashions.

68. Dr. Dio Lewis, *Our Girl* (New York: Harper & Brothers, 1871), 66–67, 72.

69. Dr. W. K. Coale, "Woman's Dress, A Cause of Uterine Displacements," *Water-Cure Journal* 12 (Dec. 1851): 105; Jackson, *American Womanhood;* Trall, *Sexual Physiology*.

70. As reported in "Shall Fashionable Women Vote?" *Revolution* (Feb. 25, 1869): 122.

71. Banner, *American Beauty,* 51–52, 55.

72. Dr. G. S. Whitman, "Words of Approval and Advice," *Water-Cure Journal* 15 (May 1853): 105.

73. Dr. William Bailey Potter, "Facts for the Thoughtful," *Sibyl* (Sept. 15, 1859): 615; Elizabeth Stuart Phelps, "Dressed to Kill," *Health Reformer* 10 (Oct. 1875): 302–3; "Fashionable Women," *Sibyl* (July 15, 1859): 589; Jane C. Wheeler, "Ill Health of American Women," *Sibyl* (Oct. 1, 1859): 629; "Ways of Shortening Life," *Sibyl* (Oct. 15, 1858): 445; *Sibyl* (Sept. 1, 1858): 422; Ellen Gould White, *Health: Or How to Live* (Battle Creek, Mich.: Steam Press, 1865), 2; "Healthfulness of Woman's Dress," *Health Reformer* 3 (Apr. 1869): 189; E. G. White Research Center, J. H. Kellogg, M.D., "The Influence of Dress in Producing the Physical Decadence of American Women," an address delivered before the Michigan State Medical Society, June 11 and 12, 1891.

74. Craik, *The Face of Fashion,* see 121–27. Valerie Steele devoted an entire chapter to the "corset controversy" in *Fashion and Eroticism,* 161–91. Elizabeth Wilson also discusses some of the important issues in the furor over the corset in *Adorned in Dreams,* 97–100.

How many women actually wore corsets or tight-laced? Because a woman wore a corset does not mean she tight-laced. Costume historian Deborah Jean Warner asserted that "countless American women laced in their waist down to 18 inches" ("Fashion, Emancipation, Reform, and the Rational Undergarment," *Dress* 4 [1978]: 25). She indicated tight-lacing to be commonplace. Historian Helene E. Roberts stated, "the wearing of the laced corset was almost universal in England and America throughout the nineteenth century" ("The Exquisite Slave: The Role of Clothes in the Making of the Victorian Woman," *Signs* 2 [Spring 1977]: 558). Roberts also implied that tight-lacing and wearing a corset were synonymous.

Was the corset a middle-class article worn to demonstrate a woman did not need to work, or did the working class or prostitutes appropriate the garment as an expression of their sexuality? This is just one of the tensions involving the corset and classes that historians continue to examine. See Wilson, *Adorned,* 99; John S. Haller and Robin M. Haller, *The Physician and Sexuality in Victorian America* (Chicago: University of Illinois Press, 1974), 173–74; and Casey Finch, "'Hooked and Buttoned Together:' Victorian Underwear and Representations of the Female Body," *Victorian Studies* 34 (Spring 1991): 343–45.

Many historians conflate corset wearing and tight-lacing into a single action, making their conclusions suspect. For some historians, the corset represented fashion's control over women; they note the demise of the corset and the practice of tight-lacing as progress and a victory for women. Roberts, "The Exquisite

Slave," 558; Warner, "Fashion, Emancipation, Reform," 24, and Haller and Haller, *The Physician,* 146–47.

According to art historian David Kunzle, nineteenth-century critics of tight-lacing were chiefly conservative men who feared female sexuality and were particularly alarmed by the "socially nomadic" women from the lower-middle and working classes who practiced tight-lacing as a form of social resistance. With and in their corsets, women were "aspiring to social power by manipulating a sexuality which the patriarchy found threatening." Kunzle even argued that the sexual assertiveness associated with the corset was a step toward the emancipation of women. Ultimately Kunzle argued that the sexual liberation of late Victorian women was a necessary step to their emancipation ("Dress Reform as Antifeminism: A Response to Helene E. Roberts's 'The Exquisite Slave: The Role of Clothes in the Making of the Victorian Woman,'" *Signs* 2 [Spring 1977]: 570–79; *Fashion and Fetishism: A Social History of the Corset, Tight-Lacing and Other Forms of Body-Sculpture in the West* [Totowa, N.J.: Rowman and Littlefield, 1982], 1, 42, 299).

75. "Report of the Proceedings of the Dress Reform Convention Held at Canastota, N.Y.," *Sibyl* 1 (Feb. 1, 1857): 113–15, 118–20.

76. Although persuasive, this interpretation was not grounded in fact. Some famous courtesans could be counted among the leaders of fashion, but they merely wore the latest and most beautiful styles as required by their profession—they did not originate them. Gerilyn Tandberg, "Sinning for Silk," *Women's Studies International Forum* (1990): 229–48; Steele, *Fashion and Eroticism.*

77. Frans H. Widstrand, "Woman's Dress," *Revolution* (Dec. 24, 1868): 391.

78. D. M. Allen, "Dress Reform Pic-Nic," *Revolution* (Nov. 4, 1869): 283.

79. Trall, *Sexual Physiology,* 262.

80. Mrs. M. Angeline Merritt, *Dress Reform Practically and Physiologically Considered* (Buffalo: Jewett, Thomas and Co., 1852), 110–11.

81. Linus Pierpont Brockett, *Woman: Her Rights, Wrongs, Privileges, and Responsibilities* (Hartford: L. Stebbins, 1869), 214.

82. In "The Democratization of Fashion: The Emergence of the Women's Dress Pattern Industry," *Journal of American History* 66 (Sept. 1979), Margaret Walsh describes the differences in women's clothing based on their income levels (300). Also see Nancy Page Fernandez, "Pattern Diagrams and Fashion Periodicals," *Dress* 13 (1987): 4–10, for a discussion of class and clothing construction. Brockett, *Woman,* 136–38.

83. Luna, "Extravagance in Dress," *Sibyl* (Feb. 15, 1860): 699; and "War upon Long Dresses," *Sibyl* (Jan. 15, 1860): 687, reprinted from the *Home Journal.*

84. See Kathy Peiss, *Cheap Amusements* (Philadelphia: Temple University Press, 1986), 62–67, for a discussion of middle-class and working-class ideas about dress in the late nineteenth century.

85. Ada Clarke, "Thoughts and Things," *New York Saturday Press,* reprinted in *Sybil* 4 (Apr. 1, 1860): 721.

86. Berg, *The Remembered Gate;* Donna A. Behnke, *Religious Issues in Nineteenth Century Feminism* (Troy, N.Y.: Whitston Publishing Co., 1982); Ginzberg, *Women and the Work of Benevolence*.

87. The exceptions to this were those health reformers working with "regular" physicians and public health regulations.

2. The First Dress Reformers

1. Background information on Owen and New Harmony comes from Donald F. Carmony and Josephine M. Elliot, "New Harmony, Indiana: Robert Owen's Seedbed for Utopia," *Indiana Magazine of History* 76 (Sept. 1980): 161–261; Webber, *Escape to Utopia;* Arthur Weinberg and Lila Weinberg, *Passport to Utopia;* Carol A. Kolmerten, *Women in Utopia: The Ideology of Gender in the American Owenite Communities* (Bloomington: Indiana University Press, 1990); George B. Lockwood, *The New Harmony Movement* (1905; rpt., New York: Augustus M. Kelly, 1970); Arthur E. Bestor, ed., *Education and Reform at New Harmony: Correspondence of William Maclure and Marie Duclos Fretageot, 1820–1833* (Indianapolis: Indiana Historical Society, 1948); Arthur Bestor, *Backwoods Utopias: The Sectarian and Owenite Phases of Communitarian Socialism in America, 1663–1829* (Philadelphia, 1950); William E. Wilson, *The Angel and the Serpent: The Story of New Harmony* (Bloomington: Indiana University Press, 1964).

2. Donald E. Pitzer and Josephine M. Elliott, "New Harmony's First Utopians, 1814–1824," *Indiana Magazine of History* 85 (Sept. 1979): 255–300.

3. Lockwood, *The New Harmony Movement,* 84–85, 189; Carmony and Elliott, "New Harmony," 168–70.

4. Lockwood quotes the new constitution and declaration of principles at length, *The New Harmony Movement,* 105–11; Carmony and Elliott, "New Harmony," 173.

5. Carmony and Elliott, "New Harmony," 174–75.

6. Robert Owen's "Farewell Address," reprinted in Lockwood, *The New Harmony Movement,* 166–73.

7. Wooster, *Communities of the Past and Present;* Anne Taylor, *Visions of Harmony: A Study in Nineteenth Century Millenarianism* (Oxford: Clarendon Press, 1987); Lockwood, *The New Harmony Movement;* Bestor, *Education and Reform at New Harmony;* Paul Brown, *Twelve Months in New Harmony* (1827; rpt., Philadelphia: Porcupine Press, 1972); Webber, *Escape to Utopia;* Weinberg and Weinberg, *Passport to Utopia;* Kolmerten, *Women in Utopia;* Wilson, *The Angel and the Serpent;* Patricia Goodwin Heiny, "The Family in New Harmony, Indiana,

During the Owenite Experiment," (Master's thesis, Indiana University, Bloomington, 1971); Rohrlich and Baruch, *Women in Search of Utopia*.

8. Lockwood, *The New Harmony Movement,* 108.

9. William Pelham, "The Letters of William Pelham," as quoted in Kolmerten, *Women in Utopia,* 56.

10. Owen's views about the excesses of fashionable dress can also be found in the *New Harmony Gazette* 1 (Oct. 15, 1825): 24; Robert Dale Owen, "Fashionable Incarceration," *Free Enquirer* 1 (Aug. 5, 1829): 321; Robert Dale Owen, *Threading My Way* (New York: G. W. Carleton & Co., 1874), 276. The *New Harmony Gazette* (1825–28) began as a way for Robert Owen to interpret his new living experiment to the outside world. Recording the progress of the New Harmony movement, the eight-page paper featured Owen's theories and social and religious topics by other community members (Mott, *A History of American Magazines, 1741–1850,* 536–38). For more information on the community newspapers, see Wilson, *The Angel and the Serpent,* 132–35.

11. *New Harmony Gazette* (June 28, 1826).

12. *New Harmony Gazette* 1 (Oct. 15, 1825): 24; Owen, "Fashionable Incarceration," 321.

13. Owen, *Threading My Way,* 276.

14. Karl Bernhard, "Travels through North America, during the Years 1825 and 1826," in Harlow Lindley, ed., *Indiana as Seen by Early Travelers* (Indianapolis: Indiana Historical Commission, 1916): 418–37, esp. 424. Sarah Pears also described the costume in Thomas Pears, ed., *New Harmony, An Adventure in Happiness: The Papers of Thomas and Sarah Pears* (Indianapolis: Indiana Historical Society, 1933).

15. Thank you to Shelly Foote for noting this similarity. See Ribeiro and Cumming, *The Visual History of Costume,* 125, 238; and Paoletti and Kregloh, "The Children's Department," 30–32.

16. Pears, *New Harmony, An Adventure in Happiness,* 82.

17. Frances Trollope, *Domestic Manners of the Americans* (New York, 1894), 59. For more information on Frances Wright's involvement with communal societies, see O. B. Emerson, "Frances Wright and Her Nashoba Experiment," *Tennessee Historical Quarterly* 6 (1947): 291–314.

18. Pears, *New Harmony, An Adventure in Happiness,* 13–14.

19. Quoted in Lockwood, *The New Harmony Movement,* 192. Lockwood's interpretation of this incident differs greatly from mine. He uses this episode to illustrate "Owen's solicitude for the welfare of the women."

20. Pears, *New Harmony, An Adventure in Happiness,* 33.

21. Ibid., 82.

22. *Expose of the Condition and Progress of the North American Phalanx: In Reply to the Inquiries of Horace Greeley, and in Answer to the Criticisms of Friends and Foes During the Past Year.* The American Utopian Adventure, Series 2. (1853; rpt., Philadelphia: Porcupine Press, 1975), 60.

23. *New Harmony Gazette* (Oct. 15, 1825): 19.

24. "Miner K. Kellogg: Recollections of New Harmony," ed. Lorna Lutes Sylvester, *Indiana Magazine of History* 64 (Mar. 1968): 39–64, esp. 58.

25. It is not clear whether Owen ever wrote about the costume worn at New Harmony. Noyes may have learned about the costume through some means other than Owen's writings, while he pursued his interest in New Harmony's experiment. Robert Allerton Parker, *A Yankee Saint: John Humphrey Noyes and the Oneida Community* (New York: G. P. Putnam's Sons, 1935), 146–47; Lockwood, *The New Harmony Movement,* 196–97; Webber, *Escape to Utopia;* Alice Felt Tyler, *Freedom's Ferment: Phases of American Social History from the Colonial Period to the Outbreak of the Civil War* (New York: Harper & Row, 1944), 186.

26. One of the few exceptions is Mary E. Tillotson's mention in *History ov the First Thirty-Five Years ov the Science Costume Movement in the United States of America* (Vineland, N.J.: Weekly Independent Book & Job Office, 1885), 89. She noted, "In the Fourieristic Community in the U.S.A. reformed garments similar to those adopted by the grate movement were used, and may have antedated the use at Oneida." Louise R. Noun in *Strong-Minded Women: The Emergence of the Woman-Suffrage Movement in Iowa* (Ames: Iowa State University Press, 1969), 16, also mentioned Robert Owen's community's costume. Recently, Kate Luck also made the connection between the Harmonite costume and later dress reform effort, in "Trouble in Eden, Trouble with Eve: Women, Trousers, and Utopian Socialism in Nineteenth-Century America," in *Chic Thrills,* ed. Juliet Ash and Elizabeth Wilson (Berkeley: University of California Press, 1993), 200–212. Also see a brief mention of early-nineteenth-century utopian dress reform in Elizabeth Wilson and Lou Taylor, *Through the Looking Glass: A History of Dress from 1860 to the Present Day* (London: BBC Books, 1989), 28.

27. Jeanette C. Lauer and Robert H. Lauer, "Sex Roles in Nineteenth-Century American Communal Societies," *Communal Societies* 3 (1983): 25; Beverly Gordon, "Dress in American Communal Societies," *Communal Societies* 5 (Fall 1985): 122–36; and Mark Holloway, *Heavens on Earth: Utopian Communities in America 1680–1880* (London: Turnstile Press, 1951), 162.

28. Nordhoff, *The Communistic Societies,* 398–99.

29. William Rufus Perkins and Barthinius L. Wick, *History of the Amana Society or Community of True Inspiration* (Iowa City: Published by the University, 1891), 74.

30. Beverly Gordon, *Shaker Textile Arts* (Hanover, N.H.: University Press of New England with the Cooperation of the Merrimack Valley Textile Museum and Shaker Community, 1980); Gordon, "Fossilized Fashion: 'Old Fashioned' Dress as a Symbol of a Separate, Work-oriented Identity," *Dress* 13 (1987): 49–59; C. Kurt Dewhurst, Betty MacDowell, and Marsha MacDowell, *Religious Folk Art in America: Reflections of Faith* (New York: E. P. Dutton, in association with the Museum of American Folk Art, 1983); Marjorie Procter-Smith, *Women in Shaker Community and Worship: A Feminist Analysis of the Uses of Religious Symbolism* (Lewiston, N.Y.: Edwin Mellen Press, 1985).

31. Elizabeth Ann Bartlett, *Sarah Grimke: Letters on the Equality of the Sexes and Other Essays* (New Haven, Conn.: Yale University Press, 1988), 70. Criticism of women and their "dress-worship" was a pervasive theme in fashion critiques by feminists. For an example, see "Women and Dress," *Revolution* (Dec. 24, 1868): 393.

32. Jackson, *American Womanhood,* 59.

33. Kate Luck focuses on this possibility in "Trouble in Eden," 200–212.

34. Ryan, *Women in Public,* 8.

3. PANTALOONS IN PRIVATE

1. Dr. Lydia Hammond Strobridge used her personal experiences as a patient, hydropathic doctor, and president of the National Dress Reform Association to spread the "all important" message of dress reform (Obituary notice of Dr. Lydia A. Strobridge, Oct. 4, 1904, Strobridge Collection, Cortland County Historical Society). Dr. Lydia Sayer Hasbrouck graduated from the Hygeia Therapeutic College in New York City, thereby becoming a hydropathic physician. Shortly before her marriage to John W. Hasbrouck, L. S. Hasbrouck assumed the editorial duties of the reform paper the *Sibyl.* According to her granddaughter, Hasbrouck took off her reform dress only once, at her granddaughter's request that Hasbrouck not wear it to her granddaughter's graduation. E. M. Ruttenber and L. H. Clark, eds., *History of Orange County, New York, with Illustrations and Biographical Sketches of Many of Its Pioneers and Prominent Men* (Philadelphia: Everts & Peck, 1881); letter from Miss Hasbrouck, and obituary notice of Lydia Sayer Hasbrouck, Hasbrouck Papers, Historical Society of Middletown and the Wallkill Precinct. Around 1838, Mary Gove Nichols took her child and deserted her first husband. She decided to devote herself to hygienic reform, to that end she lectured, wrote, and read about various health principles. In 1844 she was invited to be resident physician at the Lebanon Springs water-cure spa. M. G. Nichols and her second husband, Thomas Nichols, dabbled in many of the reforms and doctrines circulating in the mid-nineteenth century, including dress reform. Many of M. G. Nichols's articles and books on dress reform and hydropathy were the

most important in their day. John B. Blake, "Mary Gove Nichols, Prophetess of Health," *Proceedings of the American Philosophical Society* 106 (June 1962): 219–34; Philip Gleason, "From Free-Love to Catholicism: Dr. and Mrs. Thomas L. Nichols at Yellow Springs," *Ohio Historical Quarterly* 70 (Oct. 1961): 283–307; and Bertha-Monica Stearns, "Two Forgotten New England Reformers," *New England Quarterly* 6 (Mar. 1933): 59–84. Dr. Harriet N. Austin graduated from Dr. Trall's hydropathic medical school in New York City. She joined the staff of Dr. James C. Jackson's Glen Haven Water Cure. The Jackson family later adopted her as a permanent member of their family. For many years, even after she retired as a physician, she edited and wrote for the hydropathic journal, the *Laws of Life and Journal of Health* (A. O. Brunnell, *Dansville: Historical, Biographical, Descriptive* [Dansville, N.Y.: Instructor Publishing Co., 1902], 210–11).

2. James C. Jackson, "The Dress Reform Convention in June," *Sibyl* 1 (Apr. 15, 1857): 153–55.

3. Conklin, *The Jackson Health Resort,* 96, 137.

4. Donegan, *"Hydropathic Highway to Health."*

5. Quoted in ibid.,142. Gerald Carson in "Bloomers and Bread Crumbs," *New York History* 38 (July 1957): 298, stressed that Harriet Austin wore "her own *improved* version of the Bloomer costume," suggesting that the American costume appeared after the freedom dress.

6. At the turn of the century, Mabel Lee, a physical education instructor, lamented the fact that once again "bloomers . . . were to be worn only indoors." She made it one of her crusades to get the costume accepted as an appropriate garment for women to wear in outdoor sports. One of the reasons the "bloomer" gymnastic costume was relegated to indoor sports was that women participated only with other women in these activities and did not have to worry that men would see the costume (*Memories of a Bloomer Girl [1894–1924]* [American Alliance for Health, Physical Education, and Recreation, 1977], 199).

7. Tillotson, *History,* 13–17.

8. "Women's Dresses," *Water-Cure Journal* (1849): 186. The *Water-Cure Journal and Herald of Reforms* (1845–1861) was a popularly successful health reform journal. Shortly after 1850, it claimed a circulation of fifty thousand. It was established in 1845 in New York, and was, according to its own statement, devoted to physiology, pathology, hydropathy, and physical, moral, and intellectual development. It ran for fifteen years under its original title, and fifty years longer under other titles related to health and hygiene. After 1863 the journal was titled the *Herald of Health* (1863–92).

9. Tillotson, *History,* 13–17. Mrs. Suzi Donli Elliott of Bayonne, New Jersey, is another example of someone who claimed to be the pioneer trousers reformer. "Clippings: Dress Reform 1866, 1884–1913," Dr. Mary E. Walker Collection, SUL.

A woman in Wisconsin wrote to the *Lily* stating she and others had been wearing the Bloomer since 1850. "Who Are the Leaders?" *Lily* (June 1851): 45.

10. Ed. M. Richards, "A Man's Views on the Reform Dress," *Sibyl* (Aug. 15, 1859): 601–2.

11. The sparseness of the sources makes it difficult to figure out how many of the nineteenth-century communal experiments initiated some sort of dress reform; the information that is available, however, does contribute to the increase in information about dress reform. For a breakdown of the clothing practices of some communal societies, see Gordon, "Dress in American Communal Societies"; Lauer and Lauer, "Sex Roles in Nineteenth-Century American Communal Societies," 16–28.

12. Diane L. Barthel, *Amana: From Pietist Sect to American Community* (Lincoln: University of Nebraska Press, 1984); Gordon, "Dress in American Communal Societies"; Lauer and Lauer, "Sex Roles in Nineteenth-Century American Communal Societies"; and Perkins and Wick, *History of the Amana Society.*

13. John Codman, *Brook Farm: Historic and Personal Memoirs* (Boston: Arena Publishing Co., 1894), 134.

14. North American Phalanx (1843–55). William H. Dixon, *Spiritual Wives* (London: Hurst & Blackett, 1868), 223; Fredrika Bremer, "Two Visits to the North American Phalanx," *Expose of the Condition and Progress of the North American Phalanx.*

15. Codman, *Brook Farm,* 134. For more information on Brook Farm, see Zoltan Haraszti, *The Idyll of Brook Farm* (Boston: Published by the Trustees of the Public Library, n.d.); Joel Myerson, "Two Unpublished Reminiscences of Brook Farm," *New England Quarterly* 48 (1975): 253–60; and Marianne Dwight Orvis, *Letters from Brook Farm, 1844–1847* (Poughkeepsie, N.Y.: Vassar College, 1928).

16. For more information and discussions on patriarchy, see Judith M. Bennett, "Feminism and History," *Gender & History* 1 (Autumn 1989): 251–72; Christine Delphy, *Close to Home: A Materialist Analysis of Women's Oppression* (Amherst: University of Massachusetts Press, 1984); Carole Pateman, *The Sexual Contract* (Stanford, Calif.: Stanford University Press, 1988); and Gerda Lerner, *The Creation of Patriarchy* (New York: Oxford University Press, 1986).

17. "The Story of Kaweah," *Spectator* 68 (Feb. 1892): 195, as cited in Lauer and Lauer, "Sex Roles." For more information on Icaria, see Sherman B. Barnes, "An Icarian in Nauvoo," *Journal of the Illinois State Historical Society* 34 (1941): 233–44.

18. "Husbands, Wives, Fathers, Mothers," *Blackwood's Magazine* 71 (Jan. 1852): 82. *Blackwood's Magazine* was a popular British periodical which served as a model for many American magazines. Frank Luther Mott, *A History of American Magazines, 1850–1865* (Cambridge, Mass.: Harvard University Press, 1938), 130, 420–21.

19. Ibid.

20. The author opined that instead of being Elizabeth Smith Miller's idea, it was "that of her father, Gerrit Smith, that steady geyser of reform" ("That Was New York: Mrs. Bloomer's Pantaloons a la Turk," *New Yorker* 16 [June 29, 1940]: 41–42).

21. Pierrepont Noyes, *My Father's House: An Oneida Boyhood* (New York: Farrar & Rinehart, 1937), 79.

22. Many articles have been written criticizing Noyes's forceful leadership of Oneida; most historians now agree that these harsh assessments are extreme. Ernest R. Sandeen, "John Humphrey Noyes as the New Adam," *Church History* 40 (Mar. 1971) : 82–90. Sandeen did a psychological profile on Noyes and found him to be a man "deranged, besieged with sexual fantasies, and terrified of physical relationships with women." Erik Achorn, "Mary Cragin, Perfectionist Saint," *New England Quarterly* 28 (Dec. 1955): 490–518. According to Achorn, not only was Noyes "one of the strangest personalities that America ever spawned," but his fanaticism was not unlike Hitler's.

23. Pierrepont Noyes, *My Father's House*, 132–33.

24. Quoted in Kephart, *Extraordinary Groups*, 103.

25. Mandelker, *Religion, Society, and Utopia*, 122; Richard DeMaria, *Communal Love at Oneida: A Perfectionist Vision of Authority, Property and Sexual Order* (New York: Edwin Mellon Press, 1978), 158–63; and Oneida Community, *Bible Communism*, 27.

26. Stirpiculture was not synonymous with eugenics, but the two shared similarities. The word and practice of "stirpiculture" predated "eugenics" which became more common and popular. For more information on Oneida's stirpiculture experiments see Anita Newcomb McGee, "An Experiment in Human Stirpiculture," *American Anthropologist* 4 (Oct. 1891): 319–25.

27. Studies of Oneida that concentrate on gender include: Marlyn Hartzell Dalsimer, "Women and Family in the Oneida Community, 1837–1881" (Ph.D. dissertation, New York University, 1975); Foster, *Women, Family, and Utopia;* Kern, *An Ordered Love;* Rohrlich and Baruch, *Women in Search of Utopia;* Chmielewski, Kern, and Klee-Hartzell, *Women in Spiritual and Communitarian Societies;* Lauer and Lauer, "Sex Roles in Nineteenth-Century American Communal Societies"; Ellen Wayland-Smith, "The Status and Self-Perception of Women in the Oneida Community," *Communal Societies* 8 (1988): 18–53.

28. "Woman's Rights," *Circular* (Feb. 28, 1856).

29. "Woman's Position in the Community," *Circular* (Nov. 7, 1870): 266.

30. Once established, the Community's numbers stabilized with around three hundred members living in the seven branches. Only carefully screened applicants received membership acceptance, and only about two or three adults seceded each year. The branch communities of Oneida came and went; some were successful

others were not. For more information on Oneida, see Maren Lockwood Carden, *Oneida: Utopian Community to Modern Corporation* (New York: Harper & Row, 1969); DeMaria, *Communal Love at Oneida;* Walter D. Edmonds, *The First Hundred Years, 1848–1948* (New York: Oneida Ltd., 1948); Allan Estlake, *The Oneida Community* (London: George Redway, 1900); Constance Noyes Robertson, *Oneida Community Profiles* (Syracuse, N.Y.: Syracuse University Press, 1977); Robertson, ed., *Oneida Community: An Autobiography, 1851–1876* (Syracuse, N.Y.: Syracuse University Press, 1970); Morris Bishop, "The Great Oneida Love-in," *American Heritage* 20 (Feb. 1969): 14–16, 86–92; Worth Tuttle Hedden, "Communism in New York, 1848–1879," *American Scholar* 14 (Summer 1945): 283–92.

31. Francis Wayland-Smith, essay, Oneida Community Collection, SUL.

32. Ackley Noyes, *Days of My Youth,* 56, 73.

33. "Eve and Her Daughters," *Circular* (Sept. 23, 1854): 503.

34. Charlotte M. Leonard, extracts from a journal, Nov. 26, 1876, box 63, file "Leonard, Charlotte M.," Oneida Community Collection.

35. Harriet Matthews, diary, Apr. 29, 1856?, Oneida Community Collection.

36. Annie Hatch, letter, Dec. 2, 1883, Oneida Community Collection.

37. "A Community Journal," *Circular* (Mar. 19, 1863): 11.

38. "The Short Dress," *Circular* (Dec. 18, 1862): 179.

39. "A Community Journal," 11.

40. "Christian Nudists Gathering," *Herald-Times* sidebar.

41. "Paul on the Woman Question," *Circular* (Nov. 4, 1867): 267; "Ideas for Women," *Circular* (Mar. 14, 1854); "Eve and Her Daughters."

42. *First Annual Report of the Oneida Association: Exhibiting Its History, Principles, and Transactions to January 1, 1849* (Oneida Reserve: Leonard & Co., Printers, 1849); *Hand-Book of the Oneida Community* (1867); *Hand-Book of the Oneida Community; Containing a Brief Sketch of Its Present Condition, Internal Economy and Leading Principles, No. 2* (New York: Oneida Community, 1871); *Hand-Book of the Oneida Community* (New York: Office of Oneida *Circular,* 1875); and Oneida Community, *Bible Communism.*

43. References to sexual eroticism and clothing showed up with some frequency in the Oneida papers. See for example: Letter from Harriet Holton Noyes to Tirzah, Dec. 28 [1881] and Harriet Worden, diary entry, Nov. [no day] 1868, both found in the Oneida Community Collection.

44. Louis J. Kern, "Ideology and Reality: Sexuality and Women's Status in the Oneida Community," *Radical History Review* 20 (Spring–Summer 1979): 180–204, esp. 185, 199–200.

45. Corrina Ackley Noyes, *The Days of My Youth,* 74; *First Annual Report of the Oneida Association,* 8; Charlotte M. Leonard, extracts from a journal, June 6, 1876.

46. John B. Ellis, *Free Love and Its Votaries; or, American Socialism Unmasked* (San Francisco: A. L. Bancroft & Co., 1870), 209.

47. "Origin of the Short Dress Costume," *Circular* (Aug. 28, 1856): 126; "Oneida Short Dress," *Circular* (Mar. 26, 1866): 13.

48. "An Oneida Journal," *Circular* (Feb. 15, 1855): 15. In "Cycling in the 1890's," *Costume* 6 (1972): 43, Nancy Bradfield states that Mrs. Cragin and Mrs. Noyes designed their garment "on the same general lines as worn amongst the North American Indian women since the first settlement of the country, and one that had certainly existed from time immemorial in the East." Bradfield does not associate the design origins of the Oneida costume with either men or children. Her theory is highly unlikely.

49. "An Oneida Journal," 15.

50. Oneida Community, *Bible Communism,* 62. It is difficult to believe that J. H. Noyes did not induce or encourage his female followers to make the short dress, given the amount of control he had over them. Mrs. Helen Barron said, "The tyranny was so great, it was such a relief to be free." "Mrs. K. said she agreed" (Minerva S. Barron, letter, Feb. 26, 1933, Oneida Community Collection). Meanwhile Susan C. Hamilton so *"loved him from the very bottom of [her] heart"* that she probably would have done almost anything he asked of her (Sarah B. Campbell, letter to Charlotte Leonard, July 24, 1854, Oneida Community Collection [emphasis in original]). Annie Hatch viewed the Community's religious orientations as "man worship" because she did things and thought things "because Mr. N. thinks it the only way to do & think." As a member of the Community, Hatch "never felt that I could have an opinion about anything and have it respected" (Annie Hatch, letter, Dec. 2, 1883, Oneida Community Collection).

51. Historian Lawrence Foster maintained that J. H. Noyes introduced the "bloomer" as the Community costume "against the wishes of many community women."

52. "Report of the Proceedings of the Dress Reform Convention"; Laver, *Modesty in Dress,* 134–36.

53. Harriet M. Worden, *Old Mansion House Memories by One Brought Up in It* (Oneida, N.Y., 1950), 10–11.

54. "The Short Dress. Its Materials—How It Is Made—Under-Clothing—Quantity Used—Etc., Etc.," *Circular* (Jan. 10, 1870): 342–43; "Short-Dress Finance," *Circular* (June 19, 1865): 109; "Oneida Short Dress," 13.

55. Jessie C. Kinsley, "Memoir, 1914," Oneida Community Collection.

56. "A Community Journal," 11, 12; Robertson, *Oneida Community: An Autobiography,* 297–98; "Woman's Character," *Circular* (Jan. 14, 1854): 72.

57. Jessie C. Kinsley, manuscript, early summer of 1914, Oneida Community Collection.

58. Pierrepont Noyes, *My Father's House,* 79.

59. G. C. Bates, "The Beaver Island Prophet: The Trial in This City in 1851 of 'King' Strang," *Michigan Historical Collections* 32 (1903): 233.

60. Ibid., 233–34.

61. R. L. Moore, *Religious Outsiders and the Making of Americans* (New York: Oxford University Press, 1986).

62. Because Mormons keep many of their sacred rituals private, it is not possible for me to elaborate on the "endowments" or the endowment ceremonies. See C. McDannell, *Material Christianity: Religion and Popular Culture in America* (New Haven, Conn.: Yale University Press, 1995).

63. Much that has been written on Strang must be acknowledged as speculative. The background information on Strang comes from the following sources: C. Backus, "An American King," *Harper's New Monthly Magazine* 64 (1882): 553–59; Charles O. Burgess, "Green Bay and the Mormons of Beaver Island," *Wisconsin Magazine of History* 42 (1958): 39–49; Henry Colin Campbell, *Wisconsin in Three Centuries, 1634–1905* (New York: Century History Co., 1906); Doyle C. Fitzpatrick, *The King Strang Story: A Vindication of James J. Strang, the Beaver Island Mormon* (Lansing, Mich.: National Heritage, 1970); Lawrence Foster, "James J. Strang: The Prophet Who Failed," *Church History* 50 (1981): 182–92; B. Gilbert, "America's Only King Made Beaver Island His Promised Land," *Smithsonian* 26 (1995): 84–93; K. Hansen, "The Making of King Strang: A Re-examination," *Michigan History* 46 (1962): 201–19; M. L. Leach, "History of the Grand Traverse Region," *Michigan Historical Collections* 32 (1903): 14–175; H. E. Legler, *A Moses for the Mormons: Strang's City of Refuge and Island Kingdom* (Milwaukee: Printed for the Parkman Club, 1897); David Rich Lewis, "'For Life, the Resurrection, and the Life Everlasting': James J. Strang and Strangite Mormon Polygamy, 1849–1856," *Wisconsin Magazine of History* 66 (1983): 274–91; Milo Milton Quaife, *The Kingdom of Saint James: A Narrative of the Mormons* (New Haven, Conn.: Yale University Press, 1930); John Quist, "Polygamy among James Strang and His Followers," *John Whitmer Historical Association Journal* 9 (1989): 31–48; Oscar Wetherhold Riegel, *Crown of Glory: The Life of James J. Strang, Moses of the Mormons* (New Haven, Conn.: Yale University Press, 1935); M. A. Strang, ed., *The Diary of James J. Strang* (East Lansing: Michigan State University Press, 1961); *The Traverse Region, Historical and Descriptive, with Illustrations of Scenery and Portraits and Biographical Sketches of Some of Its Prominent Men and Pioneers* (Chicago: H. R. Page, 1884); Roger Van Noord, *King of Beaver Island: The Life and Assassination of James Jesse Strang* (Urbana: University of Illinois Press, 1988).

64. Klaus Hansen summarizes the argument that the title "king" was a metaphor in the nineteenth century and simply indicated the "head" of a church. Hansen agrees that the metaphor inspired Strang, but he also argues that the power Strang derived from his position as "king" was not metaphorical. Hansen, "The Making of King Strang," 204–5; James J. Strang, *The Book of the Law of the Lord* (Printed by Command of the King at the Royal Press, 1856), 6.

65. Riegel, *Crown of Glory*, 174.

66. Burgess, "Green Bay."

67. *Northern Islander* (Strangite newspaper), Mar. 4, 1852.

68. Strangite polygamy has been the central subject of most studies on Strangite Mormons. The following are a few examples: Fitzpatrick, *The King Strang Story;* Clement J. Strang, "Why I Am Not a Strangite," *Michigan History Magazine* 26 (1942); Lewis, "'For Life, the Resurrection.'" Contemporary sources also often focused on Strangite polygamy, for example see Ida Pfeiffer, *Lady's Second Journey Round the World* (New York: Harper & Brothers, 1856) and J. H. Beadle, *Polygamy: or, The Mysteries and Crimes of Mormonism* (Philadelphia: National Publishing Co., 1882).

69. Moore, *Religious Outsiders;* B. H. Roberts, *A Comprehensive History of the Church of Jesus Christ of Latter-day Saints, Century 1* (Salt Lake City: Deseret News Press, 1930).

70. *Northern Islander,* Jan. 9, 1851.

71. As quoted in Van Noord, *King of Beaver Island,* 100.

72. Riegel, *Crown of Glory; Northern Islander,* May 1851.

73. *Northern Islander,* Aug. 9,1855.

74. Strang, *The Book,* 288.

75. *Northern Islander,* May 28, 1856; May 19,1856; Feb. 14, 1856.

76. *Northern Islander,* July 1852.

77. Strang, *The Book,* 289.

78. Ibid., 290.

79. Nathan Joseph, *Uniforms and Nonuniforms: Communication through Clothing* (Westport, Conn.: Greenwood Press, 1986), 66–75.

80. Henry Munson Utley and B. M. Cutheon, *Michigan: As a Province, Territory and State, the Twenty-sixth Member of the Federal Union* (Publishing Society of Michigan, 1906), 306–7.

81. Leach, "History of the Grand Traverse Region."

82. As quoted in Quaife, *The Kingdom of Saint James*, 167.

83. *The Traverse Region,* 34.

84. Leach, "History of the Grand Traverse"; Lewis, "'For Life, the Resurrection'"; Gilbert, "America's Only King"; Riegel, *Crown of Glory.*

85. Gilbert, "America's Only King," 90.

86. Riegel, *Crown of Glory,* 259.

87. R. B. Nye, *A Baker's Dozen: Thirteen Unusual Americans* (East Lansing: Michigan State University Press, 1956); Van Noord, *King of Beaver Island.*

88. Leach, "History of the Grand Traverse," 123.

89. For examinations of frontier clothing and dress worn in the movement west, see ibid., 201–22; Marion Tinling, "Bloomerism Comes to California," *California*

History 61 (Spring 1982): 18–25; Mia Mae Feightner, "Clothing and Accessories Available to Pioneers of Southern Indiana, 1816–1830" (Master's thesis, Iowa State University at Ames, 1977); Larson, "Clothing of Pioneer Women"; Maria Barbara McMartin, "Dress of the Oregon Trail Emigrants: 1843 to 1855" (Master's thesis, Iowa State University at Ames, 1977).

90. Ruth Vickers Clayton, "Clothing and the Temporal Kingdom: Mormon Clothing Practices, 1847 to 1887" (Ph.D. dissertation, Purdue University, 1987).

91. Susa Young Gates, *The Life Story of Brigham Young* (New York: Macmillan, 1930), 300. For a similar interpretation for the origins of reform dress, see Spencer, *Brigham Young*, 85–86.

92. Much work needs to be done to uncover the history of deseret costume. Clayton has begun to discover some valuable sources but not enough to understand the use of the costume by the Latter-day Saint Mormons. Clayton, "Clothing and the Temporal Kingdom," 149–52. For some contemporary mentions of the Latter-day Saints' costume, see Mrs. Benjamin G. Ferris, *The Mormons at Home; With Some Incidents of Travel from Missouri to California, 1852–3* (New York: Dix and Edwards, 1856), 154–57; and Austin N. Ward, *Male Life among the Mormons; or the Husband in Utah,* ed. Maria Ward (New York: Derby and Jackson, 1859), 35.

93. Spencer, *Brigham Young*, 85.

94. Leonard J. Arrington, "The Economic Role of Pioneer Mormon Women," *Western Humanities Review* 9 (Spring 1955): 148; Clarissa Young Spencer recalled her father, Brigham Young, supporting her desire to wear "modest" ornaments on her clothing. Spencer, with Mabel Harmer, *Brigham Young at Home* (1940; rpt., Salt Lake City: Deseret Book Co., 1972), 84–85.

4. Pantaloons in Public

1. *Life and Writings of Amelia Bloomer,* ed. Dexter C. Bloomer (1895; rpt., Boston: Arena Publishing,1976); Banner,*American Beauty,* 86–87; Paul Fatout, "Amelia Bloomer and Bloomerism," *New York Historical Society and Quarterly* 36 (Oct. 1952): 360–73; Louise Noun, "Amelia Bloomer, A Biography: Part 1, The Lily of Seneca Falls," *Annals of Iowa* 47 (Winter 1985): 575–617; Laver, *Clothes,* 153–71; "The First of the Flappers," *Literary Digest* (May 13, 1922): 44–45; Sally Sims, "The Bicycle, the Bloomer, and Dress Reform in the 1890s" in *Dress and Popular Culture,* ed. Patricia A. Cunningham and Susan Voso Lab (Bowling Green, Ohio: Bowling Green State University Popular Press, 1991), 125–45; Shelly Foote, "Bloomers," *Costume* 5 (1980): 1–12; Frances E. Russell, "A Brief Survey of the American Dress Reform Movements of the Past, with Views of Representative Women," *Arena* 6 (Aug. 1892): 325–39; A.C.W., "Death of Mrs. Bloomer," *Notes and Queries* 8th S, 8 (July 6, 1895): 6–7;

and Judith Elaine Leslie, "Sports Fashions as a Reflection of the Changing Role of American Women in Society from 1850 to 1920" (Ph.D. dissertation, University of North Carolina at Greensboro, 1985), 39–43.

2. Gerda Lerner, *The Grimké Sisters from South Carolina* (New York: Schocken Books, 1971), 335; Alice Stone Blackwell, *Lucy Stone: Pioneer Woman Suffragist* (Norwood, Mass.: Plimpton Press, 1930), 104–13; Fatout, "Amelia Bloomer and Bloomerism," 365. Camilia was suggested as a possible name for the reform garment because of "the Volscian maiden dedicated to Diana, and as a fleet-footed follower of the chase not immobilized in a chrysalis of corset and petticoats."

3. *Life and Writings of Amelia Bloomer,* 68. *Webster's New World Dictionary* classifies bloomer as a noun and an Americanism with the following definitions: "*1* a costume for women or girls consisting of a short skirt and loose trousers gathered at the ankles: worn in the 1850's, but never popular *2* [pl.] *a)* baggy trousers gathered at the knee, formerly worn by girls and women for athletics *b)* an undergarment somewhat like this."

4. Amelia Bloomer, herself, spent a great deal of time and paper trying to convince people that she did not originate the dress named after her, with little success. Fred Davis calls the costume the "(Amelia) Bloomer costume of the mid-1850s" (*Fashion, Culture, and Identity,* 173). Among those historians and writers that have mistakenly credited Bloomer with originating the "bloomer costume" are Fatout, "Amelia Bloomer and Bloomerism"; Olive Sikes Logan, *Get Thee Behind Me, Satan! A Home-born Book of Home-truths* (New York: Adams, Victor & Co., 1872), 90–91; Bradfield, "Cycling in the 1890's," 43–44; Bertha-Monica Stearns, "Reform Periodicals and Female Reformers, 1830–1860," *American Historical Review* 37 (July 1932): 693. Lawrence Langner in *The Importance of Wearing Clothes* (New York: Hastings House, 1959, 67) not only confused Bloomer with the creator of the "Bloomer" but also dated the garment's origins to the 1870s.

5. Steele, *Fashion and Eroticism;* Banner, *American Beauty;* Jeanette C. Lauer and Robert H. Lauer, "The Battle of the Sexes: Fashion in 19th Century America," *Journal of Popular Culture* 13 (Spring 1980): 581–89. Stella Mary Newton, *Health, Art, and Reason: Dress Reformers of the 19th Century* (London: John Murray Ltd., 1974) credits Amelia Bloomer with the invention of the costume. Jane Grey Swisshelm, *Half a Century* (Chicago: Jansen, McClung & Co., 1880) named E. C. Stanton the innovator. Prof. William M. Nevin ("The Bloomer Dress," *Ladies Wreath: An Illustrated Annual* [1852]: 247–55) suggested a poetic version which owed much to classical Greece. M. D. Hoover suggested that Amelia Jenks Bloomer was interested in the reform costume because "her sister's death was largely the result of the stiff, tight corsets and heavy skirts demanded by the conventions of the times" (Bloomer Family Papers, Seneca Falls Historical Society).

6. "Who Are the Leaders?" 45.

7. The *Lily, A Ladies' Journal, Devoted to Temperance and Literature* (1849–56) was one of the earliest woman's rights papers, although it began as a temperance and literary sheet connected with the women's temperance society of Seneca Falls, New York. Amelia Bloomer founded and edited the paper. The *Lily* ceased publication in 1856. Mott, *A History of American Magazines, 1850–1865,* 50–51; Anne Mather, "A History of Feminist Periodicals, Part 1," *Journalism History* 1 (Autumn 1974): 83; Ann Russo and Cheris Kramarae, eds., *The Radical Women's Press of the 1850s* (New York: Routledge, 1991), 11–13; and Edward A. Hinck, "The Lily, 1849–1856: From Temperance to Woman's Rights," in *A Voice of Their Own: The Woman Suffrage Press, 1840–1910,* ed. Martha M. Solomon (Tuscaloosa: University of Alabama Press, 1991), 30–47.

8. "Female Attire," *Lily* 3.2 (Feb. 1851): 13.

9. "Female Attire," *Lily* 3.3 (Mar. 1851): 21.

10. It is usually stated that the spa was in Switzerland and Miller was on her honeymoon, but the spa has also been located in her home state of New York. Leila Lee Bordiga, "Bloomer Was Her Name," *New York Times Magazine* (Dec. 31, 1939): 11–15; Mary Curtis, "Amelia Bloomer's Curious Costume," *American History Illustrated* (June 1978): 11–15; Arch Merrill, *Bloomers and Bugles* (New York: American Book–Stratford Press, 1958), 6; Miriam Gurko, *The Ladies of Seneca Falls: The Birth of the Woman's Rights Movement* (New York: Schocken Books, 1974), 143; and Tinling, "Bloomerism Comes to California." M. D. Hoover states, "Mrs. Miller had brought the gown upon return from a trip to the Orient" ("Mrs. Amelia Bloomer and My Early Recollections" [no date\1948?], Bloomer Family Papers).

11. This version is favored by the descendants of the original Oneida communitarians, although they agree there is no "hard" evidence that this was how Elizabeth Smith Miller learned of the costume.

12. It is not unreasonable to assume that Miller knew of or was aware of the masculine dress adopted by Helena Maria Weber and George Sand in Europe.

13. Elizabeth Smith Miller, "Symposium on Women's Dress, Part 1," *Arena* 6 (Sept. 1892): 490, 493. The *Arena* (1889–1909) was founded and edited by Benjamin Orange Flower, an ardent dress reformer, as a social reform periodical. Frank Luther Mott, *A History of American Magazines, 1885–1905* (Cambridge, Mass.: Harvard University Press, 1957), 401–16.

14. Miller, "Symposium on Women's Dress, Part 1," 490, 493.

15. *Life and Writings of Amelia Bloomer,* 65–75. A series of articles ran in the *Lily* that discussed the Bloomer costume and the incidents which led to its adoption: Feb. 1851, 13; Mar. 1851, 21; Apr. 1851, 31; May 1851, 38; June 1851, 45; Jan. 1852. Also see "Mrs. Bloomer on Dress Reform," 43; and "Origin of the Short Dress Costume," 126.

16. Harriet N. Austin, "The Reform Dress," *Water-Cure Journal* 22 (Jan. 1857): 3; "The Demoralization of Dress," *Health Reformer* 4 (Sept. 1869): 57; Madame Demorest, "Dress and Its Relation to Health," *Herald of Health and Journal of Physical Culture* 9 (Jan. 1867): 16.

17. It appears that some women borrowed male dress or elements of male apparel as an avenue to gain power denied them elsewhere in their lives. Some dress reformers introduced features found exclusively in men's clothing into their reform garments, other women, some of whom identified themselves as dress reformers, donned male garb from head to toe. But these were exceptions.

18. At times skirt length also distinguished costumes. The most popular criteria for the length of the skirt was that a woman should be able to negotiate the stairs with ease when attired in the short dress and many women wrote of their experiences with the costume and stairs. E.H.V.F., "Dress, Disease, and Doctors," *Water-Cure Journal* 14 (Oct. 1852): 92; *Elizabeth Cady Stanton: As Revealed in Her Letters, Diary, and Reminiscences,* ed. Theodore Stanton and Harriot Stanton Blatch (New York: Harper & Brothers, 1922), 171; "Olive Logan and Woman's Dress," *Revolution* (July 8, 1869): 10; Blackwell, *Lucy Stone,* 104–13.

19. "Men's Rights Convention at ———. Extraordinary Proceedings, Exciting Scenes, and Curious Speeches. From Our Own Reporter, Chericot," *Godey's Magazine and Lady's Book* (Apr. 1852): 268–73. Also see *Yankee Notions* (1851–1852) for more examples of caricatures and poems.

20. Cunnington, *Costume in Pictures,* 101; Kemper, *Costume,* 123–24.

21. Steele, *Fashion and Eroticism,* 232–33.

22. Montague's travel writings enjoyed a new audience and popularity after *Godey's* published her letters to her sister in 1852. "Costumes of All Nations: The Toilette in Turkey," *Godey's Lady's Book* (Jan. 1852): 45.

23. Joyce Zonana, "The Sultan and the Slave: Feminist Orientalism and the Structure of *Jane Eyre,*" *Signs* 18 (Spring 1993): 593–94.

24. "Through Each Other's Eyes: Egyptian, Levantine-Egyptian, and European Women's Images of Themselves and of Each Other (1862–1920)," *Women's Studies International Forum* 12.2 (1989): 183–98.

25. *Reaches of Empire: The English Novel from Edgeworth to Dickens* (New York: Columbia University Press, 1991).

26. *Veiled Half-Truths: Western Travellers' Perceptions of Middle Eastern Women,* selected and introduced by Judy Mabro (New York: I. B. Tauris & Co., 1991), 2–6; Sarah Graham-Brown, *Images of Women: The Portrayal of Women in Photography of the Middle East 1860–1950* (New York: Columbia University Press, 1988), 118–43.

27. "Dress. The Long and Short of It," *Herald of Health* 3 (Apr. 1864): 204.

28. Craik, *The Face of Fashion,* 17.

29. Shelly Foote, personal notes to the author.

30. Craik, *Face of Fashion,* 17–43.

31. "Our Costume," *Lily* (Apr. 1851): 31; "Our Dress," and "The New Costume," *Lily* (May 1851): 38; "Our Fashion Plate," *Lily* (Jan. 1852).

32. Newton, *Health, Art, and Reason,* 4; Binder, *Muffs and Morals,* 238–39.

33. Malika Mehdid, "A Western Invention of Arab Womanhood: The 'Oriental' Female," in *Women in the Middle East: Perceptions, Realities and Struggles for Liberation,* ed. Haleh Afshar (New York: St. Martin's Press, 1993), 22–23; Alev Lytle Croutier, *Harem: The World Behind the Veil* (New York: Abbeville Press, 1989), 71–79; Billie Melman, *Women's Orients: English Women and the Middle East, 1718–1918: Sexuality, Religion and Work* (New York: Macmillan, 1992), 119–22.

34. "Our Costume," 31; "Our Dress," and "The New Costume," 38; "Our Fashion Plate."

35. One exception is the zouave uniform worn by soldiers in the U.S. Civil War. This uniform included a fez or turban headgear and full trousers similar to "Turkish trousers." See Martin Windrow and Gerry Embleton, *Military Dress of North America, 1665–1970* (New York: Charles Scribner's Sons, [1973]).

36. Other dress reformers who wore decidedly more "masculine" versions of reform apparel faced accusations of prostitution and licentiousness (Mrs. M. S. Gove Nichols, "A Lecture on Woman's Dresses," *Water-Cure Journal* 12 [Aug. 1851]: 34–36; "Dress Reform Convention," *Sibyl* 8 [June 1864]: 1241–47).

37. Mary B. Williams, "The Bloomer and Weber Dresses: A Glance at Their Respective Merits and Advantages," *Water-Cure Journal* 12 (Aug. 1851): 33.

38. "Report of the Proceedings of the Dress Reform Convention"; Laver, *Modesty in Dress,* 134–36.

39. "The 'Freedom Suit': Feminism and Dress Reform in the United States, 1848–1875," *Gender & Society* 5 (Dec. 1991): 496, 497, 501.

40. "The Shorts Gaining," *Circular* (July 24, 1865): 1.

41. Elizabeth Cady Stanton, Susan B. Anthony, and Matilda Joslyn Gage, eds., *History of Woman Suffrage,* vol. 2 (Rochester, N.Y.: Charles Mann, 1889), 470.

42. Marjorie Garber, *Vested Interests: Cross-Dressing & Cultural Anxiety* (New York: Routledge, 1992), 314.

43. Mrs. L. G. Abell, *Woman in Her Various Relations: Containing Practical Rules for American Females* (New York: R. T. Young , 1853), no page number.

44. Elizabeth Smith Miller quoted in Russell, "A Brief Survey," 326–27.

45. *Elizabeth Cady Stanton: As Revealed in Her Letters, Diary, and Reminiscences,* 172–73.

46. *Friends and Sisters: Letters between Lucy Stone and Antoinette Brown Blackwell, 1846–93,* ed. Carol Lasser and Marlene Deahl Merrill (Urbana: University of Illinois Press, 1987), 125–26.

47. Approximately 150 women and men attended the picnic. Of those, Stanton estimated that she saw ten women in "shorts," that is, the short dress and pantaloons. "Delavan, Elizabeth, Elizabeth Cady Stanton." (Written for a program of the Comment Club of Des Moines, Iowa, 1938) E. C. Stanton Papers, Seneca Falls Historical Society. Letter written on August 5, 1851, and reprinted in *Elizabeth Cady Stanton*, vol. 2, ed. Theodore Stanton and Harriot Stanton Blatch (1922; rpt., New York: Arno, *New York Times*, 1969), 32–34.

48. *A la masculine* meant no gathering or drawing in at the ankle—the cut was similar to that used on men's pants.

49. *Elizabeth Cady Stanton*, 2:172–73; Elizabeth Cady Stanton, Susan B. Anthony, and Matilda Joslyn Gage, eds. *History of Woman Suffrage*, vol. 1 (1881; rpt., New York: Source Book Press, 1970), 470.

50. Elisabeth Griffith, *In Her Own Right: The Life of Elizabeth Cady Stanton* (New York: Oxford University Press, 1984), 71; Merrill, *Bloomers and Bugles*, 9.

51. Stanton and Blatch, *Elizabeth Cady Stanton*, 2:172–73.

52. Elizabeth Smith Miller quoted in Russell, "A Brief Survey," 326–27.

53. Betty Lou Henshaw differs in her assessment of the relationship between woman's rights and dress reform. She wrote, "They [woman's rights advocates] concluded that what was needed to further and strengthen the cause of Woman's Rights was a costume that would be a symbol of the new sphere in society for which they were striving." "The Bloomer Costume: The Women's Dress Reform Movement of the 1850's" (Master's thesis, University of Colorado, 1955), 11. Sylvia D. Hoffert identified the costume as a uniform of the woman's rights cause and a test of a woman's commitment to the woman's rights cause. Hoffert, *When Hens Crow*, 23–28.

54. Kathleen Barry, *Susan B. Anthony: A Biography of a Singular Feminist* (New York: Ballantine Books, 1988): 67–68, 71–72, 810–83. Barry dates the political change in the dress to the mid-1852, I would argue that Stanton recognized the political implications of the dress much earlier, as did the press.

55. Letter from E.C.S. to Elizabeth Smith Miller, Aug. 5, 1851, reprinted in "The First of the Flappers," 45.

56. Ibid.

57. Stanton and Blatch, *Elizabeth Cady Stanton*, 2:172–73; Stanton, Anthony, and Gage, *History of Woman Suffrage*, 1:844; *Friends and Sisters*, 122.

58. Susan B. Anthony to Lucy Stone, Dec. 19, 1852, Blackwell Family Papers, Library of Congress. Blake McKelvey, "Susan B. Anthony," *Rochester History* 7 (Apr. 1945): 7.

59. Barry, *Susan B. Anthony*, 71–72.

60. Susan B. Anthony to Gerrit Smith, Dec. 25, 1855, Gerrit Smith Papers.

61. "Turkish Costume," *Harper's New Monthly Magazine* 3 (July 1851): 288.

62. "Fashions for September," *Harper's New Monthly Magazine* 3 (Sept. 1851): 575–76.

63. Gary Bunker noted that the image of the "bloomer-clad" woman proved remarkably popular. Thus the purpose of some of the caricature and satire poking fun at women in reform garb was simply to make people laugh and sell magazines ("Antebellum Caricature and Woman's Sphere," *Journal of Women's History* 3 [Winter 1992]: 6–43).

64. "The New or Proposed New Costume," *Godey's Lady's Book* 43 (Sept. 1851): 189. In 1855 the editors were much more candid in "Editors' Table" *Godey's Lady's Book* 50 (Mar. 1855): 175.

65. "The Bloomer's Complaint: A Very Pathetic Song for the Piano Forte," Lily Library, Indiana University, Bloomington, Indiana.

66. Louise Amelia Knapp Smith Clapp, *The Shirley Letters from California Mines in 1851–52* (1854–55; San Francisco: Thomas C. Russell, 1922), 142–43.

67. For another example, see Dwight Akers, "Sally Sunflower and the Bloomer: The Story of Lydia Sayer," *Yearbook* (1956): 9 (publication of the Historical Society of Middletown and the Walkill Precinct).

68. Bunker noted that when the woman's rights leaders gave up their freedom dress, the humorists refused to give up the image that had become an easily recognizable symbol of woman's rights supporters (Bunker, "Antebellum Caricature," 6–43).

69. "Woman's Rights Convention," *New York Times,* Aug. 2, 1852, 2.

70. Lori Duin Kelly, "Bipeds in Bloomers: How the Popular Press Killed the Dress Reform Movement," *Studies in Popular Culture* 8.2 (1991): 67–76.

71. Patricia Marks, *Bicycles, Bangs, and Bloomers: The New Woman in the Popular Press* (Lexington: University Press of Kentucky, 1990), 146–51; Kate Luck, "Trouble in Eden," 200–212.

72. Stanton, Anthony, and Gage, *History of Woman Suffrage,* 2:470.

73. Jean V. Matthews, historian, hypothesized that male gender identity relied on a strictly maintained sex/gender system more than female gender identity or social order ("Consciousness of Self and Consciousness of Sex in Antebellum Feminism," *Journal of Women's History* 5 [Spring 1993]: 62. Also see: Caroline Evans and Minna Thornton, "Fashion, Representation, Femininity," *Feminist Review* 38 [Summer 1991]: 48–66).

74. "Men's Rights Convention," 268–73.

75. "Well-Dressed," *Godey's Lady's Book and Magazine* 61 (Nov. 1860): 433.

76. Susan B. Anthony to Lucy Stone, Feb. 1854, in Harper, *Life and Work,* 116.

77. The citations given here demonstrate the array of critics and criticism directed at reform apparel. "Dr. Dewey on Woman's Rights," *Democratic Review* (Feb.

1852): 181–82. Abell, *Woman in Her Various Relations;* Miss F. L. Townsend, "Women in Male Attire," *Holden's Dollar Magazine* 5 (Mar. 1850): 178–79; Ellen Gould White, "The Cause in the East" in "Testimony 10 (1864)," in *Testimonies for the Church,* vol. 1: *Comprising Testimonies Numbers 1 to 14 with a Biographical Sketch of the Author* (1864; rpt., Mountain View, Calif.: Pacific Press Publishing Association, 1948), 421.

78. Ruth A. Gallaher, *Legal and Political Status of Women in Iowa* (Iowa City: State Historical Society of Iowa, 1918), 210–11.

79. Susan C. Shapiro, "The Mannish New Woman, *Punch* and Its Precursors," *Review of English Studies* 42 (Nov. 1991): 517.

80. Blackwell, *Lucy Stone,* 104–13.

81. Alma Lutz, *Susan B. Anthony: Rebel, Crusader, Humanitarian* (Boston: Beacon Press, 1960), 35; in addition a letter in *Friends and Sisters* reads, "But poor Susan did not look well in bloomers. She was a sort of scape-goat for all of us," 131.

82. Blackwell, *Lucy Stone,* 104–13.

83. Barry, *Susan B. Anthony,* 82.

84. "The First of the Flappers," 45.

85. Arlene Fanale, "Susan B. Anthony and Bloomerism," *New Women's Times* (July 15–Aug. 15, 1975): 6, 10.

86. Andrea Moore Kerr describes some of the annoyances Stone had to deal with when wearing the freedom dress (*Lucy Stone,* 63–65).

87. *Life and Writings of Amelia Bloomer,* 70.

88. Stanton and Blatch, *Elizabeth Cady Stanton,* 2:30.

89. Letter to Lucy Stone from Anthony and Stanton, Feb. 16, 1854. Blackwell, *Lucy Stone,* 104–13.

90. Elizabeth Cady Stanton to Susan B. Anthony, Feb. 19, 1854, Stanton and Blatch, *Elizabeth Cady Stanton*

91. Blackwell, *Lucy Stone,* 104–13.

92. Ibid.

93. Barry, *Susan B. Anthony,* 67–68, 71–72, 81–83.

94. Elizabeth Smith Miller, "Symposium on Women's Dress, Part 1," 494.

95. *Life and Writings of Amelia Bloomer,* 71–73; Charles Neilson Gattey, *The Bloomer Girls* (New York: Coward-McCann, 1967), 146–48.

96. Potter, "How Susan B. Anthony Keeps Young," 46–47.

97. Fanale, "Susan B. Anthony and Bloomerism," 6, 10.

98. Griffith, *In Her Own Right,* 72.

99. Merrill, *Bloomers and Bugles,* 9.

100. Letter to Elizabeth Cady Stanton from Gerrit Smith, Dec. 1, 1855, Gerrit Smith Collection.

101. *Elizabeth Cady Stanton,* 2:172–73.

102. Stanton, Anthony, and Gage, *History of Woman Suffrage,* 1:471.

103. Letter to Elizabeth Cady Stanton from Gerrit Smith, Dec. 1, 1855.

104. Octavius Brooks Frothingham, *Gerrit Smith: A Biography* (New York: G. P. Putnam's Sons, 1879), 122–26; Ralph Volney Harlow, *Gerrit Smith: Philanthropist and Reformer* (New York: Henry Holt and Co., 1939), 106–7, 376, 471–72.

105. "Report of the Proceedings of the Dress Reform"; "The Principle of Dress Reform," *Sibyl* (Jan. 15, 1857): 108–9; "The Reform Dress: Lucy Stone, Miss Anthony, and Mrs. Stanton," *Sibyl* 1.13 (Jan. 1, 1857): 100–101.

106. *New York Times,* Nov. 22, 1866 as quoted in Fatout, "Amelia Bloomer and Bloomerism," 372.

5. OUT OF THE CLOSET

1. Reprinted in *Water-Cure Journal* 13 (May 1852): 115.

2. "That Was New York," 41–42.

3. C.S., "An Illinois Bloomer," *Water-Cure Journal* 15 (June 1853): 131; Sarah E. Selby, "A Bloomer to Her Sisters," *Water-Cure Journal* 15 (June 1853): 131.

4. Mrs. E. Potter, "Is It a Duty?" *Water-Cure Journal* 15 (Apr. 1853): 82–83; "Objections to the New Costume by a Bloomer in Prairie Land," *Water-Cure Journal* 14 (Aug. 1852): 52–53.

5. Noyes, *The Days of My Youth,* 50.

6. "The Short Dress," *Circular* (Feb. 12, 1866): 382.

7. Kephart, "Experimental Family Organization," 264; Francis Wayland-Smith, essay.

8. "A Word for the Short Dress," *Circular* (Mar. 4, 1867): 404.

9. H. M. Joslyn, notes from 1915 interview, Oneida Community Collection; Noyes, *The Days of My Youth,* 50, 76; Jessie C. Kinsley, memoir, 1914, Oneida Community Collection.

10. Adela Elizabeth Richards Orpen, *Memories of the Old Emigrant Days in Kansas, 1862–1865* (New York: Harper & Brothers, 1928), 132–33. No last name was given for Olive.

11. Jones, *Woman's Dress,* 12.

12. Ibid., 21.

13. "Random Thoughts for Dress Reform," *Sibyl* 3 (Aug. 1, 1858): 406.

14. As social and intellectual historian Martha H. Verbrugge and others have argued, "definitions of health carried far more than biological information," and are culturally constructed (Verbrugge, *Able-Bodied Womanhood*).

15. "Dress Reform Convention," *Lily* (May 1, 1856): 67; "The Dress Reform Constitution," *Sibyl* 1 (Sept. 15, 1856): 46; "Dress Reform Convention," *Water-Cure Journal* 21 (Apr. 1856): 81.

16. "Mrs. Bloomer on Dress Reform," *Sibyl* 1 (Sept. 15, 1856): 43.

17. The NDRA shunned the name of "Bloomer." The members felt compelled to pass a resolution that disclaimed their association with "Bloomer." Ironically, the word was prevalent in the songs and poems written by members and performed at conventions. See Charlotte Austin Joy, "Suggestions to Women Who Are Interested in the Dress Reform," *Water-Cure Journal* 21 (May 1856): 114–15; "Resolutions," *Sibyl* 1(Sept. 1, 1856): 37.

18. Joy, "Suggestions to Women Who Are Interested in the Dress Reform."

19. "Dress Reform Resolutions," *Sibyl* 1(Sept. 1, 1856): 37.

20. "Letters Read at the Convention," *Sibyl* 2 (July 1, 1857): 195, 198.

21. Austin, "The Reform Dress," 3; Mary E. Walker, *Hit* (New York: American News Co., 1871), 83–84.

22. "Letter 6, 1864. (To Brother and Sister Lockwood, September 1864)," *Manuscript Releases from the Files of the Letters and Manuscripts Written by Ellen G. White* (Silver Spring, Md.: E. G. White Estate, 1990), 5:380.

23. "Report of the Proceedings of the Dress Reform Convention"; Laver, *Modesty in Dress,* 134–36.

24. Mary E. Tillotson, *Progress vs. Fashion: An Essay on the Sanitary and Social Influences of Woman's Dress* (Vineland, N.J.: 1873), 16.

25. Austin, "The Reform Dress," 3.

26. Ibid.

27. "Miss Austin in New York in the American Costume," *Laws of Life* 3 (Feb. 1860): 23.

28. Harriet Austin, "A Response to Fannie's Letter in the February No.," 79.

29. "Dress Reform Convention" *Health Reformer* 4 (Sept. 1869): 57.

30. Walker, *Hit,* 83–84.

31. I have counted more than four hundred names in the official rolls printed in the *Sibyl.* "List of Dress Reformers" (July 15, 1859): 588–89; "List of Dress Reformers" (Sept. 1, 1858): 420–21.

32. "The Canastota Convention," *Sibyl* 1 (Jan. 15, 1857): 109; "Dress Reform Convention," *Sibyl* 1 (Jan. 1, 1857): 101; "A Dress Reform Ball," *Sibyl* (Dec. 1, 1857): 273–74.

33. For more information on the *Sibyl* as a reform periodical, see Russo and Kramarae, *The Radical Women's Press of the 1850s;* Kesselman, "Lydia Sayer Hasbrouck and *The Sibyl.*"

34. "Our Title Head—Our Aim," *Sibyl* (July 1, 1856): 3; *Whig Press* (Oct. 14, 1857); "To The Reform Public," *Sibyl* (July 1, 1856): 4.

35. The *Laws of Life* and the *Water-Cure Journal* also reported on the NDRA's activities, but not to the extent or detail of the *Sibyl.*

36. Jackson, "The Dress Reform Convention in June."

37. "Dress Reform Convention," *Sibyl* 1 (Dec. 15, 1856): 90.

38. Jackson did preside over the 1863 meeting when Dr. Harriet Austin was unable to perform her presidential duties. "National Dress Reform Association," *Sibyl* (July 1863): 1153–60.

39. "Dress Reform Convention," *Sibyl* (Jan. 1, 1857): 101.

40. Letter from Hopedale, Massachusetts reprinted in "Report of the Proceedings of the Dress Reform Convention."

41. "Dress Reform Convention," *Sibyl* 4 (July 1, 1859): 577–84.

42. Mary Gove Nichols, "The New Costume, and Some Other Matters," *Water-Cure Journal* 12 (Aug. 1851): 30.

43. Nichols, "A Lecture on Woman's Dresses," 34–36.

44. The dress reformers were not alone in their desire to separate American fashions from French fashions. The *Auburn Advertiser* supported a change in women's dress, though not the American costume, because it would relieve women "from the barborous and tyrannous Parisian fashions, by which they are now oppressed and enslaved." *Auburn Advertiser* reprinted in the *Sibyl* 2 (July 1, 1857): 198. Using a similar line of reasoning, the *International Magazine of Literature, Art, and Science* favored the short dress as an "American fashion," created for "American taste, and suited to [American] climate and habits" ("The Bloomer Costume," *International Magazine of Literature, Art, and Science* 4 [Sept. 1851]: 243).

45. "Dress Reform Convention," *Sibyl* 4 (July 1, 1859): 577–84.

46. "Report of the Proceedings of the Dress Reform Convention"; "The Principle of Dress Reform," 108–9; "The Reform Dress: Lucy Stone, Miss Anthony, and Mrs. Stanton."

47. "National Dress Reform Association," *Sibyl* 4 (June 15, 1860): 761–62.

48. Mrs. O. P. M'Cune, M.D. "Dress," *Herald of Health and Journal of Physical Culture* 9 (Apr. 1867): 181.

49. "The Auburn Convention," *Sibyl* (Aug. 1, 1859): 598–99. The organizers of the convention read letters containing slave images to those in attendance. One writer related fashion to the "chains" worn by slaves and bemoaned the "debasing servility" of fashion that made woman the "menial, the slave, the vain votary of fashion." Then she begged her "brothers and sisters" to "cast away" the chains that fettered them.

50. "National Dress Reform Association," *Sibyl* (Apr. 1863): 1132.

51. "Report of the Annual Dress Convention," *Sibyl* (May 15, 1861): 940–41; "Letters from Dress Reformers," *Sibyl* (July 1863): 1158–59.

52. Letter to Gerrit Smith from James C. Jackson, May 8, 1865, Gerrit Smith Collection.

53. Numbers, *Prophetess of Health: Ellen G. White,* 134.

54. Numbers writes eloquently of the difficulties in writing religious history that balances the secular with the divine. Nevertheless, his emphasis on secular influences on E. G. White over religious or divine inspiration resulted in a discussion of dress that divided it on religious and health issues (ibid., xi–xii, 134–46).

55. "Simplicity of Dress," *Review and Herald* (Jan. 14, 1861): 56.

56. "Fashions of the Present Age," *Review and Herald* 12 (Oct. 21, 1858): 169.

57. "The Dress Question," *Review and Herald* (Sept. 23, 1858): 142.

58. James White, "Report From Bro. White," *Advent Review and Sabbath Herald* 29 (Jan. 15, 1867): 66–67.

59. "Our Uses of the Visions of Sr. White," *Review and Herald* 35 (Feb. 15, 1870): 64–65.

60. Ellen G. White, "Extremes in Dress," in "Testimony 10," in *Testimonies for the Church,* 1:421.

61. Ellen Gould White, "The Cause in the East" 1:421.

62. Mrs. S. W. Dodds, M.D., "Dress Reform and Health Reform in Kansas," *Health Reformer* 4 (Feb. 1870): 157.

63. "The Demoralization of Dress," 57.

64. "Woman's Right to Right Treatment," *Health Reformer* 4 (Jan. 1870): 122.

65. "Horace Greeley on Fashion," *Health Reformer* 4 (Nov. 1869): 84.

66. "Woman's Right to Right Treatment," 122.

67. "Gail Hamilton on Long Dresses," *Health Reformer* 5 (Jan. 1871): 127.

68. For more information on the Seventh-day Adventists' opinion of the woman's rights women and their choice of dress, see "Woman's Right to a Womanly Dress," *Health Reformer* 5 (Jan. 1871): 124; "Woman's Right to Dress Decently," *Health Reformer* 4 (Feb. 1870): 144–45.

69. For more information on the position of women in the Seventh-day Adventist Church, see Malcolm Bull and Keith Lockhart, *Seeking a Sanctuary: Seventh-day Adventism and the American Dream* (San Francisco: Harper & Row, 1989), esp. 179–92.

70. Arthur L. White, *Ellen G. White: The Early Years,* Vol. 1: *1827–1862* (Washington, D.C.: Review and Herald Publishing Association, 1985), 469. For more information on Ellen G. White's position on the status of women, see William Fagal, "Ellen White and the Role of Women in the Church," EGW papers, Ellen G. White Research Center, Berien Springs, Michigan.

71. Ellen G. White, "Reform in Dress" in "Testimony 11," in *Testimonies for the Church,* 1:465.

72. Ibid.

73. Linden, *The Last Trump,* 317; Numbers, *Prophetess of Health;* Staff of the Ellen G. White Estate, *A Critique of the Book* Prophetess of Health (Takoma Park, Washington, D.C.: Ellen G. White Estate, 1976).

74. Ellen G. White, *Testimonies for the Church,* vol. 4: *Compromising Testimonies Numbers 26 to 30* (1875–81; rpt., Mountain View, Calif.: Pacific Press Publishing Association, 1948), 634.

75. White, *Testimonies,* 1:465–66.

76. "Business Proceedings," *Review and Herald* 29 (May 28, 1867): 283–84.

77. White, "Report from Bro. White."

78. D. M. Canright, *Review and Herald* (June 18, 1867): 9; C. O. Taylor, "The Reform Dress," *Advent Review and Sabbath Herald* 30 (Sept. 3, 1867): 188.

79. Ellen G. White, "Testimony 12 (1867)," *Testimonies for the Church* 1:520–27.

80. E.G.W., "A Few Suggestions," *Health Reformer* 3 (Sept. 1868): 42–43.

81. The pamphlet was reprinted in the *Review and Herald* (Apr. 14, 1868), and the *Health Reformer* (Aug. 1868). E. G. White may have been reacting to earlier discussions on modest dress, which exhorted women to avoid calling attention to themselves through their clothing. See Albert Stone, "Modest Apparel," *Review and Herald* 19 (Apr. 1, 1862): 141.

82. "The Dress Reform" pamphlet at the Ellen G. White Research Center, 4–5, 8–11.

83. Dodds, "Dress Reform and Health Reform in Kansas," 155–58.

84. Dr. S. W. Dodds, "Dress Reform in the West," *Health Reformer* 5 (July 1870): 16. More research needs to be done to find the less-known and less-documented attempts at dress reform organizations in all states.

85. M. J. Cottrell, "In Answer to Our Prayers," *Review and Herald* 31 (Feb. 25, 1868): 166–67.

86. White, *Testimonies,* 4:637, 648.

87. Rev. T. DeWitt Talmage, *Woman, Her Power and Privileges. A Series of Sermons* (New York: J. S. Ogilvie, 1888), 57. The Seventh-day Adventists occasionally noted biblical references to dress. See "Trailing Dresses Condemned," *Health Reformer* 3 (July 1868): 3.

88. *Friends and Sisters,* 125.

89. Jackson, *American Womanhood,* 61.

6. "I'm Coming Out as a Bloomer"

1. Merab Hotchkiss Dresser, "Health and Dress Reform," *Sibyl* (Apr. 1, 1860): 723.

2. Hiram A. Reid, "A Bloomer in Boston," *Sibyl* (Aug. 1, 1859): 599.

3. For an example of a dress reformer who was considered an "odd girl," see "The Home of Gerrit Smith," *Sibyl* (Sept. 15, 1859): 615.

4. "Henry Ward Beecher on Bloomerism," *Water-Cure Journal* 19 (Jan. 1855): 9; "The Short Dress," *Circular* (Dec. 18, 1862).

5. "The Progress of Dress Reform," *Sibyl* 1 (Feb. 15, 1857): 125–26.

6. Several articles aimed at farmers' wives encouraged women to wear short dresses. For example, see Helen L. Manning, "Comfortable and Healthy Costumes for Farmers' Wives," *Kansas Farmer* (Aug. 6, 1890): 6; "Interesting to Farmers' Wives," *Prairie Farmer* 5 (May 3, 1860): 277; Mrs. F. D. Gage, "A Chapter from a House Keeper's Diary," *Prairie Farmer* 7 (Jan. 3, 1861): 10; "The American Costume," *Prairie Farmer* 6 (Sept. 27, 1860): 202.

7. Nevin, "The Bloomer Dress," 249, 251, 253, 255.

8. "From Margaret E. Bennett," *Sibyl* 8 (June 1864): 1243–47.

9. Mrs. N. Whittlesy, "Undaunted and True," *Sibyl* (Sept. 1, 1858): 423.

10. "That Was New York," 41–42; "The Short Dress," *Circular* (Mar. 6, 1865): 403–4.

11. "Henry Ward Beecher," *Water-Cure Journal* 19 (Jan. 1855): 9.

12. "Principle of Right," *Sibyl* (Apr. 1, 1858): 343.

13. L.A.B., "A Voice from Illinois," *Water-Cure Journal* 15 (May 1853): 106.

14. Women who wore "worn-out" finery were often ridiculed. Soiled and spotted silk and wool dresses could not be washed. Wash dresses or washable dresses, which were less affected by fashion, were worn for housework. Print fabrics were preferred to conceal soiling.

15. Janet Robertson, *The Magnificent Mountain Women: Adventures in the Colorado Rockies* (Lincoln: University of Nebraska Press, 1990), 2–6; J. A. Archibald, "A Journey to Pike's Peak and New Mexico," *Sibyl* 3 (Apr. 1, 1859): 529–31; *Mountain Charley or the Adventures of Mrs. E. J. Guerin, Who Was Thirteen Years in Male Attire,* introduction by Fred W. Mazzulla and William Kostka (1861; rpt., Norman: University of Oklahoma Press, 1968).

16. Recently historians have begun to explore the different experiences of men and women in the West. John Mack Faragher, *Women and Men on the Overland Trail* (New Haven, Conn.: Yale University Press, 1979); Julie Roy Jeffrey, *Frontier Women: The Trans-Mississippi West, 1840–1880* (New York: Hill and Wang, 1979); Sandra L. Myres, *Westering Women and the Frontier Experience 1800–1915* (Albuquerque: University of New Mexico Press, 1982); Glenda Riley, *The Female Frontier: A Comparative View of Women on the Prairie and the Plains* (Lawrence: University Press of Kansas, 1988); Lillian Schlissel, *Women's Diaries of the Westward Journey,* expanded ed. (New York: Schocken Books, 1992); Joanna L. Stratton, *Pioneer Women: Voices from the Kansas Frontier* (New York: Simon and Schuster, 1981).

17. For a detailed description of what a woman might wear on the overland trail, see McMartin, "Dress of the Oregon Trail Emigrants"; Julie A. Campbell and Brenda Brandt, "'No Seamstresses, No Ready-Made Clothing': Clothing Consumption on the American Frontier, 1850–1890," *Clothing and Textiles Research Journal* 3 (Spring 1994): 16–19.

18. Jeffrey, *Frontier Women,* 38–39; Faragher, *Women and Men,* 105–8; Schlissel, *Women's Diaries,* 85, 98, 105, 125, 128.

19. Kate Stephens, *Life at Laurel Town in Anglo-Saxon Kansas* (Lawrence: Alumni Association of the University of Kansas, 1920), 76–77. For more information on the clothing women wore on the frontier, see Feightner, "Clothing and Accessories"; Larson, "Clothing of Pioneer Women"; Carol Anne Dickson, "Patterns for Garments: A History of the Paper Garment Pattern Industry in America to 1976" (Ph.D. dissertation, Ohio State University, 1979); Sally Ingrid Helvenston,

"Feminine Response to a Frontier Environment as Reflected in the Clothing of Kansas Women: 1854–1895" (Ph.D. dissertation, Kansas State University, 1985).

20. Jeffrey, *Frontier Women,* 73.

21. Riley, *The Female Frontier;* Faragher, *Men and Women;* Schlissel, *Women's Diaries.* Some frontier women remarked about the absence of white clothing on the frontier—no clean water for laundering.

22. Faragher remarks that "in 1852 a large number of emigrant women adopted Amelia Bloomer's reformed dress style as a more sensible traveling costume." *Men and Women,* 106. Historians debate the popularity of the costume on the overland trail.

23. "Albert D. Richardson's Letters on the Pike's Peak Gold Region," ed. Louise Barry, *Kansas Historical Quarterly* 12 (Feb. 1943): 23.

24. "The Oregon and California Letters of Bradford Ripley Alden," *California Historical Society Quarterly* 28 (Sept. 1949): 202.

25. Miriam Davis Colt also noticed that when the wagon train arrived in towns, her costume did not go without notice. *Went to Kansas: Being a Thrilling Account of an Ill-Fated Expedition* (Watertown [N.Y.]: L. Ingalls & Co., 1862), 65, 165–67.

26. "Sherman Was There: The Recollections of Major Edwin A. Sherman," *California Historical Society Quarterly* 24 (Mar. 1945): 67–69.

27. Clapp, *The Shirley Letters,* 322, 330.

28. Mrs. Francis H. Sawyer, "Overland to California," as quoted in Faragher, *Women and Men,* 106.

29. Several historians noted this trend. Julie Roy Jeffrey, *Frontier Women*; Glenda Riley, *The Female Frontier,* 109.

30. "Sherman Was There: The Recollections of Major Edwin A. Sherman," *California Historical Society Quarterly* 24 (June 1945): 165.

31. Orpen, *Memories of the Old Emigrant Days in Kansas,* 132.

32. Stephens, *Life at Laurel Town,* 105.

33. Quoted in Dee Brown, *Wondrous Times on the Frontier* (Little Rock, Ark.: August House, 1991), 274–75.

34. "The Rocky Mountain Bloomers," *Water-Cure Journal* 13 (Jan. 1852): 19.

35. Orpen, *Memories,* 132. Myres, *Westering Women,* 125.

36. Riley, *The Female Frontier,* 185.

37. Brown, *The Gentle Tamers,* 139. Also reprinted in Julia Cooley Altrocchi, "Paradox Town: San Francisco in 1851," *California Historical Society Quarterly* (1932): 31–46.

38. Schlissel discusses "bloomers" as a fashion, and notes that "fashion" was something beyond the economic grasp of most women. *Women's Diaries,* 104–6.

39. Quoted in the *Alta California* and reprinted in Altrocchi, "Paradox Town," 40.

40. Edith Drinker, "Science and Long Skirts," *Water-Cure Journal* 20 (July 1855): 7.

41. "The Short Dress," *Circular* (Mar. 6, 1865): 403–4.

42. Harriet Beecher Stowe, "Sojourner Truth, the Libyan Sibyl," *Atlantic Monthly* 11.66 (1863): 473–81.

43. Fatima B. Cheney, "Reforms and Reformers," *Sibyl* (Oct. 15, 1858): 445. This may account for the discrepancies in the lists of dress reformers.

44. D.D., "Beauty in Dress," *Sibyl* (Nov. 15, 1858): 463; Fannie, "Chit-Chat," *Sibyl* (Dec. 1, 1859): 661; and M. A. Hunter, "Self Reform—Dress Reform," *Sibyl* (Nov. 1, 1859): 646.

45. "The Right Spirit," *Water-Cure Journal* 15 (Jan. 1853): 11; Dresser, "Health and Dress Reform," 723.

46. Jones, *Woman's Dress,* 24.

47. M. L. Perry, "Weak-Minded Men and Women," *Health Reformer* 3 (Feb. 1869): 155.

48. R. C. Alexander, "Concerning Dress Reform," *Sibyl* (Nov. 1, 1858): 451.

49. Elizabeth Brown Pryor, *Clara Barton: Professional Angel* (Philadelphia: University of Pennsylvania Press, 1987), 179–81; Percy H. Epler, *The Life of Clara Barton* (New York: Macmillan, 1917), 216–19.

50. For some examples of early attempts to introduce formal exercise to women, see Dorothy S. Ainsworth, *The History of Physical Education in Colleges for Women,* New York: A. S. Barnes and Co., 1930; Helen L. Manning, "Comfortable and Healthy Costume for Farmers' Wives," 6, reprinted from *Farmers' Review;* Cogan, *All-American Girl;* Paula D. Welch and Harold A. Lerch, *History of American Physical Education and Sport* (Springfield, Ill.: Charles C. Thomas, 1981); Borish, "The Robust Woman and the Muscular Christian"; Borish, "Farm Females, Fitness, and the Ideology of Physical Health."

51. Sport dress was more a twentieth-century phenomenon, although it had its roots in the late nineteenth century. See Lee Hall, *Common Threads: A Parade of American Clothing* (Boston: Little, Brown and Co., 1992), 221–36; Patricia Campbell Warner, "Clothing as Barrier: American Women in the Olympics, 1900–1920," *Dress* 24 (1997): 55–68; Warner, "The Gym Suit: Freedom at Last," in *Dress in American Culture* (Bowling Green, Ohio: Bowling Green State University Popular Press, 1993); Warner, "The Gym Slip: The Origins of the English Schoolgirl Tunic," *Dress* 22 (1995): 45–58.

52. Jennifer A. Hargreaves argues that women's sports developed in a totally separate sphere than men's ("Playing Like Gentlemen while Behaving Like Ladies: Contradictory Features of the Formative Years of Women's Sport," *British Journal of Sports History* 2 [May 1985]: 46). See also Jihang Park, "Sport, Dress Reform, and the Emancipation of Women in Victorian England: A Reappraisal," *International Journal of the History of Sport* 6 (May 1989): 16–20.

53. Phillis Cunnington and Alan Mansfield, *English Costume for Sports and Outdoor Recreation from the Sixteenth to the Nineteenth Centuries* (New York: Barnes and

Noble, 1969), 357–58. Also see *The Gallery of English Costume: Costume for Sport* (Published for the Art Galleries Committee of the Corporation of Manchester, 1963).

54. Welch and Lerch, *History of American Physical Education,* 225.

55. Ann Buerman Wass and Clarita Anderson, "What Did Women Wear to Run?" *Dress* 17 (1990): 169–84.

56. M'Cune, "Dress," 181.

57. "The Health of American Women," *North American Review* 135 (Dec. 1882): 503–10.

58. Warner, "Public and Private," 48–55.

59. Foote, "Bloomers," 11. Valerie Steele agrees that "a modification of the Bloomer costume was widely adopted as gymnasium dress" (*Fashion and Eroticism,* 157).

60. Numerous dress reformers wrote to the *Sibyl* or wrote their own pamphlets with suggestions on how to design and make a reform dress. See "A Few Words about Costume," *Sibyl* (Sept. 15, 1859): 621; H. J. Noyes, "Patterns For Dresses," *Sibyl* (Sept. 1, 1858): 422; "The Dress Reform," *Health Reformer* 2 (Mar. 1968): 129–31; G.W.H., "Something Strange," *Health Reformer* 5 (July 1870): 14; Hannah, "Letter to a Friend," *Health Reformer* 5 (Dec. 1870): 114; Austin, "The Reform Dress," 3; "The Short Dress. Its Materials—How It Is Made—Under-Clothing—Quantity Used—Etc., Etc.," 342–43; "Short Dress Finance," *Circular* (June 19, 1865): 109.

61. Illustrations of these garments would clarify how they differed from one another. Unfortunately, few are available, and written descriptions make the costumes sound remarkably similar to other reform apparel.

62. Merritt, *Dress Reform Practically and Physiologically Considered,* 86–90. On pages 90–91, Merritt lists four "different styles or modifications of the reform dress."

63. Ellen Beard Harman, M.D., "The Premium Dress," *Herald of Health* 6 (Sept. 1865): 74.

64. Williams, "The Bloomer and Weber Dresses," 33.

65. Letter to Reform Dress Association, May 18, 1857, Gerrit Smith Collection.

66. "A Chapter on Dress: Home-Talk by J.H.N.," *Circular* (Aug. 25, 1855): 122.

67. Vern L. Bullough and Bonnie Bullough, *Cross Dressing, Sex, and Gender* (Philadelphia: University of Pennsylvania Press, 1993), 166.

68. The tales of these remarkable women who lived a portion of their lives as men can be found in Mary Chaney Hoffman, "Whips of the Old West," *American Mercury* 84 (Apr. 1957): 107–10; *Mountain Charley;* Roseanne Smith, "Women Who Wanted to Be Men," *Coronet* 42 (Sept. 1957): 62–66; Bullough and Bullough, *Cross Dressing; New York Times,* Feb. 21, 22, 24, 1882; Sylvia G. L. Dannett, *She Rode with the Generals: The True and Incredible Story of Sarah Emma Seelye, Alias Franklin Thompson* (New York: Thomas Nelson and Sons, 1960); S. Emma E. Edmonds, *Nurse and Spy in the Union Army* (Hartford: W. S. Williams & Co., 1865); C. Kay Larson, "Bonny Yank and Ginny Reb," *Minerva* 8 (Spring 1992); Loreta

Janeta Velazquez, *The Woman in Battle: A Narrative of the Exploits, Adventures, and Travels of Madame Loreta Janeta Velazquez, Otherwise Known as Lieutenant Harry T. Buford, Confederate States Army,* ed. C. J. Worthington (Hartford: T. Belknap, 1876); Janet E. Kaufman, "'Under the Petticoat Flag': Women in the Confederate Army," *Southern Studies* 23.4 (1984); Richard Hall, *Patriots in Disguise: Women Warriors of the Civil War* (New York: Paragon House, 1993).

69. *Washington Post,* Feb. 23, 1919.

70. Helen Beal Woodward, *The Bold Women* (New York: Farrar, Strauss, and Young, 1953).

71. Charles McCool Snyder, *Dr. Mary Walker: The Little Lady in Pants* (New York: Arno Press, 1974).

72. Much of the background information on Walker comes from the following sources: James A. Brussel, M.D., "Pants, Politics, Postage, and Physic," *Psychiatric Quarterly Supplement* 35 (1961): 332–45; Mrs. John A. Logan, *The Part Taken by Women in American History* (Wilmington, Del.: Perry-Nalle Publishing Co., 1912); Lida Poynter, "Dr. Mary Walker, M.D. Pioneer Woman Physician," *Medical Woman's Journal* 53 (Oct. 1946): 43–51; Charles McCool Snyder, *Oswego: From Buckskin to Bustles* (Port Washington, N.Y.: Ira J. Friedman, 1968); Snyder, *Dr. Mary Walker;* Susan C. Waters, "The Invincible Doctor Walker," *New York Alive* (Nov.–Dec. 1983): 30–33.

73. There is controversy among Walker's biographers about her medical skills. During the Civil War she lost her first appointment because of questions surrounding her medical competency. It is not clear whether the controversy stemmed in part from the type of medicine she practiced, which was one of the alternative medical sects then being used in the United States. Civil War physicians were not noted for their skill, and Walker may have been no worse, and perhaps better, than some of her male counterparts. Elizabeth D. Leonard, *Yankee Women: Gender Battles in the Civil War* (New York: W. W. Norton, 1994). Also see Allen D. Spiegel and Peter B. Suskind, "Mary Edwards Walker, M.D.: A Feminist Physician a Century ahead of Her Time," *Journal of Community Health* 21 (June 1996): 211–35.

74. *Sibyl* (Nov. 1862).

75. Woodward, *The Bold Women*.

76. *New York Times,* Sept. 21, 1869.

77. In 1917 a government review board withdrew Walker's medal, along with the medals of nine hundred other Civil War veterans. The board claimed Walker's medal had been improperly awarded because of the question of her status as a contract doctor. Walker refused to relinquish her medal and vowed to wear it every day. The award was later reinstated. *New York Times,* June 4, 1977.

78. Accounts of Walker's arrests can be found in *New York Times* (June 14, 1866; Dec. 6, 1878); *Circular* (June 18, 1866, June 25, 1866).

79. *New York Times,* June 26, 1881.

80. I have searched the congressional records looking for some mention of Walker and pants; Walker does appear in the *Congressional Record* for seeking a pension and arguing for suffrage. The Dr. Mary Edwards Walker Collection at Syracuse University Library does not contain information to support the story. Walker's February 23, 1919, obituary in the *Washington Post* has several headlines, including "Woman Whom Congress Let Don Male Garb Dies." The body of the notice does not elaborate on the suggestive headline. Walker's *New York Times* obituary also contains the same misinformation (Feb. 23, 1919, 18).

81. *Oswego Palladium,* Nov. 4, 1880.

82. *New York Times,* Sept. 7, 1876; Oct. 26, 1913. Also see Kathleen De Grave, *Swindler, Spy, Rebel: The Confidence Woman in Nineteenth-Century America* (Columbia: University of Missouri Press, 1995), 126, 171

83. No doubt Walker was alluding to her own arrests and dress (Walker, *Hit,* 65).

84. Ibid., 64, 65.

85. Tillotson, *History*.

86. Mann, *A Few Thoughts of the Power and Duties of Woman,* 16.

87. Historian Eric Lott has explored castration theories in his study of men dressed as women in nineteenth-century minstrel shows. Lott speculates that the "blackface cross-dresser" converted male gender anxiety into comic pleasure. The portrayal of a woman with a penis—that is, a male cross-dresser—deflated the threatening and "castrating" power of women because they "proved" that feminization did not take away masculinity, that is, the penis. If Lott's historical application of psychoanalytic theory is correct, then perhaps the converse is also true. The cross-dressing woman—the woman in male clothing—then suggests the possibility of the penisless man, and is therefore a source of anxiety because she reinforces the "castrating" power of women (Eric Lott, *Love and Theft: Blackface Minstrelsy and the American Working Class* [New York: Oxford University Press, 1993]).

88. *American Whig Review,* Oct. 1848, 374–75.

89. Gretchen van Slyke, "Who Wears the Pants Here? The Policing of Women's Dress in Nineteenth-Century England, Germany, and France," *Nineteenth-Century Contexts* 17.1 (1993): 20.

90. *Congressional Record,* July 4, 1898.

91. Linden F. Edwards, "Dr. Mary Edwards Walker (1832–1919): Charlatan or Martyr?" *Ohio State Medical Journal* 54 (1958); *New York Times,* Mar. 8, 1887.

92. *New York Times,* Aug. 17, 1911. Woodward, *Bold Women,* 290; Havelock Ellis, *Studies in the Psychology of Sex: Sexual Inversion* (Philadelphia: F.A. Davis Co., 1908), 133–43.

93. *New York Times,* Feb. 2, 1882, 3.

94. *New York Times,* June 13, 1982.

95. Allison Lockwood, "Pantsuited Pioneer of Women's Lib, Dr. Mary Walker," *Smithsonian Magazine* (Mar. 1977): 113–16.

96. "The Bloomer Costume," *International Magazine of Literature, Art, and Science; Harper's New Monthly Magazine* (June 1851–July 1851): 288.

97. "Dr. Holmes on Trail Dresses," *Health Reformer* 10 (Nov. 1875): 333. "The Bloomer Costume," 288.

98. Lott, *Love and Theft*, 26, 160–61; Shirley Staples, *Male-Female Comedy Teams in American Vaudeville, 1865–1932* (Ann Arbor, Mich.: UMI Research Press, 1984), 12–13, 149; Rosemary Hawthorne, *Oh . . . Knickers! A Brief History of "Unmentionables"* (London: Bachman & Turner, 1985), 76–79.

99. Fannie, "Chit-Chat," 661.

100. *International Magazine of Literature, Art, and Science* 4 (Nov. 1851): 563.

101. Olive Logan, "A Word about Dress," *Revolution* (June 3, 1869): 337.

102. *International Magazine of Literature, Art, and Science* 4 (Nov. 1851): 563.

103. Faith Rochester speculated that "Thousands of prostitutes wear, and long have worn, the fashionable dress," in "Dot and I Again: Our Talk About Dress," *Revolution* (Dec. 23, 1869): 389–90. Also see Peiss, *Cheap Amusements*, 63–66; and Tandberg, "Sinning for Silk."

104. Nichols, "A Lecture on Woman's Dresses" 34–36; "Dress Reform Convention," *Sibyl* 8 (June 1864): 1241–47.

105. For discussions on dress reform in the South, see Dr. Mary Walker, "Letter from Dr. Walker," *Sibyl* (Nov. 1862): 1092; B, "The New Social Propositions," *Southern Literary Messenger* 20 (May 1854): 294–306; Gerilyn G. Tandberg, "Towards Freedom in Dress for Nineteenth Century Women," *Dress* 11 (1985): 11–12.

106. *Friends and Sisters*, 105.

107. Reports such as this one that used vague language to recount the numbers of women wearing reform garments contributed to the confusion over the number of dress reformers. "There are many others in our State [Rhode Island] who wear it as a working dress, and I am personally acquainted with a goodly number in the "Bay State" (Mass) who wear it much of the time" ("To the Friends of Dress Reform," *Sibyl* 8 [June 1864]: 1243–47).

7. What Happened to Dress Reform?

1. The *New York Truth* was a newspaper that had several lives. Its 1891 reorganization resulted in a paper strong on social satire, high society news, and sophisticated fiction (Mott, *A History of American Magazines, 1885–1905*, 83–85).

2. Letter to Gerrit Smith from James C. Jackson, May 8, 1865; "National Dress Reform Association," *Union and Advertiser* (June 21, 1865): 2; "The Dress

Reformers,"2; "The Dress Reform Convention," *Union and Advertiser* (June 23, 1865): 2; "To the Editors of the Rochester Press," *Union and Advertiser* (June 26, 1865): 2; "The National Dress Reform Association and the Rochester Meeting," *Union and Advertiser* (June 27, 1865): 2; "Dr. Jackson and the Dress Reformers," *Union and Advertiser* (June 28, 1865): 2; "About Costume—Dress Not a Rochester 'Institution,'" *Union and Advertiser* (June 30, 1865): 2.

3. "National Dress Reform Association," *Union and Advertiser* (June 21, 1865): 2.

4. Ibid.

5. "The National Dress Reform Association and Rochester," 2; "The Dress Reformers," *Union and Advertiser* (June 22, 1865): 2.

6. "Secretary's Report of the Dress Reform Convention," *Sibyl* (Mar. 1, 1859).

7. "Dr. Jackson and the Dress Reformers," 2.

8. "National Dress Reform Associaton," *Union and Advertiser* (June 21, 1865): 2.

9. "The Suspension of *The Sibyl*," *Sibyl* (Apr. 1864): 1228; "Dress Reform Convention," *Sibyl* (Mar. 1864): 1220.

10. Ellen G. White, "Simplicity in Dress," originally written in 1877, published in *Review and Herald* (Mar. 20, 1958): 12–13.

11. Arthur L. White, *Ellen G. White: The Australian Years,* Vol. 4: *The Australian Years, 1891–1900* (Washington, D.C.: Review and Herald Publishing Association, 1983), 332; Arthur L. White, *Ellen G. White: The Progressive Years,* Vol. 2: *1863–1875* (Washington, D.C.: Review and Herald Publishing Association, 1986), 184.

12. White, *The Australian Years,* 332–33.

13. Ibid. White's response has appeared in a number of publications. For example, see "The Spirit of Prophecy and Dress Reform," *Ministry* (Dec. 1940): 27–31, or Francis D. Nichol, *Ellen G. White and Her Critics* (Takoma Park, Washington, D.C.: Review and Herald Publishing, 1951), 158.

14. "Letter to J. H. Haughey, July 4 1897," *Manuscript Releases.*

15. Ibid.

16. Tirzah Crawford Herrick Miller, diary, Jan. 25, 1874, Oneida Community Collection.

17. Kephart, *Extraordinary Groups,* 97; Carden, *Oneida,* 89–104; Constance Noyes Robertson, *Oneida Community: The Breakup, 1876–1881* (Syracuse, N.Y.: Syracuse University Press, 1972).

18. Carden, *Oneida,* 89–104.

19. Noyes, *The Days of My Youth,* 85–86.

20. Ibid.

21. Francis Wayland-Smith, letter to Noyes, July 19, 1879, Oneida Community Collection.

22. Francis Wayland-Smith, letter to Noyes, July 19, 1879.

23. Emma Jones, letter to Harriet, Jan. 23, 1880, Oneida Community Collection (emphasis in original).

24. Karen J. Blair, *The Clubwoman as Feminist: True Womanhood Redefined, 1868–1914* (New York: Holmes & Meier, 1980), 32–36; Abba Goold Woolson, ed., *Dress Reform: A Series of Lectures Delivered in Boston, on Dress as It Affects the Health of Women* (Boston: Roberts Brothers, 1874), iii–xviii.

25. Reigel, *American Feminists,* 398–99; Mary Ann Powell, "Ladies with Legs: An Historical Survey of the Social Acceptability of Pants on Women, 1851–1976," (Master's thesis, University of Texas at Austin, 1977), 28–29; Deborah Jean Warner, "Fashion, Emancipation, Reform," 25; Sally Buchanan Kinsey, "A More Reasonable Way to Dress," in *"The Art that Is Life:" The Art and Crafts Movement in America, 1875–1920,* ed. Wendy Kaplan (Boston: Museum of Fine Arts, Boston, 1987), 358–69.

26. Warner, "Fashion, Emancipation, Reform," 25–26. Marion Harland gave some information on health corsets in *Eve's Daughters; or, Common Sense for Maid, Wife, and Mother* (New York: John R. Anderson & Henry S. Allen, 1882), 351–52. And the *Revolution* came out in support of the "Health Corset" ("The Health Corset," *Revolution* [Nov. 11, 1869]: 292).

27. See for example Ada S. Ballin, *The Science of Dress in Theory and Practice* (London: Sampson Low, Marston, Searle, & Rivington, 1885).

28. Mary E. Tillotson, *History ov the First Thirty-Five Years ov the Science Costume Movement,* 37–40.

29. Elizabeth Stuart Phelps, *What to Wear?* (Boston: James R. Osgood and Co., 1873).

30. Sims, "The Bicycle, the Bloomer," 126; Bradfield, "Cycling in the 1890's," 43–47; Leslie, "Sports Fashions," 101–14, 155–56.

31. Mary Kathleen Saxon, "Aesthetic Dress of the Nineteenth Century: Principles and Practices," (Master's thesis, University of Texas at Austin, 1981); Eva Olney Farnsworth, *The Art & Ethics of Dress: As Related to Efficiency and Economy* (San Francisco: Paul Elder & Co., 1915); Rabbi Joseph Leiser, "Simplicity: A Law of Nature," *Craftsman* 2 (Aug. 1902): 224–31; "Dress and Its Relation to Life," *Craftsman* 11 (Nov. 1906): 269–71; "The Right to Beauty," *Craftsman* 12 (Apr. 1907): 124–32.

32. Joel H. Kaplan and Sheila Stowell, *Theatre and Fashion: Oscar Wilde to the Suffragettes* (Cambridge: Cambridge University Press, 1994); Alicia Finkel, "A Tale of Lilies, Sunflowers, and Knee-Breeches: Oscar Wilde's Wardrobe for His American Tour," *Dress* 15 (1989): 4–15.

33. Russell, "A Brief Survey"; Elizabeth Smith Miller, "Symposium on Women's Dress, Part 1," 488–95; Miller, "Symposium on Women's Dress, Part 2" *Arena* 6 (Oct. 1892): 621–35; Frances E. Russell, "Freedom in Dress for Women," *Arena* 8 (June 1893): 70–77; Frances E. Russell, "Woman's Dress," *Arena* 3 (Feb. 1891): 352–60; B. O. Flower, "Fashion's Slaves," *Arena* 4 (Sept. 1891): 401–30; Josette H. Rabun and Mary Frances Drake, "Warmth in Clothing: A Victorian Perspective," *Dress* 9 (1983): 24–31; Twelves, "An Investigation of the Impact of the Dress Reform Movement."

34. The special Committee on Dress Reform was a committee formed by the National Council of Women. The National Council of Women was a federation of a number of women's societies that came together for the World's Columbian Exposition of 1893, held in Chicago.

35. Patricia Cunningham, "Annie Jenness Miller and Mabel Jenness: Promoters of Physical Culture and Correct Dress," *Dress* 16 (1990): 48–61.

36. For some examples, see Anna G. Noyes, "A Practical Protest against Fashion," *Independent* 63 (Aug. 29, 1907): 503–9; I.M.T., "Nina Wilcox Putnam," *American Magazine* 75 (May 1913): 34–36; Nina Wilcox Putnam, "Fashion and Feminism," *Forum* 52 (Oct. 1914): 580–84; Putnam, "Ventures and Adventures in Dress Reform," *Saturday Evening Post* (Oct. 7, 1922): 15, 93–94; Ethel Ronzone, "Standardized Dress," *Journal of Home Economics* 10 (Sept. 1918): 426–28; Mary Alden Hopkins, "Woman's Rebellion against Fashions," *New Republic* (Aug. 16, 1922): 331–32; "Personal Glimpses: To-day's Morals and Manners—The Side of "The Girls," *Literary Digest* 70 (July 9, 1921): 35–37, 42; Barbara Burman and Melissa Leventon, "The Men's Dress Reform Party 1929–37," *Costume* 21 (1987): 75–87.

Epilogue

1. Penelope Byrde, *A Visual History of Costume: The Twentieth Century* (London: B. T. Batsford), 44; Wilson, *Adorned in Dreams,* 162–64; Anne Hollander, *Sex and Suits: The Evolution of Modern Dress* (New York: Alfred A. Knopf, 1994), 145; Powell, "Ladies with Legs," 108–9; Steele, *Fashion and Eroticism;* James C. Bayles, "The New Woman," *Independent* 70 (May 4, 1911): 956–57.

2. Steele, *Fashion and Eroticism,* 238–41.

3. Ribeiro and Cumming, *The Visual History of Costume,* 214; Wilson, *Adorned in Dreams,* 164; Hollander, *Sex and Suits*; Christopher Breward, *The Culture of Fashion: A New History of Fashionable Dress* (Manchester: Manchester University Press, 1995).

4. Powell, "Ladies with Legs," 281.

5. For just a few of the examples where the question of who wears the pants in the White House is asked, see "Elizabeth Dole: Frontrunning First Lady Says She's No Hillary," *Agence France Presse,* Mar. 10, 1996; "Only Hillary Can Go to China," *Washington Times,* Sept. 1, 1995; "Can Clinton Get the Venus Vote? Women Worry He's from Mars," *Washington Post,* May 21, 1995; "Does Hillary Clinton Have Too Much Power?" *San Francisco Chronicle,* June 30, 1994.

6. "Who Wears the Pants?" *Atlanta Journal and Constitution,* Sept. 27, 1995.

7. "Legislative Update: Who Wears the Pants in Your Business?" *California Employment Law Monitor* 5.6 (Nov. 1994).

8. Smith and Peiss, *Men and Women.*

Bibliography

Primary Sources

MANUSCRIPT COLLECTIONS

The Ellen G. White Research Center, Seventh-day Adventist Theological Seminary. Andrews University. Berien Springs, Michigan.

Ellen G. White Papers.

Lily Library, Indiana University. Bloomington, Indiana.

Sheet Music Collection.

Cortland County Historical Society. Cortland, New York.

Amelia Bloomer Papers.

Dr. Lydia Strobridge Papers.

Dr. Mary Walker Papers.

State of Wisconsin Historical Society. Madison, Wisconsin.

Historical Society of Middletown and the Wallkill Precinct. Middletown, New York.

Lydia Sayer Hasbrouck Papers.

New Harmony Workingmen's Institute Library and Museum. New Harmony, Indiana.

Madison County Historical Society. Oneida, New York.

Gerrit Smith Collection.

Oneida Community Mansion House. Oneida, New York.

Seneca Falls Historical Society. Seneca Falls, New York.

Amelia Bloomer Papers.

Susan B. Anthony Papers.

The George Arents Research Library at Syracuse University. Syracuse, New York.

Gerrit Smith Collection.

Oneida Community Collection.
Dr. Mary E. Walker Collection.

PERIODICALS

Advent Review and Sabbath Herald, also called *Review and Herald,* 1851–.
The American Magazine, 1913.
American Whig Review, 1848.
Arena, 1889–1909.
Atkinson's Casket, 1832.
Atlantic Monthly, 1878.
Banner of Light, 1862–67.
Bibliotheca Sacra, 1853.
Craftsman, 1902–7.
Cortland County Republican, 1859.
Cortland Standard, 1945.
Daily Journal of Oneida Community, vols. 1–3; *The O.C. Daily,* vols. 4–5 (Reprint, Philadelphia: Porcupine Press, 1975).
Democratic Review, 1854.
Eclectic Magazine, 1859.
Forum, 1914.
Frank Leslie's Illustrated Newspaper, 1857.
The Free Church Circular (Oneida), 1850–51.
The Free Enquirer, 1829–35.
Good Companion, 1880.
The Health Reformer, 1866–75.
Herald of Health, 1863–92.
Holden's Dollar Magazine, 1850.
The Independent, 1907.
International Magazine of Literature, Art, and Science, 1851.
The Journal of Home Economics, 1918.
Kansas Farmer, 1890.
The Ladies Wreath: An Illustrated Annual, 1852.
Laws of Life, 1858–93.
The Lily, 1849–52.
Middletown Whig Press, 1861.
New Harmony Gazette, 1825–28.
The New Republic, 1922.
New York Times.
New York Tribune.
Notes and Queries, 1883–1903.

The Oneida Circular, 1851–76.

The Prairie Farmer, 1860–61.

The Quarterly Review, 1847.

The Revolution, 1868–70.

Rochester Union and Advertiser, 1863–65.

Sartain's Union Magazine of Literature and Art, 1851.

The Saturday Evening Post, 1922.

The Sibyl, A Review of the Tastes, Errors, and Fashions of Society, 1856–64.

The UNA: A Paper Devoted to the Elevation of Woman, 1853–55.

The Water-Cure Journal, 1845–61.

Yankee Notions, 1850s.

PUBLISHED SOURCES

Abell, Mrs. L. G. Woman in Her Various Relations: Containing Practical Rules for American Females. New York: R. T. Young, 1853.

Backus, C. "An American King." Harper's New Monthly Magazine 64 (1882): 553–59.

Ballin, Ada S. The Science of Dress in Theory and Practice. London: Sampson Low, Marston, Searle & Rivington, 1885.

Ballou, Adin. History of the Hopedale Community. Lowell, Mass.: Thompson & Hill, 1897.

Bartlett, Elizabeth Ann. Sarah Grimké: Letters on the Equality of the Sexes and Other Essays. New Haven, Conn.: Yale University Press, 1988.

Bates, G. C. "The Beaver Island Prophet: The Trial in This City in 1851 of 'King' Strang." Michigan Historical Collections 32 (1903): 225–35.

Beadle, J. H. Polygamy: or, the Mysteries and Crimes of Mormonism. Philadelphia: National Publishing Co., 1882.

Bernhard, Karl. "Travels through North America, during the Years 1825 and 1826." In Indiana as Seen By Early Travelers, ed. Harlow Lindley. Indianapolis: Indiana Historical Commission, 1916: 418–37.

Bestor, Arthur E., ed. Education and Reform at New Harmony: Correspondence of William Maclure and Marie Duclos Fretageot. Indianapolis: Indiana Historical Society, 1948.

Bloomer, Amelia. Life and Writings of Amelia Bloomer, ed. Dexter C. Bloomer. 1895. Reprint, Boston: Arena Publishing Co.,1976.

Blum, Stella, ed. Fashion and Costumes from Godey's Lady's Book. New York: Dover, 1985.

Bremer, Fredrika. Two Visits to the North American Phalanx. 1858. Reprint, Philadelphia: Porcupine Press, 1975.

Brockett, Linus Pierpont. Woman's Work in the Civil War, a Record of Heroism, Patriotism and Patience. Philadelphia: Ziegler, McCurdy & Co., 1867.

———. *Woman: Her Rights, Wrongs, Privileges, and Responsibilities*. Hartford: L. Stebbins, 1869.

Brown, Paul. *Twelve Months in New Harmony*. 1827. Philadelphia: Porcupine Press, 1972.

Burgess, Lauren Cook, ed. *An Uncommon Soldier: The Civil War Letters of Sarah Rosetta Wakeman, alias Pvt. Lyons Wakeman, 153rd Regiment, New York State Volunteers, 1862–1864*. Pasadena, Md.: Minerva Center, 1994.

Clapp, Louise Amelia Knapp Smith. *The Shirley Letters from California Mines in 1851–52*. 1854–55. Reprint, San Francisco: Thomas C. Russell, 1922.

Clark, Uriah. *Plain Guide to Spiritualism. A Handbook*. Boston: William White & Co., 1863.

Codman, John. *Brook Farm*. Boston, 1844.

———. *Brook Farm: Historic and Personal Memoirs*. Boston: Arena Publishing Co., 1894.

Colt, Mrs. Miriam Davis. *Went to Kansas: Being a Thrilling Account of an Ill-Fated Expedition*. Watertown [N.Y.]: L. Ingalls & Co., 1862.

Cooley, Benjamin Franklin [?]. *Summary Exposition of the Social Theory of the Dissenters, Called Perfectionists*. Worcester: Printed for the Publisher, 1850.

Dixon, William H. *Spiritual Wives*. London: Hurst & Blackett, 1868.

Edmonds, S. Emma E. *Nurse and Spy in the Union Army*. Hartford: W. S. Williams & Co., 1865.

Ellis, John B. *Free Love and Its Votaries; or, American Socialism Unmasked*. San Francisco: A. L. Bancroft & Co., 1870.

Ellis, Havelock. *Studies in the Psychology of Sex: Sexual Inversion*. Philadelphia: F. A. Davis Co., 1908.

Exposé of the Conditions and Progress of the North American Phalanx: in Reply to the Inquiries of Horace Greeley, and in Answer to the Criticisms of Friends and Foes During the Past Year. The American Utopian Adventure, Series 2. 1853. Reprint, Philadelphia: Porcupine Press, 1975.

Farnsworth, Eva Olney. *The Art and Ethics of Dress: As Related to Efficiency and Economy*. San Francisco: Paul Elder & Co., 1915.

Ferris, Mrs. Benjamin G. *The Mormons at Home; With Some Incidents of Travel from Missouri to California, 1852–3*. New York: Dix & Edwards, 1856.

First Annual Report of the Oneida Association: Exhibiting Its History, Principles, and Transactions to January 1, 1849. Oneida Reserve: Leonard & Co., 1849.

Gage, Matilda Joslyn. *Who Planned the Tennessee Campaign of 1862? or Anna Ella Carroll vs. Ulysses S. Grant*. National Citizen Tract No. 1.

Grip's Historical Souvenir of Cortland. Cortland, N.Y.: Standard Press, 1899.

Guerin, Elsa Jane. *Mountain Charley or the Adventures of Mrs. E. J. Guerin, Who Was Thirteen Years in Male Attire*. 1861. Reprint, Norman: University of Oklahoma Press, 1968.

Hand-Book of the Oneida Community; With a Sketch of Its Founder, and an Outline of Its Constitution and Doctrine. Wallingford, Conn.: Office of *The Circular,* 1867.

Hand-Book of the Oneida Community; Containing a Brief Sketch of Its Present Condition, Internal Economy and Leading Principles, No. 2. New York: Oneida Community, 1871.

Hand-Book of the Oneida Community. New York: Office of Oneida *Circular,* 1875.

Hanoford, Phebe. *Daughters of America: Women of the Century Illustrated.* Augusta, Maine: True and Co., 1882.

Harland, Marion. *Eve's Daughters; or, Common Sense for Maid, Wife, and Mother.* New York: John R. Anderson & Henry S. Allen, 1882.

Hawthorne, Nathaniel. *The American Notebooks.* New Haven, Conn.: Yale University Press, 1932.

Holley, Marietta. *My Opinions and Betsey Bobbet's.* Hartford: American Publishing Co., 1873.

Jackson, James C. *American Womanhood: Its Peculiarities and Necessities.* Dansville, N.Y.: Austin, Jackson & Co., 1870.

———. *The Sexual Organism and Its Healthful Management.* 1861. Reprint, New York: Arno Press, 1974.

Jones, Mrs. M. M. *Woman's Dress; Its Moral and Physical Relations.* New York: Miller, Wood & Co., 1865.

Keatley, J. H. "Amelia Bloomer." *Annals of Iowa* 12 (July 1874): 190–94.

Lasser, Carol, and Marlene Deahl Merrill, eds. *Friends and Sisters: Letters between Lucy Stone and Antoinette Brown Blackwell, 1846–93* (Urbana: University of Illinois Press, 1987).

Lewis, Dio. *The New Gymnastics for Men, Women, and Children.* 10th ed. Boston: Fields, Osgood & Co., 1869.

———. *Our Girls.* New York: Harper & Brothers, 1871.

Logan, Olive Sikes. *Get Thee Behind Me, Satan! A Home-born Book of Home-truths.* New York: Adams, Victor & Co., 1872.

Mann, Horace. *A Few Thoughts of the Power and Duties of Woman, Two Lectures.* Syracuse, N.Y.: Hall, Mills & Co., 1853.

Merritt, Mrs. M. Angeline. *Dress Reform Practically and Physiologically Considered.* Buffalo: Jewett, Thomas and Co., 1852.

Moore, Madeline. *The Lady Lieutenant: The Strange and Thrilling Adventures of Miss Madeline Moore.* Philadelphia: Barclay & Co., 1862.

Mutual Criticism. Oneida, N.Y.: Office of the American Socialist, 1876, r.p. 1975.

Nichols, Dr. Thomas. *Forty Years of American Life,* Vol. 2. London: John Maxwell and Co., 1864.

Nordhoff, Charles. *The Communistic Societies of the United States: From Personal Visit and Observation.* 1875. Reprint, New York: Schocken Books, 1973.

Noyes, Corinna Ackley. *The Days of My Youth.* Kenwood, N.Y.: The Mansion, 1960.

Noyes, John Humphrey. *Dixon and His Copyists. A Criticism*. Published by the Oneida Community, 1874.

———. *History of American Socialisms*. Introduction by Mark Holloway. Philadelphia: J. B. Lippincott & Co., 1870.

———. *Home-Talks*. 1875. Reprint, New York: AMS Press, 1975.

———. *Male Continence; Self-Control in Sexual Intercourse*. Published by the Oneida Community, no date.

Noyes, Pierrepont. *My Father's House: An Oneida Boyhood*. New York: Farrar & Rinehart, 1937.

Oneida Community. *Bible Communism: A Compilation from the Annual Reports and Other Publications of the Oneida Association and Its Branches*. Brooklyn, N.Y.: Published at the Office of *The Circular*, 1853.

The Oneida Community: A Familiar Exposition of Its Ideas and Practical Life in a Conversation with a Visitor. Wallingford, Conn.: *The Circular* Office, 1865.

Orpen, Adela Elizabeth Richards. *Memories of the Old Emigrant Days in Kansas, 1862–1865*. New York: Harper & Brothers, 1928.

Orvis, Marianne Dwight. *Letters From Brook Farm, 1844–1847*. Poughkeepsie, N.Y.: Vassar College, 1928.

Owen, Robert Dale. *Threading My Way*. New York: G. W. Carleton & Co., 1874.

Pears, Thomas, ed. *New Harmony, An Adventure in Happiness: The Papers of Thomas and Sarah Pears*. Indianapolis: Indiana Historical Society, 1933.

Pfeiffer, Ida. *Lady's Second Journey Round the World*. New York: Harper & Brothers, 1856.

Phelps, Elizabeth Stuart. *What to Wear?* Boston: James R. Osgood and Co., 1873.

Progressive Annual for 1862, Comprising an Almanac, a Spiritualist Register, and a General Calender of Reform. New York: A. J. Davis, 1862.

Reade, Charles. *The Course of True Love Never Did Run Smooth*. London: Richard Bentley, 1857.

Rich, Jane Kinsley, ed. *A Lasting Spring: Jessie Catherine Kinsley, Daughter of the Oneida Community*. Syracuse, N.Y.: Syracuse University Press, 1983.

Robertson, Constance Noyes, ed. *Oneida Community: An Autobiography, 1851–1876*. Syracuse, N.Y.: Syracuse University Press, 1970.

Ruttenber, E. M., and L. H. Clark, eds. *History of Orange County, New York, with Illustrations and Biographical Sketches of Many of Its Pioneers and Prominent Men*. Philadelphia: Everts & Peck, 1881.

Shew, Joel, M.D. *The Water-Cure Manual; A Popular Work*. New York: Fowlers and Wells, 1850.

Shew, Mrs. M. L. *Water-Cure for Ladies*. New York: Wiley and Putnam, 1844.

Stanton, Elizabeth Cady. *Elizabeth Cady Stanton: As Revealed in Her Letters, Diary, and Reminiscences*. Theodore Stanton and Harriot Stanton Blatch, eds. New York: Harper & Brothers, 1922.

Stanton, Theodore, and Harriot Stanton Blatch, eds. *Elizabeth Cady Stanton*, 2 vols. 1922. Reprint, New York: Arno & The New York Times, 1969.

———. *Eighty Years and More (1815–1897)*. New York: European Publishing Co., 1898.

Stanton, Elizabeth Cady, Susan B. Anthony, and Matilda Joslyn Gage. *History of Woman Suffrage*, 2 vols. Rochester, N.Y.: Charles Mann, 1889.

Stephens, Kate. *Life at Laurel Town in Anglo-Saxon Kansas*. Lawrence: Alumni Association of the University of Kansas, 1920.

Strang, James. *The Book of the Law of the Lord*. N.d. Reprint, Burlington, Wis.: Voree Press, 1949.

Swisshelm, Jane Grey. *Half a Century*. 2d ed. Chicago: Jansen, McClung & Co., 1880.

Talmage, Rev. T. DeWitt. *Woman, Her Power and Privileges. A Series of Sermons*. New York: J. S. Ogilvie, 1888.

Tillotson, Mary E. *History ov the First Thirty-Five Years ov the Science Costume Movement in the United States of America*. Vineland, N.J.: Weekly Independent Book & Job Office, 1885.

———. *Progress vs. Fashion. An Essay on the Sanitary & Social Influences of Woman's Dress*. Vineland, N.J.: 1873.

Trall, R. T. *The Hydropathic Encyclopedia: A System of Hydropathy and Hygiene*. New York: Fowlers and Wells, 1853.

———. *Sexual Physiology: A Scientific and Popular Exposition*. 28th ed. New York: M. L. Holbrook, 1881.

Trollope, Anthony. *The Three Clerks*. London: John Long, 1903.

Trollope, Frances. *Domestic Manners of the Americans*. New York, 1894.

Walker, Mary E., M.D. *Hit*. New York: American News Co., 1871.

———. *Unmasked, or The Science of Immorality*. Philadelphia: Wm. H. Boyd, 1878.

Watson, Wingfield. *Prophetic Controversy No. 4: Mr. Strang Proved to Have Been Always an Honorable Man*. No publication information available; circa 1897.

White, Ellen G. *Manuscript Releases: From the Files of the Letters and Manuscripts Written by Ellen G. White*. Vol. 5. Silver Spring, Md.: E. G. White Estate, 1990.

———. *Testimonies for the Church*. Vol. 1: *Comprising Testimonies Numbers 1 to 14. With a Biographical Sketch of the Author*. 1864. Reprint. Mountain View, Calif.: Pacific Press Publishing Association, 1948.

———. *Testimonies for the Church*. Vol. 2: *Comprising Testimonies Numbers 15 to 20*. 1875–81. Reprint. Mountain View, Calif.: Pacific Press Publishing Association, 1948.

———. *Testimonies for the Church*. Vol. 4: *Compromising Testimonies Numbers 26 to 30*. 1875–81. Reprint, Mountain View, Calif.: Pacific Press Publishing Association, 1948.

Velazquez, Loreta Janeta. *The Woman in Battle: A Narrative of the Exploits, Adventures, and Travels of Madame Loreta Janeta Velazquez, Otherwise Known as Lieutenant Harry T. Buford, Confederate States Army,* ed. C. J. Worthington. Hartford: T. Belknap, 1876.

Woolson, Abba Goold, ed. *Dress Reform: A Series of Lectures Delivered in Boston, on Dress as It Affects the Health of Women.* Boston: Roberts Brothers, 1874.

Worden, Harriet M. *Old Mansion House Memories by One Brought Up in It.* Kenwood, Oneida, N.Y., 1950.

Secondary Sources

BOOKS AND DISSERTATIONS

Abzug, Robert H. *Cosmos Crumbling: American Reform and the Religious Imagination.* New York: Oxford University Press, 1994.

Ainsworth, Dorothy S. *The History of Physical Education in Colleges for Women.* New York: A. S. Barnes and Co., 1930.

Albanese, Catherine L. *Nature Religion in America: From the Algonkian Indians to the New Age.* Chicago: University of Chicago Press, 1990.

Angle, Paul M. *A Pictorial History of the Civil War Years.* Garden City, N.Y.: Doubleday, 1967.

Anthony, Katherine. *Susan B. Anthony: Her Personal History and Her Era.* Garden City, N.Y.: Doubleday, 1954.

Arnold, Janet. *Patterns of Fashion: Englishwomen's Dresses and Their Construction, c. 1660–1860.* New York: Drama Book, 1964.

———. *Patterns of Fashion: Englishwomen's Dresses and Their Construction, c. 1860–1940.* New York: Drama Book, 1966.

Banner, Lois. *American Beauty.* Chicago: University of Chicago Press, 1983.

———. *Elizabeth Cady Stanton: A Radical for Woman's Rights.* Boston: Little, Brown and Co., 1980.

Barry, Kathleen. *Susan B. Anthony: A Biography of a Singular Feminist.* New York: Ballantine Books, 1988.

Barthel, Diane L. *Amana: From Pietist Sect to American Community.* Lincoln: University of Nebraska Press, 1984.

Barton, Lucy. *Historic Costume for the Stage.* Boston: Walter H. Baker Co., 1963.

Batterberry, Michael, and Ariane Batterberry. *Fashion: The Mirror of History.* New York: Greenwich House, 1977.

Behnke, Donna A. *Religious Issues in Nineteenth Century Feminism.* Troy, N.Y.: Whitston Publishing Co., 1982.

Berg, Barbara J. *The Remembered Gate: Origins of American Feminism.* New York: Oxford University Press, 1978.

Binder, Pearl. *Muffs and Morals*. New York: William Morrow and Co., n.d.

Birney, Catherine N. *The Grimke Sisters. Sarah and Angelina Grimke*. Boston: Lee and Shepard, 1885.

Black, J. Anderson, and Madge Garland. *A History of Fashion*. New York: William Morrow and Co., 1980.

Blackwell, Alice Stone. *Lucy Stone: Pioneer Woman Suffragist*. Norwood, Mass.: Plimpton Press, 1930.

Blair, Karen J. *The Clubwoman as Feminist: True Womanhood Redefined, 1868–1914*. New York: Holmes & Meier, 1980.

Bledstein, Burton J. *The Culture of Professionalism: The Middle Class and the Development of Higher Education in America*. New York: W. W. Norton & Co., 1978.

Boynton, Bonnie Veazey. "The Relationship between Women's Rights Movements and Fashion Changes." Master's thesis, Florida State University, 1974.

Brandon, Ruth. *Singer and the Sewing Machine: A Capitalist Romance*. London: Barrie & Jenkins, 1977.

Braude, Ann. *Radical Spirits: Spiritualism and Women's Rights in Nineteenth Century America*. Boston: Beacon Press, 1989.

Breward, Christopher. *The Culture of Fashion: A New History of Fashionable Dress*. Manchester: Manchester University Press, 1995.

Brown, Dee. *The Gentle Tamers: Women of the Old Wild West*. Lincoln: University of Nebraska Press, 1968.

———. *Wondrous Times on the Frontier*. Little Rock, Ark.: August House, 1991.

Brunnell, A. O. *Dansville; Historical, Biographical, Descriptive*. Dansville, N.Y.: Instructor Publishing Co., 1902?

Bull, Malcolm, and Keith Lockhart. *Seeking a Sanctuary: Seventh-day Adventism and the American Dream*. San Francisco: Harper & Row, 1989.

Bullough, Vern L. *Sexual Variance in Society and History*. New York: John Wiley & Sons, 1976.

Bullough, Vern L., and Bonnie Bullough. *Cross Dressing, Sex, and Gender*. Philadelphia: University of Pennsylvania Press, 1993.

Bunker, Gary L., and Davis Bitton. *The Mormon Graphic Image, 1834–1914: Cartoons, Caricatures, and Illustrations*. Salt Lake City: University of Utah Press, 1983.

Byrde, Penelope. *The Male Image: Men's Fashion in Britain 1300–1970*. London: B. T. Batsford, 1979.

Cable, Mary. *The Little Darlings: A History of Child Rearing in America*. New York: Charles Scribner's Sons, 1972.

Cahn, Susan K. *Coming On Strong: Gender and Sexuality in Twentieth-Century Women's Sport*. Cambridge, Mass: Harvard University Press, 1994.

Calvert, Karin. *Children in the House: The Material Culture of Early Childhood, 1600–1900*. Boston: Northeastern University Press, 1992.

Campbell, Henry Colin. *Wisconsin in Three Centuries, 1634–1905*. New York: Century History Co., 1906.

Carden, Maren Lockwood. *Oneida: Utopian Community to Modern Corporation*. New York: Harper & Row, 1969.

Carson, Gerald. *Cornflake Crusade*. New York: Rinehart & Co., 1957.

Cayleff, Susan E. *Wash and Be Healed: The Water-Cure Movement and Women's Health*. Philadelphia: Temple University Press, 1987.

Chafe, William H. *Women and Equality*. New York: Oxford University Press, 1977.

Clayton, Ruth Vickers. "Clothing and the Temporal Kingdom: Mormon Clothing Practices, 1847 to 1887." Ph.D. dissertation: Purdue University, 1987.

Clinton, Catherine. *The Other Civil War: American Women in the Nineteenth Century*. New York: Hill and Wang, 1984.

Cogan, Frances B. *All-American Girl: The Ideal of Real Womanhood in Mid-Nineteenth-Century America*. Athens: University of Georgia Press, 1989.

Commanger, Henry Steele. *The Era of Reform, 1830–1860*. Princeton, N.J.: D. Van Nostrand Co., 1960.

Conklin, William D., compiler. *The Jackson Health Resort: Pioneer in Its Field: As Seen by Those Who Knew It Well*. Dansville, N.Y.: 1971.

Coon, Anne C., ed. *Hear Me Patiently: The Reform Speeches of Amelia Jenks Bloomer*. Westport, Conn.: Greenwood Press, 1994.

Cooper, Grace Rogers. *The Sewing Machine: Its Invention and Development*. Washington, D.C.: Smithsonian Institution Press, 1976.

Craik, Jennifer. *The Face of Fashion: Cultural Studies in Fashion*. New York: Routledge, 1994.

Credle, Mariotte James. "The Effect of Woman's Club Activity on the Dress Reform Movement of the Late Nineteenth Century." Master's thesis, University of North Carolina at Greensboro, 1984.

Cross, Whitney R. *The Burned-over District: The Social and Intellectual History of Enthusiastic Religion in Western New York, 1800–1850*. New York: Harper & Row, 1950.

Croutier, Alev Lytle. *Harem: The World behind the Veil*. New York: Abbeville Press, 1989.

Cunnington, C. Willett, and Phillis Cunnington. *History of Underclothes*. London: Michael Joseph, 1951.

Cunnington, Phillis. *Costume in Pictures*. London: Herbert Press, 1964.

Cunnington, Phillis, and Anne Buck. *Children's Costume in England: From the Fourteenth to the End of the Nineteenth Century*. London: Adam & Charles Black, 1978.

Cunnington, Phillis, and Alan Mansfield. *English Costume for Sports and Outdoor Recreation from the Sixteenth to the Nineteenth Centuries*. New York: Barnes and Noble, 1969.

Dalsimer, Marlyn Hartzell. "Women and Family in the Oneida Community, 1837–1881." Ph.D. dissertation, New York University, 1975.

Dannett, Sylvia G. L. *She Rode with the Generals: The True and Incredible Story of Sarah Emma Seelye, Alias Franklin Thompson*. New York: Thomas Nelson and Sons, 1960.

Davis, David Brion, ed. *Ante-bellum Reform*. New York: Harper & Row, 1967.

De Grave, Kathleen. *Swindler, Spy, Rebel: The Confidence Woman in Nineteenth-Century America*. Columbia: University of Missouri Press, 1995.

de Marly, Diana. *Dress in North America: Vol. 1, The New World, 1492–1800*. New York: Holmes & Meier, 1990.

———. *Fashion for Men: An Illustrated History*. New York: Holmes & Meier, 1985.

———. *The History of Haute Couture, 1850–1950*. London: B.T. Batsford, 1990.

DeMaria, Richard. *Communal Love at Oneida: A Perfectionist Vision of Authority, Property and Sexual Order*. New York: Edwin Mellon Press, 1978.

Devor, Holly. *Gender Blending: Confronting the Limits of Duality*. Bloomington: Indiana University Press, 1989.

Dickson, Carol Anne. "Patterns for Garments: A History of the Paper Garment Pattern Industry in America to 1976." Ph.D. dissertation, Ohio State University, 1979.

Donegan, Jane B. *"Hydropathic Highway to Health": Women and the Water-Cure in Antebellum America*. New York: Greenwood Press, 1986.

Douglas, Ann. *The Feminization of American Culture*. New York: Alfred A. Knopf, 1977.

DuBois, Ellen Carol. *Feminism and Suffrage: The Emergence of an Independent Women's Movement in America, 1848–1869*. Ithaca, N.Y.: Cornell University Press, 1978.

Earle, Alice Morse. *Two Centuries of Costume in America, MDCXX–MDCCCXX*, vol 2. New York: Benjamin Blom, 1903; r.p. 1968.

Edmonds, Walter D. *The First Hundred Years, 1848–1948*. New York: Oneida Ltd., 1948.

Epler, Percy H. *The Life of Clara Barton*. New York: Macmillan, 1917.

Epstein, Julia, and Kristina Straub. *Body Guards: The Cultural Politics of Gender Ambiguity*. New York: Routledge, 1991.

Estlake, Allan. *The Oneida Community*. London: George Redway, 1900.

Ewing, Elizabeth. *History of Children's Costume*. London: B. T. Batsford, 1977.

———. *Underwear: A History*. New York: Theatre Arts Books, 1972.

Feightner, Mia Mae. "Clothing and Accessories Available to Pioneers of Southern Indiana, 1816–1830." Master's thesis, Iowa State University at Ames, 1977.

Finley, Ruth E. *The Lady of Godey's: Sarah Josepha Hale*. Philadelphia: J. B. Lippincott Co., 1931.

Fitzpatrick, Doyle C. *The King Strang Story: A Vindication of James J. Strang, the Beaver Island Mormon*. Lansing, Mich.: National Heritage, 1970.

Fogarty, Robert S. *All Things New: American Communes and Utopian Movements 1860–1914*. Chicago: University of Chicago Press, 1990.

———. *American Utopianism*. Itasca, Ill.: F. E. Peacock, 1972.

———, ed. *Special Love/Special Sex: An Oneida Community Diary*. Syracuse, N.Y.: Syracuse University Press, 1994.

Foster, Lawrence. *Religion and Sexuality: The Shakers, the Mormons, and the Oneida Community*. Urbana: University of Illinois Press, 1984.

———. *Women, Family, and Utopia: Communal Experiments of the Shakers, the Oneida Community, and the Mormons*. Syracuse, N.Y.: Syracuse University Press, 1991.

Frothingham, Octavius Brooks. *Gerrit Smith: A Biography*. New York: G. P. Putnam's Sons, 1879.

The Gallery of English Costume: Costume for Sport. Published for the Art Galleries Committee of the Corporation of Manchester, 1963.

Garber, Marjorie. *Vested Interests: Cross-Dressing & Cultural Anxiety*. New York: Routledge, 1992.

Gates, Susa Young. *The Life Story of Brigham Young*. New York: Macmillan, 1930.

Gattey, Charles Neilson. *The Bloomer Girls*. New York: Coward-McCann, 1967.

Ginzberg, Lori D. *Women and the Work of Benevolence: Morality, Politics, and Class in the 19th-Century United States*. New Haven, Conn.: Yale University Press, 1990.

Gordon, Beverly. *Shaker Textile Arts*. Hanover, N.H.: University Press of New England with the Cooperation of the Merrimack Valley Textile Museum and Shaker Community, Inc., 1980.

Graham, Abbie. *Ladies in Revolt*. New York: Womans Press, 1934.

Graham, Roy E. *Ellen G. White: Co-Founder of the Seventh-day Adventist Church*. New York: Peter Lang, 1985.

Graham-Brown, Sarah. *Images of Women: The Portrayal of Women in Photography of the Middle East 1860–1950*. New York: Columbia University Press, 1988.

Graybill, Ronald D. "The Power of Prophecy: Ellen G. White and the Women Religious Founders of the Nineteenth Century." Ph.D. dissertation, Johns Hopkins University, 1983.

Griffith, Elisabeth. *In Her Own Right: The Life of Elizabeth Cady Stanton*. New York: Oxford University Press, 1984.

Grossbard, Judy. "Style Changes in American Women's Sportswear from 1881–1910." Ph.D. dissertation, Florida State University, 1990.

Guttmann, Allen. *Women's Sports: A History*. New York: Columbia University Press, 1991.

Hall, Carrie A. *From Hoopskirts to Nudity*. Caldwell, Idaho: Caxton Printers, 1946.

Hall, Lee. *Common Threads: A Parade of American Clothing*. Boston: Little, Brown and Co., 1992.

Hall, Richard. *Patriots in Disguise: Women Warriors of the Civil War*. New York: Paragon House, 1993.

Haller, John S., and Robin M. Haller. *The Physician and Sexuality in Victorian America*. Chicago: University of Illinois Press, 1974.

Halttunen, Karen. *Confidence Men and Painted Women: A Study of Middle-Class Culture in America, 1830–1870*. New Haven, Conn.: Yale University Press, 1982.

Hansen, Karen V. *A Very Social Time: Crafting Community in Antebellum New England*. Berkeley: University of California Press, 1996.

Haraszti, Zoltan. *The Idyll of Brook Farm*. Boston: Published by the Trustees of the Public Library, n.d..

Harlow, Ralph Volney. *Gerrit Smith: Philanthropist and Reformer*. New York: Henry Holt and Co., 1939.

Harper, Ida Husted. *The Life and Work of Susan B. Anthony*. Vol. 1. 1889. Reprint, New York: Arno, 1969.

Hawthorne, Rosemary. *Oh . . . Knickers! A Brief History of "Unmentionables."* London: Bachman & Turner, 1985.

Hayden, Dolores. *Seven American Utopias: The Architecture of Communitarian Socialism, 1790–1975*. Cambridge, Mass.: MIT Press, 1976.

Hedden, Worth Tuttle. *Wives of High Pasture*. Garden City, N.Y.: Doubleday, Doran & Co., 1944.

Helvenston, Sally Ingrid. "Feminine Response to a Frontier Environment as Reflected in the Clothing of Kansas Women: 1854–1895." Ph.D. dissertation, Kansas State University, 1985.

Henshaw, Betty Lou. "The Bloomer Costume: The Women's Dress Reform Movement of the 1850's." Master's thesis, University of Colorado, 1955.

Hersh, Blanche Glassman. "The Slavery of Sex: Feminist-Abolitionists in Nineteenth Century America." Ph.D. dissertation, University of Illinois at Chicago Circle, 1975.

Hewitt, Nancy A. *Women's Activism and Social Change: Rochester, New York 1822–1872*. Ithaca, N.Y.: Cornell University Press, 1984.

Hinds, William Alfred. *American Communities and Co-operative Colonies*. Chicago: Charles H. Kerr & Co., 1908.

Hine, Robert V. *California's Utopian Colonies*. San Marino, Calif.: Huntington Library, 1953.

Hoffert, Sylvia D. *When Hens Crow: The Woman's Rights Movement in Antebellum America*. Bloomington: Indiana University Press, 1995.

Holbrook, Stewart H. *Dreamers of the American Dream*. Garden City, N.Y.: Doubleday, 1957.

Hollander, Anne. *Seeing through Clothes*. New York: Avon Books, 1978.

———. *Sex and Suits: The Evolution of Modern Dress*. New York: Alfred A. Knopf, 1994.

Holloway, Mark. *Heavens on Earth: Utopian Communities in America 1680–1880*. London: Turnstile Press, 1951.

Hotchkiss, Valerie R. *Clothes Make the Man: Female Cross Dressing in Medieval Europe*. New York: Garland, 1996.

James, Edward T., Janet Wilson James, and Paul S. Boyer, eds. *Notable American Women, 1607–1950: A Biographical Dictionary*. Vol. 2. Cambridge, Mass.: Belknap Press of Harvard University, 1971.

Jeffrey, Julie Roy. *Frontier Women: The Trans-Mississippi West, 1840–1880*. New York: Hill and Wang, 1979.

Joseph, Nathan. *Uniforms and Nonuniforms: Communication through Clothing*. New York: Greenwood Press, 1986.

Kaplan, Joel H. and Sheila Stowell. *Theatre and Fashion: Oscar Wilde to the Suffragettes*. Cambridge: Cambridge University Press, 1994.

Kartchner, Grace Joan. "Dresses of Mormon Girls, Ages One to Twelve, in the Great Salt Lake and Utah Valleys from 1847 to 1896." Master's thesis, Oregon State University, 1975.

Kemper, Rachel H. *Costume*. New York: Newsweek Books, 1977.

Kephart, William M. *Extraordinary Groups: The Sociology of Unconventional Lifestyles*. New York: St. Martin's Press, 1976.

Kern, Louis J. *An Ordered Love: Sex Roles and Sexuality in Victorian Utopias — the Shakers, the Mormons, and the Oneida Community*. Chapel Hill: University of North Carolina, 1981.

Kerr, Andrea Moore. *Lucy Stone: Speaking Out for Equality*. New Brunswick, N.J.: Rutgers University Press, 1992.

Kidwell, Claudia B. *Cutting a Fashionable Fit*. Washington, D.C.: Smithsonian Institution Press, 1979.

Kidwell, Claudia Brush, and Valerie Steele, eds. *Men and Women: Dressing the Part*. Washington, D.C.: Smithsonian Institution Press, 1989.

Klaw, Spencer. *Without Sin: The Life and Death of the Oneida Community*. New York: Penguin Press, 1993.

Kolmerten, Carol A. *Women in Utopia: The Ideology of Gender in the American Owenite Communities*. Bloomington: Indiana University Press, 1990.

Kriebl, Karen Joyce. "From Bloomers to Flappers: The American Women's Dress Reform Movement, 1840–1920." Ph.D. dissertation, Ohio State University, 1998.

Kunciov, Robert, ed. *Mr. Godey's Ladies: Being a Mosaic of Fashions & Fancies*. Princeton, N.J.: Pyne Press, 1971.

Kunzle, David. *Fashion and Fetishism: A Social History of the Corset, Tight-Lacing and Other Forms of Body-Sculpture in the West*. Totowa, N.J.: Rowman and Littlefield, 1982.

Larson, Joyce Marie. "Clothing of Pioneer Women of Dakota Territory, 1861–1889." Master's thesis, South Dakota State University, 1978.

Land, Gary, ed. *Adventism in America*. Grand Rapids, Mich.: William B. Eerdmans Publishing Co., 1986.

Lauer, Jeanette C., and Robert H. Lauer. *Fashion Power: The Meaning of Fashion in American Society*. Englewood Cliffs, N.J.: Prentice-Hall, 1981.

Laver, James. *Clothes*. London: Burke Publishing Co., 1952.

———. *A Concise History of Costume*. London: Thames and Hudson, 1969.

———. *Modesty in Dress*. London: William Heinemann, 1969.

Leach, William. *True Love and Perfect Union: The Feminist Reform of Sex and Society*. New York: Basic Books, 1982.

LeCompte, Mary Lou. *Cowgirls of the Rodeo: Pioneer Professional Athletes*. Urbana: University of Illinois Press, 1993.

Lee, Mabel. *Memories of a Bloomer Girl (1894–1924)*. American Alliance for Health, Physical Education, and Recreation, 1977.

Leonard, Elizabeth D. *Yankee Women: Gender Battles in the Civil War*. New York: W. W. Norton, 1994.

Leslie, Judith Elaine. "Sports Fashions as a Reflection of the Changing Role of American Women in Society from 1850 to 1920." Ph.D. dissertation, University of North Carolina at Greensboro, 1985.

Linden, Ingemar. *The Last Trump: An Historico-genetical Study of Some Important Chapters in the Making and Development of the Seventh-day Adventist Church*. Las Vegas, Nev.: Peter Lang, 1978.

Lipovetsky, Gilles. *The Empire of Fashion: Dressing Modern Democracy*. Catherine Porter, trans. Princeton, N.J.: Princeton University Press, 1994.

Lockwood, George B. *The New Harmony Movement*. 1905. Reprint, New York: Augustus M. Kelley, 1970.

Lott, Eric. *Love and Theft: Blackface Minstrelsy and the American Working Class*. New York: Oxford University Press, 1993.

Lumpkin, Katharine Du Pre. *The Emancipation of Angelina Grimké*. Chapel Hill: University of North Carolina Press, 1974.

Lutz, Alma. *Susan B. Anthony: Rebel, Crusader, Humanitarian*. Boston: Beacon Press, 1960.

Mabro, Judy. *Veiled Half-Truths: Western Travellers' Perceptions of Middle Eastern Women*. New York: I.B. Tauris & Co., 1991.

McMartin, Maria Barbara. "Dress of the Oregon Trail Emigrants: 1843 to 1855." Master's thesis, Iowa State University at Ames, 1977.

Mandelker, Ira L. *Religion, Society, and Utopia in Nineteenth Century America*. Amherst: University of Massachusetts Press, 1984.

Marks, Patricia. *Bicycles, Bangs, and Bloomers: The New Woman in the Popular Press*. Lexington: University Press of Kentucky, 1990.

Maynard, Margaret. *Fashioned from Penury: Dress as Cultural Practice in Colonial Australia*. New York: Cambridge University Press, 1994.

Melder, Keith E. *Beginnings of Sisterhood: The American Woman's Rights Movement, 1800–1850*. New York: Schocken Books, 1977.

Melman, Billie. *Women's Orients: English Women and the Middle East, 1718–1918: Sexuality, Religion and Work*. New York: Macmillan, 1992.

Merrill, Arch. *Bloomers and Bugles*. New York: American Book–Stratford Press, Inc., 1958.

Meyer, Donald. *The Positive Thinkers: A Study of the American Quest for Health, Wealth and Personal Power from Mary Baker Eddy to Norman Vincent Peale*. Garden City, N.Y.: Doubleday, 1965.

Mintz, Steven. *Moralists and Modernizers: America's Pre–Civil War Reformers*. Baltimore: Johns Hopkins University Press, 1995.

Morantz-Sanchez, Regina. *Sympathy and Science: Women Physicians in American Medicine*. New York: Oxford University Press, 1985.

Mott, Frank Luther. *A History of American Magazines, 1850–1865*. Cambridge, Mass.: Harvard University Press, 1938.

———. *A History of American Magazines, 1741–1850*. Cambridge, Mass.: Harvard University Press, 1957.

———. *A History of American Magazines, 1885–1905*. Cambridge, Mass.: Harvard University Press, 1957.

Murphy, Lamar Riley. *Enter the Physician: The Transformation of Domestic Medicine, 1760–1860*. Tuscaloosa: University of Alabama Press, 1991.

Myres, Sandra L. *Westering Women and the Frontier Experience 1800–1915*. Albuquerque: University of New Mexico Press, 1982.

Newell, Linda King, and Valeen Tippetts Avery. *Mormon Enigma: Emma Hale Smith*. Garden City, N.Y.: Doubleday, 1984.

Newton, Stella Mary. *Health, Art & Reason: Dress Reformers of the 19th Century*. London: John Murray, 1974.

Nichol, Francis D. *Ellen G. White and Her Critics*. Tacoma Park, Washington, D.C.: Review and Herald Publishing Association, 1951.

Nissenbaum, Stephen. *Sex, Diet, and Debility in Jacksonian America: Sylvester Graham and Health Reform*. Westport, Conn.: Greenwood Press, 1980.

Noun, Louise R. *Strong Minded Women: The Emergence of the Woman-Suffrage Movement in Iowa*. Ames: Iowa State University Press, 1969.

Numbers, Ronald L. *Prophetess of Health: A Study of Ellen G. White*. New York: Harper & Row, 1976.

———. *Prophetess of Health: Ellen G. White and the Origins of Seventh-day Adventist Health Reform*. Knoxville: University of Tennessee Press, 1992.

Nye, R. B. *A Baker's Dozen: Thirteen Unusual Americans*. East Lansing: Michigan State University Press, 1956.

Ortner, Sherry B., and Harriet Whitehead. *Sexual Meanings: The Cultural Construction of Gender and Sexuality*. New York: Cambridge University Press, 1981.

Oved, Yaacov. *Two Hundred Years of American Communes*. New Brunswick, N.J.: Transaction Books, 1988.

Parker, Gail, ed. *The Oven Birds*. New York: Doubleday, 1972.

Parker, Robert Allerton. *A Yankee Saint: John Humphrey Noyes and the Oneida Community*. New York: G. P. Putnam's Sons, 1935.

Parsons, Frank Alvah. *The Art of Dress*. New York: Doubleday, Doran & Co., 1928.

Pattee, Fred Lewis. *The Feminine Fifties*. New York: D. Appleton-Century Co., 1940.

Perkins, William Rufus, and Barthinius L. Wick. *History of the Amana Society or Community of True Inspiration*. Iowa City: Published by the University, 1891.

Powell, Mary Ann. "Ladies With Legs: An Historical Survey of the Social Acceptability of Pants on Women, 1851–1976." Master's thesis, University of Texas at Austin, 1977.

Procter-Smith, Marjorie. *Women in Shaker Community and Worship: A Feminist Analysis of the Uses of Religious Symbolism*. Lewiston, N.Y.: Edwin Mellen Press, 1985.

Pryor, Elizabeth Brown. *Clara Barton: Professional Angel*. Philadelphia: University of Pennsylvania Press, 1987.

Quaife, Milo Milton. *The Kingdom of Saint James: A Narrative of the Mormons*. New Haven, Conn.: Yale University Press, 1930.

Radcliffe, Pamela M. "Pre-Raphaelite Influences on Women's Dress in the Victorian Era." Ph.D. dissertation, Florida State University, 1990.

The Radical Women's Press of the 1850s. Ann Russo and Cheris Kramarae, eds. New York: Routledge, 1991.

Reid, George W. *A Sound of Trumpets: Americans, Adventists, and Health Reform*. Washington, D.C.: Review and Herald Publishing Association, 1982.

Ribeiro, Aileen. *Dress and Morality*. New York: Holmes & Meier, 1986.

Riegel, Oscar Wetherhold. *Crown of Glory: The Life of James J. Strang, Moses of the Mormons*. New Haven, Conn.: Yale University Press, 1935.

Riegel, Robert E. *American Feminists*. Lawrence: University of Kansas Press, 1963.

Riley, Glenda. *The Female Frontier: A Comparative View of Women on the Prairie and the Plains*. Lawrence: University Press of Kansas, 1988.

Roberts, B. H. *A Comprehensive History of the Church of Jesus Christ of Latter-day Saints, Century I*. Salt Lake City: Deseret News Press, 1930.

Robertson, Constance Noyes. *Oneida Community Profiles*. Syracuse, N.Y.: Syracuse University Press, 1977.

———. *Oneida Community: The Breakup, 1876–1881*. Syracuse, N.Y.: Syracuse University Press, 1972.

Robertson, Janet. *The Magnificent Mountain Women: Adventures in the Colorado Rockies*. Lincoln: University of Nebraska Press, 1990.

Robinson, Dores Eugene. *The Story of Our Health Message*. 1943. Reprint, Nashville: Southern Publishing Association, 1955.

Roche, Daniel. *The Culture of Clothing: Dress and Fashion in the 'Ancien Regime'*. Jean Birrell, trans. New York: Cambridge University Press, 1994.

Rose, Clare. *Children's Clothes since 1750*. London: B. T. Batsford, 1989.

Rose, June. *The Drawings of John Leech*. London: Art and Technic, 1950.

Rosencranz, Mary Lou. *Clothing Concepts: A Social Psychological Approach*. New York: Macmillan, 1972.

Rudofsky, Bernard. *Are Clothes Modern?* Chicago: Paul Theobald, 1947.

Ryan, Mary P. *Cradle of the Middle Class: The Family in Oneida County, New York, 1790–1865*. Cambridge: Cambridge University Press, 1981.

———. *Women in Public: Between Banners and Ballots, 1825–1880*. Baltimore: Johns Hopkins University Press, 1990.

Said, Edward. *Orientalism*. New York: Vintage Books, 1979.

Saxon, Mary Kathleen. "Aesthetic Dress of the Nineteenth Century: Principles and Practices." Master's thesis, University of Texas at Austin, 1981.

Schlissel, Lillian, Byrd Gibbens, and Elizabeth Hampsten. *Far from Home: Families of the Westward Journey*. New York: Schocken Books, 1989.

Scott, Anne Firor. *Natural Allies: Women's Associations in American History*. Urbana: University of Illinois Press, 1992.

Sears, Hal D. *The Sex Radicals*. Lawrence: Regents Press of Kansas, 1977.

Shryock, Richard Harrison. *Medicine in America: Historical Essays*. Baltimore: Johns Hopkins University Press, 1966.

Sklar, Kathryn Kish. *Catherine Beecher: A Study in American Domesticity*. New York: W. W. Norton & Co., 1976.

Smith, Barbara Clark, and Kathy Peiss. *Men and Women: A History of Costume, Gender, and Power*. Washington, D.C.: National Museum of American History, 1989.

Smith-Rosenberg, Carroll. *Disorderly Conduct: Visions of Gender in Victorian America*. New York: Alfred A. Knopf, 1985.

Snyder, Charles McCool. *Oswego: From Buckskin to Bustles*. Port Washington, N.Y.: Ira J. Friedman, 1968.

———. *Dr. Mary Walker: The Little Lady in Pants*. New York: Arno Press, 1974.

Sokolow, Jayme A. *Eros and Modernization: Sylvester Graham, Health Reform, and the Origins of Victorian Sexuality in America*. Rutherford, N.J.: Fairleigh Dickinson University Press, 1983.

Sontag, Susan. *Illness as Metaphor*. New York: Vintage Books, 1979.

Spalding, Arthur Whitefield. *Origin and History of Seventh-day Adventists*. Vol. 1. Washington, D.C.: Review and Herald Publishing Association, 1961.

Spencer, Clarissa Young with Mabel Harmer. *Brigham Young at Home*. 1940. Reprint, Salt Lake City: Deseret Book Co., 1972.

Spurlock, John C. *Free Love: Marriage and Middle-Class Radicalism in America, 1825–1860*. New York: New York University Press, 1988.

Staples, Shirley. *Male-Female Comedy Teams in American Vaudeville, 1865–1932*. Ann Arbor, Mich.: UMI Research Press, 1984.

Starr, Paul. *The Social Transformation of American Medicine*. New York: Basic Books, 1982.

Steele, Valerie. *Fashion and Eroticism*. New York: Oxford University Press, 1985.

———. *Paris Fashion: A Cultural History*. New York: Oxford University Press, 1988.

Stoehr, Taylor. *Free Love in America: A Documentary History*. New York: AMS Press, 1979.

Stratton, Joanna L. *Pioneer Women: Voices from the Kansas Frontier*. New York: Simon and Schuster, 1981.

Strouse, Jean. *Alice James: A Biography*. Boston: Houghton Mifflin Co., 1980.

Symes, Lillian, and Travers Clement. *Rebel America*. New York: Harper & Brothers, 1934.

Tarrant, Naomi E. A. *The Rise and Fall of the Sleeve, 1825–1840*. [Edinburgh] Royal Scottish Museum, 1983.

Taylor, Anne. *Visions of Harmony: A Study in Nineteenth-Century Millenarianism*. Oxford: Clarendon Press, 1987.

Temin, Peter. *The Jacksonian Economy*. New York: W. W. Norton & Co., 1969.

Thom, W. DeCourcy. *A Brief History of Panics and Their Periodical Occurrence in the United States,* 3d ed. New York: August M. Kelley, 1966.

Thomas, Robert David. *The Man Who Would Be Perfect: John Humphrey Noyes and the Utopian Impulse*. N.p.: University of Pennsylvania Press, 1977.

Thompson, C. J. S. *The Mysteries of Sex: Women Who Posed as Men and Men Who Impersonated Women*. New York: Causeway Books, 1974.

The Traverse Region, Historical and Descriptive, with Illustrations of Scenery and Portraits and Biographical Sketches of Some of Its Prominent Men and Pioneers. Chicago: H. R. Page & Co., 1884.

Tseelon, Efrat. *The Masque of Femininity: The Presentation of Woman in Everyday Life*. London: Sage Publications, 1995.

Twelves, Valerie. "An Investigation of the Impact of the Dress Reform Movement: A Case Study of Reform Movements in the Years 1890 to 1920." Master's thesis, Cornell University, 1969.

Tyler, Alice Felt. *Freedom's Ferment: Phases of American Social History from the Colonial Period to the Outbreak of the Civil War.* New York: Harper & Row, 1944.

Utley, Henry Munson, and Byron M. Cutcheon. *Michigan: As a Province, Territory and State, the Twenty-Sixth Member of the Federal Union.* Publishing Society of Michigan, 1906.

Van Noord, Roger. *King of Beaver Island: The Life and Assassination of James Jesse Strang.* Urbana: University of Illinois Press, 1988.

Verbrugge, Martha H. *Able-Bodied Womanhood: Personal Health and Social Change in Nineteenth-Century Boston.* New York: Oxford University Press, 1988.

Walsh, Mary Roth. *"Doctors Wanted: No Women Need Apply": Sexual Barriers in the Medical Profession, 1835–1975.* New Haven, Conn.: Yale University Press, 1977.

Walters, Ronald G. *American Reformers, 1815–1860.* New York: Hill and Wang, 1978.

Watts, Margaret Woodson. "The Evolution of Pants as an Outerwear Garment for Women." Master's thesis: University of Missouri, Columbia, 1969.

Waugh, Norah. *Corsets and Crinolines.* New York: Theatre Arts Books, 1981.

———. *The Cut of Men's Clothes, 1600–1900.* New York: Theatre Arts Books, 1964.

———. *The Cut of Women's Clothes, 1600–1930.* New York: Theatre Arts Books, 1968.

Webber, Everett. *Escape to Utopia: The Communal Movement in America.* New York: Hastings House, 1959.

Weimann, Jeanne Madeline. *The Fair Women: The Story of the Woman's Building, World's Columbian Exposition, Chicago 1893.* Chicago: Academy Chicago, 1981.

Weinberg, Arthur, and Lila Weinberg. *Passport to Utopia: Great Panaceas in American History.* Chicago: Quadrangle Books, 1968.

Weiss, Harry B., and Howard R. Kemble. *The Great American Water-Cure Craze.* Trenton: Post Times Press, 1967.

Welch, Paula D., and Harold A. Lerch. *History of American Physical Education and Sport.* Springfield, Ill.: Charles C. Thomas, 1981.

Wheelwright, Julie. *Amazons and Military Maids: Women Who Dressed as Men in Pursuit of Life, Liberty and Happiness.* Boston: Pandora Press, 1989.

White, Arthur L. *Ellen G. White: The Early Years:* Vol. 1, *1827–1862.* Washington, D.C.: Review and Herald Publishing Association, 1985.

———. *Ellen G. White: The Progressive Years:* Vol. 2, *1863–1875.* Washington, D.C.: Review and Herald Publishing Association, 1986.

———. *Ellen G. White: The Australian Years,* Vol. 4, *1891–1900.* Washington, D.C.: Review and Herald Publishing Association, 1983.

White, Eugene, ed. *Crashes and Panics: The Lessons from History*. Homewood, Ill.: Dow Jones–Irwin, 1990.

Whitman, Alden, ed. *American Reformers*. New York: H. W. Wilson, Co., 1985.

Whorton, James C. *Crusaders for Fitness: The History of American Health Reformers*. Princeton, N.J.: Princeton University Press, 1982.

Williams, Susan Reynolds. "In the Garden of New England: Alice Morse Earle and the History of Domestic Life." Ph.D. dissertation, University of Delaware, 1992.

Wilson, Elizabeth. *Adorned in Dreams: Fashion and Modernity*. Berkeley: University of California Press, 1985.

Wilson, Elizabeth, and Lou Taylor. *Through the Looking Glass: A History of Dress from 1860 to the Present Day*. London: BBC Books, 1989.

Wilson, William E. *The Angel and the Serpent: The Story of New Harmony*. Bloomington: Indiana University Press, 1964.

Wolf, Naomi. *The Beauty Myth: How Images of Beauty Are Used against Women*. New York: William Morrow and Co., 1991.

Women in Search of Utopia: Mavericks and Mythmakers. Ruby Rohrlich and Elaine Hoffman Baruch, eds. New York: Schocken Books, 1984.

Women in Spiritual and Communitarian Societies in the United States. Wendy E. Chmielewski, Louis J. Kern, and Marlyn Klee-Hartzell, eds. Syracuse, N.Y.: Syracuse University Press, 1993.

Wooster, Ernest S. *Communities of the Past and Present*. Newllano, La.: Llano Colonist, 1924.

Young, Agatha. *The Women and the Crisis: Women of the North in the Civil War*. New York: McDowell, Obolensky, 1959.

Young, Marguerite. *Angel in the Forest*. New York: Reynolds & Hitchcock, 1945.

ARTICLES

Achorn, Erik. "Mary Cragin, Perfectionist Saint." *New England Quarterly* 28 (December 1955): 490–518.

Akers, Dwight. "Sally Sunflower and the Bloomer: The Story of Lydia Sayer." *Yearbook* (1956): 3–19, publication of the Historical Society of Middletown and the Walkill Precinct.

Albanese, Catherine L. "Physic and Metaphysic in Nineteenth-Century America: Medical Sectarians and Religious Healing." *Church History* 55 (December 1986): 489–502.

Aldrich, Clarence B. "The Evolution of Gymnasium Clothing for Women." *Journal of Health and Physical Education* 1 (October 1930): 15–17, 47.

Altrocchi, Julia Cooley. "Paradox Town: San Francisco in 1851." *California Historical Society Quarterly* (1932): 31–46.

Arrington, Leonard J. "The Economic Role of Pioneer Mormon Women." *Western Humanities Review* 9 (Spring 1955): 145–64.

Ash, Martha Montague. "The Social and Domestic Scene in Rochester, 1840–1860." *Rochester History* 18 (April 1956): 1–20.

Banner, Lois. "The Fashionable Sex, 1100–1600." *History Today* 42 (April 1992): 37–44.

Barnes, Sherman B. "An Icarian in Nauvoo." *Journal of the Illinois State Historical Society* 34 (1941): 233–44.

"Beaches and Bloomers: Bathing and Boating in Cincinnati Waters." *Cincinnati Historical Society Bulletin* 30, 2 (1972): 130–45.

Bennett, Judith M. "Feminism and History." *Gender & History* 1 (Autumn 1989): 251–72.

Bigger, Darold. "Ellen White and the Dress Reform Movement of the 19th Century." (May 1970) Unpublished paper, Andrews University, Seventh-day Adventist Theological Seminary, E. G. White Research Center.

Bishop, Morris. "The Great Oneida Love-in." *American Heritage* 20 (February 1969): 14–16, 86–92.

Blackwood, Evelyn. "Sexuality and Gender in Certain Native American Tribes: The Case of Cross-Gender Females." *Signs* 10 (Autumn 1984): 27–42.

Blake, John B. "Mary Gove Nichols, Prophetess of Health." *Proceedings of the American Philosophical Society* 106 (June 1962): 219–34.

———. "Women and Medicine in Ante-Bellum America." *Bulletin of the History of Medicine* 39 (March-April 1965): 99–123.

"Bloomer Girl." *New York Theatre Critics' Reviews 1944* 5 (October 30, 1944): 118–21.

"Bloomers Jeered by Men in 1850 Would Amuse and Amaze Today." *Cortland Democrat* (May 12, 1933).

Bordiga, Leila Lee. "Bloomer Was Her Name." *New York Times Magazine* (December 31, 1939): 11–15.

Borish, Linda J. "Farm Females, Fitness, and the Ideology of Physical Health in Antebellum New England." *Agricultural History* 64, 3 (1990): 17–30.

———. "The Robust Woman and the Muscular Christian: Catharine Beecher, Thomas Higginson, and Their Vision of American Society, Health and Physical Activities." *International Journal of the History of Sport* 4 (September 1987): 139–54.

Bradfield, Nancy. "Cycling in the 1890's." *Costume* 6 (1972): 43–47.

Branch, E. Douglas. "*The Lily* & The Bloomer." *Colophon, A Book Collector's Quarterly* 12 (1932).

Brobeck, Stephen. "Images of the Family." *Journal of Psychohistory* 5 (Summer 1977): 81–106.

Brussel, James A., M.D. "Pants, Politics, Postage, and Physic." *Psychiatric Quarterly Supplement* 35 (1961): 332–45.

Brydon, Diana. "'Empire Bloomers': Cross-Dressing's Double Cross." *Essays on Canadian Writing* 54 (Winter 1994): 23–46.

Bunker, Gary L. "Antebellum Caricature and Woman's Sphere." *Journal of Women's History* 3 (Winter 1992): 6–43.

Burgess, Charles O. "Green Bay and the Mormons of Beaver Island." *Wisconsin Magazine of History* 42 (Autumn 1958): 39–49.

Burman, Barbara, and Melissa Leventon. "The Men's Dress Reform Party 1929–37." *Costume* 21 (1987): 75–87.

Butler, Jonathon M. "Prophecy, Gender, and Culture: Ellen Gould Harmon [White] and the Roots of Seventh-day Adventism." *Religion and American Culture* 1 (Winter 1991): 3–29.

Carmony, Donald F., and Josephine M. Elliot. "New Harmony, Indiana: Robert Owen's Seedbed for Utopia." *Indiana Magazine of History* 76 (September 1980): 161–261.

Carson, Gerald. "Bloomers and Bread Crumbs." *New York History* 38 (July 1957): 294–308.

Castel, Albert. "Mary Walker: Samaritan or Charlatan?" *Civil War Times Illustrated* 33 (May-June 1994): 40–43, 62–64.

Chandler, Robert. "Eliza Ann Hurd DeWolf: An Early Case for Cross-Dressing." *Californians* 11, 2 (1993): 28–30.

Clausius, Gerhard P. "The Little Soldier of the 95th: Albert D. J. Cashier," *Journal of the Illinois State Historical Society* 51 (Winter 1958): 380–87.

Connelly, Dolly. "Bloomers and Blouses Plus Waving Alpenstocks." *Smithsonian* 7, 7 (1976): 126–31.

Cook, Sharon Anne. "'Do Not . . . Do Anything that You Cannot Unblushingly Tell Your Mother': Gender and Social Purity in Canada." *Social History* [Canada] 30, 60 (1997): 215–38.

Covington, Dale W. "Shaker Trouser Design Aspects." *Shaker Messenger* 15 (March 1994): 23–26.

Cunningham, Patricia. "Annie Jenness Miller and Mabel Jenness: Promoters of Physical Culture and Correct Dress." *Dress* 16 (1990): 48–61.

Curtis, Mary. "Amelia Bloomer's Curious Costume." *American History Illustrated* (June 1978): 11–15.

Cyr, Paul Albert. "The Progress of Bloomerism." *Spinner: People and Culture in Southeastern Massachusetts* 5 (1996): 134–41.

Davis, Rodney O. "Private Albert Cashier: As Regarded by His/Her Comrades." *Illinois Historical Journal* 82 (Summer 1989): 108–12.

DeCunzo, Lu Ann. "Reform, Respite, Ritual: An Archaeology of Institutions. The Magdalen Society of Philadelphia, 1800–1850." *Historical Archaeology* 29, 3 (1995): 1–168.

"Dr. Mary Walker's Eccentric Dress Drew Attention from Her Real Achievements." *Literary Digest* 60 (March 15, 1919): 94.

Dougherty, Edward P. "Then and Now." *Sunday Record* (August 31, 1975): 66.

Douglas, Ann [Wood]. "'The Fashionable Diseases': Women's Complaints and Their Treatment in Nineteenth-Century America." *Journal of Interdisciplinary History* 4 (Summer 1973): 25–52.

"Dress Reform for Women Rendered Probable by the Bicycle Costume." *JAMA: The Journal of the American Medical Association* 276 (August 21, 1996): 522C.

Dubrow, Gail Lee. "Claiming Public Space for Women's History in Boston: A Proposal for Preservation, Public Art, and Public Historical Interpretation." *Frontiers* 13, 1 (1992): 111–48.

Edwards, Linden F. "Dr. Mary Edwards Walker (1832–1919); Charlatan or Martyr?" *Ohio State Medical Journal* 54 (1958): 1296–98.

Emerson, O. B. "Frances Wright and Her Nashoba Experiment." *Tennessee Historical Quarterly* 6 (1947): 291–314.

Epstein, Julia. "Either/Or—Neither/Both: Sexual Ambiguity and the Ideology of Gender." *Genders* 7 (Spring 1990): 99–142.

Evans, Caroline, and Minna Thornton. "Fashion, Representation, Femininity." *Feminist Review* 38 (Summer 1991): 48–66.

Farrell-Beck, Jane, Patricia Haviland, and Thelma Harding. "Sewing Techniques in Women's Outerwear, 1800–1869." *Clothing and Textiles Research Journal* 4, 2 (1985–86).

Fatout, Paul. "Amelia Bloomer and Bloomerism." *New York Historical Society and Quarterly* 36 (October 1952): 360–73.

Fernandez, Nancy Page. "Innovations for Home Dressmaking and the Popularization of Stylish Dress." *Journal of American Culture* 17 (Fall 1994): 23–34.

———. "Pattern Diagrams and Fashion Periodicals." *Dress* 13 (1987): 4–10.

Finch, Casey. "'Hooked and Buttoned Together:' Victorian Underwear and Representations of the Female Body." *Victorian Studies* 34 (Spring 1991): 337–64.

Finkel, Alicia. "A Tale of Lilies, Sunflowers, and Knee-Breeches: Oscar Wilde's Wardrobe for His American Tour." *Dress* 15 (1989): 4–15.

"The First of the Flappers." *Literary Digest* (May 13, 1922): 44–45.

Fischer, Gayle Veronica. "Dressing to Please God: Pants-wearing Women in Mid-Nineteenth-Century Religious Communities." *Communal Societies: Journal of the Communal Studies Association* 15 (1995): 55–74.

———. "A Matter of Wardrobe? Mary Edwards Walker, a Nineteenth-Century American Cross-Dresser." *Fashion Theory* (Fall 1998).

———. "The Obedient and Disobedient Daughters of the Church: Strangite Mormon Dress as a Mode of Control." In *Culture, Religion and Dress,* ed. Linda Boynton Arthur. Oxford: Berg Publishers, 1998.

————. "'Pantalets' and 'Turkish Trowsers': Designing Freedom in the Mid-Nineteenth-Century United States." *Feminist Studies* (Spring 1997).

————. "'She Ought to Be a Female-man': Dress Reform in the Oneida Community, 1848–1879." *Mid-America* 77 (Fall 1995).

Foote, Shelly. "Bloomers." *Costume* 5 (1980): 1–12.

Foster, Lawrence. "James J. Strang: The Prophet Who Failed." *Church History* 50 (June 1981): 182–92.

Fulmer, Robert. "Mystery Zouaves: Unknown Soldiers in Baggy Pants." *Military Images* 16 (1995): 26–29.

Gleason, Philip. "From Free-Love to Catholicism: Dr. and Mrs. Thomas L. Nichols at Yellow Springs." *Ohio Historical Quarterly* 70 (October 1961): 283–307.

Gordon, Beverly. "Dress in American Communal Societies." *Communal Societies* 5 (Fall 1985): 122–36.

————. "Fossilized Fashion: 'Old Fashioned' Dress as a Symbol of a Separate, Work-oriented Identity." *Dress* 13 (1987): 49–59.

————. "Meanings in Mid-Nineteenth Century Dress: Images from New England Women's Writings." *Clothing and Textiles Research Journal* 10 (Spring 1992): 44–53.

————. "Textiles and Clothing in the Civil War: A Portrait for Contemporary Understanding." *Clothing and Textiles Research Journal* 5 (Spring 1987): 41–47.

Greaves, Halbert S. "Doctrine on Dress." *Utah Humanities Review* 2 (January 1948): 44–53.

Gregorich, Barbara. "Blues, Bloomers, and Bobbies." *Pennsylvania Heritage* 19, 3 (1993): 32–37.

Grundy, Pamela. "Bloomers and Beyond: North Carolina Women's Basketball Uniforms, 1901–1997." *Southern Cultures* 3, 3 (1997): 52–67.

Gubar, Susan. "Blessings in Disguise: Cross-Dressing as Re-Dressing for Female Modernists." *Massachusetts Review* (Autumn 1981): 477–508.

Hansen, Klaus. "The Making of King Strang: A Re-examination." *Michigan History* 46 (September 1962): 201–19.

Harris, R. Curtis. "Bloomers Unlimited." *Seven Valley Villager* (October 30, 1961).

Hedden, Worth Tuttle. "Communism in New York, 1848–1879." *American Scholar* 14 (Summer 1945): 283–92.

Helvenston, Sally I. "Ornament or Instrument? Proper Roles for Women on the Kansas Frontier." *Kansas Quarterly* 18.3 (1986): 35–49.

Hoder-Salmon, Marilyn. "Myrtle Archer McDougal: Leader of Oklahoma's 'Timid Sisters.'" *Chronicles of Oklahoma* 60, 3 (1982): 332–43.

Hoffman, Mary Chaney. "Whips of the Old West." *American Mercury* 84 (April 1957): 107–10.

Hogeland, Ronald. "The Female Appendage: Feminine Lifestyles in America, 1820–1860." *Civil War History* 17 (1971): 101–14.

"The Household Conducted by Mrs. Nellie M. Rich." Robert Burchfield and Linda K. Kerber, eds. *Palimpsest* 61 (March-April 1980): 42–55.

Howard-Filler, Saralee R. "Woman A Wheel." *Michigan History* 64, 5 (1980): 33–35.

Jordan, Philip D. "The Bloomers in Iowa." *Palimpsest* 20 (1939): 295–309.

Kelly, Lori Duin. "Bipeds in Bloomers: How the Popular Press Killed the Dress Reform Movement." *Studies in Popular Culture* 8, 2 (1991): 67–76.

Kephart, William M. "Experimental Family Organization: An Historico-Cultural Report on The Oneida Community." *Marriage and Family Living* 25 (August 1963): 261–71.

Kern, Louis J. "Ideology and Reality: Sexuality and Women's Status in the Oneida Community." *Radical History Review* 20 (Spring-Summer 1979): 180–204.

Kesselman, Amy. "The 'Freedom Suit': Feminism and Dress Reform in the United States, 1848–1875." *Gender & Society* 5 (December 1991): 495–510.

———. "Lydia Sayer Hasbrouck and *The Sibyl*: Bloomers, Feminism and the Laws of Life." *OCHS Journal* 14 (November 1985): 39–44.

Kidwell, Claudia B. "Women's Bathing and Swimming Costume in the United States." *Contributions from the Museum of History and Technology: Bulletin 250*. Washington, D.C.: 1969.

Kinsey, Sally Buchanan. "A More Reasonable Way to Dress." In *"The Art That Is Life:" The Arts and Crafts Movement in America, 1875–1920,* ed. Wendy Kaplan. Boston: Museum of Fine Arts, 1987, 358–69.

Kunzle, David. "Dress Reform as Antifeminism: A Response to Helene E. Roberts's 'The Exquisite Slave: The Role of Clothes in the Making of the Victorian Woman.'" *Signs* 2 (Spring 1977): 570–79.

Lauer, Jeanette C., and Robert H. Lauer. "The Battle of the Sexes: Fashion in 19th Century America." *Journal of Popular Culture* 13 (Spring 1980): 581–89.

———. "Sex Roles in Nineteenth-Century American Communal Societies." *Communal Societies* 3 (1983): 16–28.

Legan, Marshall Scott. "Hydropathy in America: A Nineteenth Century Panacea." *Bulletin of the History of Medicine* 45 (1971): 267–80.

Lewis, David Rich. "'For Life, the Resurrection, and the Life Everlasting': James J. Strang and Strangite Mormon Polygamy, 1849–1856." *Wisconsin Magazine of History* 66 (Summer 1983): 274–91.

Lockwood, Allison. "Pantsuited Pioneer of Women's Lib, Dr. Mary Walker." *Smithsonian Magazine* (March 1977): 113–18.

Luck, Kate. "Trouble in Eden, Trouble with Eve: Women, Trousers & Utopian Socialism in Nineteenth-Century America." In Juliet Ash and Elizabeth Wilson, eds. *Chic Thrills: A Fashion Reader.* Berkeley: University of California Press, 1993, 200–12.

"Mary Edwards Walker." *Lesbian News* 22 (May 1997): 56.

McCall, Laura. "'The Reign of Brute Force Is Now Over'" A Content Analysis of *Godey's Lady's Book*, 1830–1860." *Journal of the Early Republic* 9 (Summer 1989): 217–36.

McGee, Anita Newcomb. "An Experiment in Human Stirpiculture." *American Anthropologist* 4 (October 1891): 319–25.

McGovern, James R. "The American Woman's Pre–World War I Freedom in Manners and Morals." *Journal of American History* 40 (September 1968): 315–33.

McKelvey, Blake. "Susan B. Anthony." *Rochester History* 7 (April 1945): 1–24.

Marieskind, Helen. "The Women's Health Movement: Past Roots." In *Seizing Our Bodies,* ed. Claudia Dreifus. New York: Vintage Books, 1978, 3–12.

Martin, Lawrence. "The Genesis of *Godey's Lady's Book*." *New England Quarterly* 1 (January 1928): 41–70.

Mather, Anne. "A History of Feminist Periodicals, Part I." *Journalism History* 1 (Autumn 1974): 82–85.

Matthews, Jean V. "Consciousness of Self and Consciousness of Sex in Antebellum Feminism." *Journal of Women's History* 5 (Spring 1993): 61–78.

Mehdid, Malika. "A Western Invention of Arab Womanhood: The 'Oriental' Female." In *Women in the Middle East: Perceptions, Realities and Struggles for Liberation,* ed. Haleh Afshar. New York: St. Martin's Press, 1993.

Monro, D. H. "Godwin, Oakeshott, and Mrs. Bloomer." *Journal of the History of Ideas* 35, 4 (1974): 611–24.

Morgan, Dale L. "A Bibliography of the Church of Jesus Christ of Latter Day Saints [Strangite]." *Western Humanities Review* 5 (Winter 1950–51): 43–114.

Noun, Louise. "Amelia Bloomer, A Biography: Part I, The Lily of Seneca Falls." *Annals of Iowa* 47 (Winter 1985): 575–617.

———. "Amelia Bloomer, A Biography: Part II, The Suffragist of Council Bluffs." *Annals of Iowa* 47 (Spring 1985): 575–621.

Numbers, Ronald L., and David R. Larson. "The Adventist Tradition." In *Caring and Curing: Health and Medicine in the Western Religious Traditions* (New York: Macmillan, 1986), 447–67.

Numbers, Ronald L., and Janet S. Numbers. "The Psychological World of Ellen White." *Spectrum* 14 (August 1983): 21–31.

Park, Jihang. "Sport, Dress Reform and the Emancipation of Women in Victorian England: A Reappraisal." *International Journal of the History of Sport* 6 (May 1989): 10–30.

Park, Roberta J. "'Embodied Selves': The Rise and Development of Concern for Physical Education, Active Games and Recreation for American Women, 1776–1865." *Journal of Sport History* 5 (Summer 1978): 5–33.

———. "Harmony and Cooperation: Attitudes toward Physical Education and Recreation in Utopian Social Thought and American Communitarian Experiments, 1825–1865." *Research Quarterly* 45, 3 (1973): 276–92.

Phillips, Janet, and Peter Phillips. "History from Below: Women's Underwear and the Rise of Women's Sport." *Journal of Popular Culture* 27 (1993): 129–48.

Poynter, Lida. "Dr. Mary Walker, M.D. Pioneer Woman Physician." *Medical Woman's Journal* 53 (October 1946): 43–51.

Prager, Emily. "Jurassic Beach: Bloomers, Bustles, Bows." *New York Times,* July 23, 1995, 33.

Quist, John. "Polygamy among James Strang and His Followers." *John Whitmer Historical Association Journal* 9 (1989): 31–48.

Rabun, Josette H., and Mary Frances Drake. "Warmth in Clothing: A Victorian Perspective." *Dress* 9 (1983): 24–31.

Riegel, Robert E. "Women's Clothes and Women's Rights." *American Quarterly* 25 (Fall 1963): 390–401.

Roberts, Helene E. "The Exquisite Slave: The Role of Clothes in the Making of the Victorian Woman." *Signs* 2 (Spring 1977): 554–69.

Rolley, Katrina. "Cutting a Dash: The Dress of Radclyffe Hall and Una Troubridge." *Feminist Review* 35 (Summer 1990): 54–66.

Sandeen, Ernest R. "John Humphrey Noyes as the New Adam." *Church History* 40 (March 1971): 82–90.

Sawyer, Corinnne Holt. "Men in Skirts and Women in Trousers, from Achilles to Victoria Grant: One Explanation of a Comedic Paradox." *Journal of Popular Culture* 21, 2 (1987): 1–18.

Schroeder, Fred E. H. "Feminine Hygiene, Fashion and the Emancipation of American Women." *American Studies* 18 (Fall 1976): 101–10.

Selman, Bertha L. "Early History of Women in Medicine." *Medical Woman's Journal* 53 (January 1946): 44–48.

Shapiro, Susan C. "The Mannish New Woman, *Punch* and Its Precursors." *Review of English Studies* 42 (November 1991): 510–22.

Shryock, Richard Harrison. "Sylvester Graham and the Popular Health Movement, 1830–1870." *Mississippi Valley Historical Review* 18 (September 1931): 172–83.

Sibbald, John R. "Camp Followers All." *American West* 3, 2 (1966): 56–67.

Sims, Sally. "The Bicycle, the Bloomer and Dress Reform in the 1890s." In Patricia A. Cunningham and Susan Voso Lab, eds. *Dress and Popular Culture*. Bowling Green, Ohio: Bowling Green State University Popular Press, 1991, 125–45.

Sklar, Kathryn Kish. "All Hail to Pure Cold Water!" *American Heritage* 26 (December 1974): 64–69, 100–101.

Smith, Rosanne. "Women Who Wanted to Be Men." *Coronet* 42 (September 1957): 62–66.

Smith-Rosenberg, Carroll, and Charles Rosenberg. "The Female Animal: Medical and Biological Views of Woman and Her Role in Nineteenth Century America." *Journal of American History* 60 (June 1973): 332–56.

Stearns, Bertha-Monica. "Reform Periodicals and Female Reformers, 1830–1860." *American Historical Review* 37 (July 1932): 678–99.

———. "Two Forgotten New England Reformers." *New England Quarterly* 6 (March 1933): 59–84.

Steele, Valerie. "'Le Corset': A Material Culture Analysis of a Deluxe French Book." *Yale Journal of Criticism* 11 (Spring 1998): 29–39.

Strang, Clement J. "Why I Am Not a Strangite." *Michigan History Magazine* 26 (Autumn 1942): 457–79.

Stull, James N. "The Maidenform Campaigns: Reaffirming the Feminine Ideal." *Connecticut Review* 14 (Spring 1992): 1–7.

Tandberg, Gerilyn G. "Sinning for Silk." *Women's Studies International Forum* 13, 3 (1990): 229–48.

———. "Towards Freedom in Dress for Nineteenth Century Women." *Dress* 11 (1985): 11–30.

"That Was New York: Mrs. Bloomer's Pantaloons a la Turk." *New Yorker* 16 (June 29, 1940): 39–43.

Tinling, Marion. "Bloomerism Comes to California." *California History* 61 (Spring 1982): 18–25.

Torrens, Kathleen M. "All Dressed Up with No Place to Go: Rhetorical Dimensions of the Nineteenth Century Dress Reform Movement." *Women's Studies in Communication* 20 (Fall 1997): 189–210.

Trautman, Pat. "Personal Clothiers: A Demographic Study of Dressmakers, Seamstresses, and Tailors." *Dress* 5 (1979): 84–88.

Vail, Robert W. Glenroie. "*The Lily*." *New York Historical Society Quarterly* 36 (1952).

van Slyke, Gretchen. "Who Wears the Pants Here? The Policing of Women's Dress in Nineteenth-Century England, Germany, and France." *Nineteenth-Century Contexts* 17, 1 (1993): 17–33.

Vertinsky, Patricia. "Rhythmics: A Sort of Physical Jubilee: A New Look at the Contributions of Dio Lewis." *Canadian Journal of History of Sport and Physical Education* 9, 1 (1978): 31–41.

Vicinus, Martha. "'They Wonder to which Sex I Belong': The Historical Roots of the Modern Lesbian Identity." *Feminist Studies* 18 (Fall 1992): 467–98.

Vick, Margaret S. "The Oneida Community's Mansion House." *Classic America* 2 (Winter 1987): 18–23, 32–33.

Walkup, Fairfax Proudfit. "The Sunbonnet Woman: Fashions in Utah Pioneer Costume." *Utah Humanities Review* 1 (July 1947): 201–22.

Walsh, Margaret. "The Democratization of Fashion: The Emergence of the Women's Dress Pattern Industry." *Journal of American History* 66 (September 1979): 299–313.

Warner, Deborah Jean. "Fashion, Emancipation, Reform, and the Rational Undergarment." *Dress* 4 (1978): 24–29.

Warner, Patricia Campbell. "Clothing as Barrier: American Women in the Olympics, 1900–1920." *Dress* 24 (1997): 55–68.

———. "The Gym Suit: Freedom at Last." In *Dress in American Culture*. Bowling Green State University Popular Press, 1993.

———. "The Gym Slip: The Origins of the English Schoolgirl Tunic." *Dress* 22 (1995): 45–58.

———. "Public and Private: Men's Influence on American Women's Dress for Sport and Physical Education." *Dress* 14 (1988): 48–55.

Wass, Ann Buermann, and Clarita Anderson. "What Did Women Wear to Run?" *Dress* 17 (1990): 69–84.

Waters, Susan C. "The Invincible Doctor Walker." *New York Alive* (November-December 1983): 30–33.

Wayland-Smith, Ellen. "The Status and Self-Perception of Women in the Oneida Community." *Communal Societies* 8 (1988): 18–53.

Weimann, Jeanne Madeline. "Fashion and the Fair." *Chicago History* 12, 3 (1983): 48–56.

Welch, Paula. "The Relationship of the Women's Rights Movement to Women's Sport and Physical Education in the United States 1848–1920." *Proteus* 3, 1 (1986): 34–40.

Welter, Barbara. "The Cult of True Womanhood, 1820–1860." *American Quarterly* 16 (1966): 151–74.

"Who's Wearing the Pants?" *Time* 147 (January 8, 1996): 27.

Wood, Genevieve Smith. "Woman's Dress Reform Was Hot Issue in Middletown Paper 100 Years Ago." *Middletown Times Herald* (date illegible): 38.

Index

Economics: of clothing and fashion, 23, 29; cost of trying reform dress, 138, 141; depressions during nineteenth century, 2, 19; effects on fashion, 19, 185 nn. 40, 41, 216n. 38; in utopian communities, 10, 34–36

Economy community, 42

Ellis, John B., 58

Entertainment, 156

Equal rights. *See* Woman's rights

European fashions, 17–18; antifashion criticism of, 90; and nationalism behind American costume, 121, 212n. 44

Exercise, 40, 173, 175, 195n. 6

Fabric: innovations in, 23; of men's *vs.* women's clothes, 3; for reform outfits, 61, 117, 129; of women's clothes, 18, 29

Farms, reform dress for work on, 135–37, *136*

Fashion, 215n. 14; and antifashion, 23–30; confusion of reform dress as trend in, 96, 141; costs of following, 23, 35–36, 184n. 31, 185n. 40, 216n. 38; criticism of, 47, 69–70, 125–26, 129–30, 172, 212n. 44; criticisms of, 188nn. 64, 67; cultural borrowing in, 86–87; evolution of, 3, 20, 166, 172–73, 175, 185n. 41; features incorporated into Turkish outfit, 95; gendered, 3–5, 17–23; influences on, 19–20, 184n. 31, 186n. 50; in magazines, 100–101, 140–41, 156, 184n. 30; at New Harmony community, 36–41; power and prestige through, 87; simplified, 42, 75–76, 165; and social class, 24–25, 155–56; as social ill, 1, 3, 26, 29–30, 55–56; women's opinion of, 16, 20, 44. *See also* Children's clothing; Dress reform outfits; Men's clothing

Finney, Charles Grandison, 9

Foote, Shelly, 87

Freedom, 83; in artistic dress, 172–73; in fashions of the Twenties, 175; as motive for dress reform, 82, 87, 91–92, 123, 153–54

Freedom dress, *80,* 92, 195n. 5, 203n. 2; origin of, 82–91, 203n. 2, 204nn. 10–12; press coverage of, 94–96; woman's rights advocates stop wearing, 90, 101–8; woman's rights advocates wearing, 79–109

Frontier: clothing on, 216n. 21; reform dress on, 96–98, 136–42, 216n. 22

Garber, Marjorie, 90

Gates, Susa Young, 75

Gender distinctions, in clothing, 3, 154, 176; for children, 61, 187n. 53; desire to maintain, 117, 128, 155; in dress reform outfits, 37, 57–58; and gender identity, 28, 42

Gender equality, and dress reform at New Harmony, 35–38

Gender identity, 5, 16, 24, 220n. 87; and fear of women's pants-wearing, 99–101, 108–9, 153, 155; instability of, 5, 208n. 73; and sex-distinctiveness of clothing, 28, 42

Gender relations, 127; effects of women's clothing on, 28–29; men maintaining power in, 38–40, 59–61, 77, 153–54; in NDRA, 120–21, 162–64; at Oneida Community, 56–57; power in, 3–5, 16–17, 153–54

Gender roles: effects of dress on, 17–23; emphasis on femininity, 14, 20; interaction with fashion, 18–19, 22–23; in public fears of women in pantaloons, 83–85; separate spheres model of, 12–13, 79, 140; in utopian communities, 10, 37–38, 52, 54; wanting to maintain on frontier, 137–41

Gilbert, Theodosia, 48–49, 92

Glen Haven Water Cure, 91–92, 116

Godey's Lady's Book and Magazine, 96, 100, 184n. 30

Gordon, Beverly, 42

Graham, Sylvester, 11

Grand League and Covenant of the Ladies, 25

Marriage: at Oneida Community, 54, 167; polygamy of Mormons, 66–68; Robert Owen's criticism of, 34, 39

Martin, Rachel and Grace, 148

Matthews, Harriet, 56

Matthews, Jean V., 100, 208n. 73

Medicine, alternative, 15, 181n. 12, 194n. 1; and health reform, 10–12; women as doctors of, 141, 149, 219n. 73. *See also* Hydropathy

Men, 144; in dress reform movement, 41, 47–48, 52–53, 116, 162–64; efforts to defeat dress reform, 98–102; fear of feminization of, 84–85; influence on women's body ideals, 145–46; NDRA trying to attract, 119–21; reactions to women's Mormon dress, 66, 72; reactions to women's reform outfits, 58, 101, 107, 133–34; reactions to women's reform outfits on the frontier, 136, 139–40; reasons for supporting dress reform, 77, 107; reform outfits for at Oneida Community, 59, 61; in women's clothing, 176

Men's clothing, 22–23, 71, 187n. 55; elements in dress reform outfits, 117, 206n. 36; fashion in, 3, 56; and gender roles, 3–4; monopoly over pants, 89, 99, 176–77; in origin of reform outfit style, 83–85, 87–90; superiority over women's, 3–4, 83, 87; women wearing, 82, 147–55, *152*, 158, 205n. 17. *See also* Pantaloons

Merritt, M. Angeline, 29, 146

Middle East: influence on reform outfits, 50–51; influence on U.S. fashions, 18, 40

Miller, Alfred E., 149

Miller, Annie J., 172–73

Miller, Elizabeth Smith, 15, *105;* and origin of reform outfit, 81–82, 89, 91, 204nn. 10–12; wearing freedom dress, 79, 104, 107

Miller, J. D., 137

Millerites, 14

Modern Times community, 51

Modernization, during nineteenth century, 1–2

Modesty, 49, 186n. 48; as goal of fashion, 19–20, 24; and hair length, 61–62; as moral obligation, 28–29; and Seventh Day Adventist dress reform, 125–26, 128–29, 214n. 80; and sin, 56–57

Montague, Lady Mary Worley, 85

Morality. *See* Modesty

Mormons, 63–64; deseret costume of, 75–76, 202n. 92; Strangites, 12, 62–75; Utah *vs.* Strangite, 66–67

Mott, Lucretia, 15

Murray, John, 19

Nash, Olive, 167

National Council of Women, 224n. 34

National Dress Reform Association (NDRA), 13, 49, 114–23; demise of, 161–64; and divisiveness within dress reform movement, 90, 143, 211n. 17; Jackson in, 92, 212n. 38

National Organization for Women (NOW), 106

National Social Science Sisterhood, 170

Nationalism, behind American costume, 121, 212n. 44

Native Americans, 51, 199n. 48

Nature, 10–12, 172–73

Nevin, William M., 135

New Harmony community, 33–45, 192n. 10, 193n. 25

Newspapers. *See* Press

Newton, Stella Mary, 87

Nichols, Mary Gove, 11, 48, 77, 121, 157, 194n. 1

North American Phalanx community, 39, 51–52

Noyes, Corinna Ackley, 55–56

Noyes, Harriet Holton, 58–60, 199n. 48

Noyes, Helen C., 15–16

Noyes, John Humphrey, *168;* and dress reform, 40–43, 48, 53–62, 193n. 25, 199n. 50; interaction with other reform leaders, 15–16; leadership of Oneida by, 166–67, 197n. 22

Noyes, Pierrepont, 62

Nudity, of Garden of Eden, 57

Pantaloons and Power
was designed and composed by Christine Brooks
at The Kent State University Press
in 10/13 Granjon with display type in Arepo;
printed on 50-pound Supple Opaque stock,
and notch paper bound in signatures
by Thomson-Shore, Inc. of Dexter, Michigan;
and published by
The Kent State University Press
Kent, Ohio 44242